Evaluation Research Methods

SECOND EDITION

VOLUMES IN THE SAGE FOCUS EDITIONS

Evaluation Research Methods:
A BASIC GUIDE

SECOND EDITION

MATERIALS PURCHASED
WITH TITLE III FUNDS

LEONARD RUTMAN

SAGE PUBLICATIONS
Beverly Hills   London   New Delhi

For information address:

SAGE Publications, Inc.
275 South Beverly Drive
Beverly Hills, California 90212

SAGE Publications India Pvt. Ltd.
C-236 Defence Colony
New Delhi 110 024, India

SAGE Publications Ltd
28 Banner Street
London EC1Y 8QE, England

Printed in the United States of America

Library of Congress Cataloging in Publication Data
Main entry under title:

Evaluation research methods.

  (Sage focus editions ; v. 3)
  Includes bibliographies and index.
  1. Evaluation research (Social action programs)—
Addresses, essays, lectures. I. Rutman, Leonard.
II. Series.
H62.E85   1984   361.6'1'072   84-8293
ISBN 0-8039-2336-8
ISBN 0-8039-2337-6 (pbk.)

FIRST PRINTING

CONTENTS

PREFACE

In the summer of 1976, I organized a training institute on evaluation research at Carleton University in Ottawa. The generous grant by the Department of National Health and Welfare made it possible to bring leaders in the field to conduct two- or three-day seminars on various topics. These people summarized the content of the seminars in articles that were included in the first edition of *Evaluation Research Methods* (1977).

The first edition sold extremely well, with adoptions at about 150 universities. Its success was due largely to the manner in which recognized experts provided practical guidance on how to plan, conduct, and utilize evaluation research. This revised edition has the same aim as its predecessor. However, this book includes substantial changes and major additions to the first edition, reflecting developments in the field since the mid-1970s. Two are modified versions of chapters in the previous edition—research design and data analyses. The others, which cover essentially the same topics as in the first edition, are new and were written specifically for this book.

The impressive group of authors who contributed to this book have been most cooperative in accepting editorial advice. Each of them had other major commitments when they worked on the articles for this book. Yet they found the time and energy to meet my expectations. I am flattered that they agreed to make a contribution and pleased with the caliber of their efforts.

Sage Publications has been a great friend to the field of evaluation research, and I have enjoyed my long-standing association with them. I am thankful for the support and encouragement that I have received from them over the years. I thank them, because working on it was a source of great pleasure.

Leonard Rutman
Price Waterhouse

1

INTRODUCTION

Leonard Rutman

The field of program evaluation has been under considerable stress in the 1980s. The level of interest in program evaluation has declined significantly in the past few years in the United States. Many social programs with built-in evaluation requirements have been transferred to the states. There is no longer major social experimentation as occurred in the previous two decades, and the demand for evaluating ongoing programs has declined.

In contrast, there appears to be growing interest in program evaluation in other countries and among international agencies. For example, the federal government in Canada has set a requirement for departments and agencies to undertake the periodic evaluation of all programs on a regular basis. Practically every major department has established formal evaluation units, and studies are being undertaken to guide decision-making of the deputy head and cabinet committees.

Stress in the field of program evaluation is not limited to the level of demand for such activity. In addition, the focus and methods of evaluation are under debate. There are many dimensions to this debate. More and more attention is being paid to the relevance of program evaluation for decision-making, even if this is at the expense of scientific rigor. Short-term evaluations (of less than three months' duration) are increasingly popular for addressing specific issues of concern to decision makers. Growing attention is being paid to the problems of program implementation as opposed to the focus on outcomes. Qualitative methods have gained greater acceptance. Ongoing performance measurement systems, which in the past were limited to information on resources consumed and outputs produced, are being modified to include measures of program process and outcomes. The idea of doing *evaluation research* to advance knowledge is far less compelling a reason for undertaking a study than *program evaluation* to meet the information needs of decision makers.

It is beyond the scope of this book to address adequately the various approaches to program evaluation. Evaluators can consult the specialized literature to familiarize themselves with these various approaches. This book is concerned with the type of program evaluation that is used to determine the effectiveness of programs, and the dominant approach of the past forms the core of this book. However, the articles do attempt to broaden this approach to some extent by including recent developments in the field.

DEFINING PROGRAM EVALUATION

Program evaluation has no uniform and consistently applied definition. The term has become the subject of a variety of interpretations in relation to its purposes, scope, and methodology. The definition adopted for this book is the following: *Program evaluation entails the use of scientific methods to measure the implementation and outcomes of programs for decision-making purposes.*

In recent years I have tended to use the term "program evaluation" because my interest has been in examining large-scale programs. Some contributors prefer the term "evaluation research." Both terms are used because, essentially, they refer to the same thing.

PROGRAM EVALUATION FOCUSES ON PROGRAM STRUCTURE

In contrast to various other kinds of analysis that might be attempted to examine the quality of program management, evaluation draws attention to the significant structural elements of the program—program components, outputs, objectives, and effects. The concept of a program and its elements are described below.

Program: What Is It?

A program, in our practical terms, is an intervention or set of activities mounted to achieve external objectives—that is, to meet some recognized social need or to solve an identified problem. For example, manpower training programs aim at increasing the employability of their clients while at the same time meeting employers' needs for workers trained in specific skills. Parole services attempt to reduce recidivism, the return of offenders to crime and additional incarceration. Mental health programs may be dedicated to improving the social functioning of individuals. Child welfare programs try to prevent child neglect and to reintegrate weakened or broken families.

Programs are, above all, the embodiment of ideas about means of achieving desired objectives. How ideas get implemented and their impact are the dual concerns of program evaluation. How is the program being carried out? Is the program being implemented in the prescribed manner? Is the target population being reached? What are the outcomes of the program? How could the program be delivered more effectively to the client population? These are among the key questions addressed by an evaluation.

Program Components

Typically, programs can be broken down into several components. Program evaluation cannot provide a global assessment of various types of services that differ substantially and are directed toward different objectives. So we look for the components that would be suitable units for evaluations. The rule is that the selected component should be able to be linked to its own external objectives. Here are some examples of components for particular programs:

- Sheltered workshop program: (a) supervised employment, (b) counseling, (c) life skills training, and (d) job placement service.
- Child protection program: (a) casework, (b) group work, (c) educational sessions, (d) volunteer services, and (e) drop-in center.
- Parole: (a) individual supervision, (b) group work with alcoholics, (c) family treatment, (d) job placement, and (e) "big brothers" for parolees.

Program Outputs

Program outputs are the services delivered by the program. Examples of outputs are number of individuals served, number of counseling sessions, client contacts or contacts on their behalf (e.g., with other agencies), number of referrals, and number of educational sessions with community groups. The quantification of program outputs makes possible the calculation of workloads and the level of efficiency. Evaluations can examine the extent to which increasing workloads (such as assigning more clients to workers) affects outcomes. For example, how would increasing the size of caseloads for probation officers affect the attainment of the objectives of this program? This kind of analysis can be used to increase the cost-effectiveness of programs.

Program Objectives

Program objectives are the formally stated ends to whose achievement the program's resources are directed. Such objectives are typically mandated by legislatures, boards of directors, and often by the funding agency. Managers are expected to direct resources and program activities toward the achievement of these objectives.

Program objectives are often stated in vague terms—for example, improve social functioning, increase community integration, and enhance individual fulfillment. Clarification and practical definition of objectives are essential for both program management and subsequent evaluation.

Program Effects

Effects are the unintended consequences of the program's components. Some may be desirable; others may not. Let's take a social assistance program, for example. Negative (unintended) effects could include such outcomes as dependency of clients on welfare payments, disincentives to gainful employment, or stigma experienced by clients ("welfare bums"). An evaluation can be used to examine these effects in order to find out how pervasive they are and to what extent the program is really responsible for their occurrence.

LINKAGES: THE GLUE OF PROGRAM STRUCTURE

Linkages are the connections between the program's components and its outputs, plus the connections to the hierarchy of objectives and effects. Take, for example, a family counseling component of an urban welfare program. Its output is measured by the number of clients counseled. Its immediate objective is to reduce anxiety. Intermediate objectives might include better family relations, with ultimate objectives of better functioning on the job and improved social relations generally.

Linkages are the expression of the logic of the program structure. Evaluation pays great attention to such cause-and-effect relations. It discovers such relations and either verifies or denies their validity. Evaluations oriented toward program implementation are useful for identifying such possible linkages between program components, outputs, objectives, and effects. Such evaluations thus are used to develop models of the program's structure and underlying logic. Linkages considered plausible can be tested in outcome-oriented evaluations.

PROGRAM EVALUATION IS CONCERNED WITH IMPLEMENTATION AS WELL AS OUTCOMES

Program evaluation need not restrict itself to program outcomes. It can also address the implementation processes of the program.

Program implementation studies attempt to describe how the program is being carried out. They help the program manager understand the manner in which program activities are being delivered: The aim is to use the findings to modify program activities to have the best chance of achieving specified objectives. Such studies are useful for subsequent evaluation of effectiveness, inspiring confidence that the evaluation will be focused on program components that are in fact susceptible to being implemented in the prescribed manner.

Attention to program implementation is important as part of effectiveness evaluations. Failure to look at program implementation presents a dilemma. Was the program poorly implemented, or was it truly ineffective? Unless the evaluation documents the manner in which the program was implemented, the goodness of the idea underlying the program cannot be differentiated from the quality of program administration.

Studies that deal with both program processes and outcomes are especially useful because they focus attention on areas for decision by the manager. They permit the manager to draw conclusions about the manner in which the program was implemented (e.g., length, frequency and types of interviews or sessions) and about the outcomes or results obtained. In such cases, examination of program processes explains how the program's activities relate (or do not relate) to the outcomes. The manager is then able to use findings to change programs in ways shown to produce the best results.

SCIENTIFIC METHODS: OPTIONS ON RIGOR

"Scientific methods" refers to objective and systematic methods of conducting an evaluation. But a scientific approach, with a minimum of subjective elements, itself comprises many different levels of rigor.

There is a wide range of possible options on rigor for each conceivable situation, but the extreme positions are easily explained. At the subjective end of the continuum are evaluations based on intuition and judgment backed by little or no hard evidence. From day to day in their work, managers are always evaluating their programs in this way. They have their own perceptions. They get feedback from their staff, complaints from their clients, and comments from members of outside monitors or funding agencies. They also have the most detailed knowledge of program finances. They often reflect on the quality of service being received by clients, come to conclusions, and take action to improve the delivery of the program. I am not suggesting that intuition and judgment should be curtailed. However, such a subjective evaluation is not the type dealt with in this book.

At the scientific end of the evaluation continuum are evaluations carried out with rigorous scientific methods predicated on the achievement of maximum objectivity—in other words, on the achievement of demonstrable and supportable results from the evaluation analysis. This often, but not necessarily, imples a heavy component of quantitative research and inference from so-called facts. Because of the methodology used, the inferences are assumed to be credible and "actionable." Even within the scientific approaches to evaluation, however, the question of options on rigor remains: How much is enough? An important consideration is the purpose of the evaluation and the type of information required by the decision makers. Part of the answer comes from the economics of the evaluation itself. How much rigor can we afford? What would it mean to the validity of the results? Is some initially suggested plan feasible, or should we look for more economical methods? That is, in short, a cost-benefit question in this respect.

Various kinds of generally accepted approaches are available for the collection of qualitative or quantitative data, and there are various types of appropriate research designs. The approach should be tailored to the purpose of the evaluation and the characteristics of the program. It should take into account the state-of-the-art on research, cost, and whatever political, legal, ethical, and administrative constraints that condition the evaluation effort.

PROGRAM EVALUATION INCLUDES BOTH PERIODIC STUDIES AND ONGOING MONITORING SYSTEMS

Many program managers think of an evaluation as a study done at intervals under suitable terms of reference. In this scenario, the program waits for some indeterminate period—perhaps several years—for the next evaluation. In other words, this perception lends itself to periodic, one-shot studies. The mounting disenchantment with program evaluation is due at least partly to the problems associated with periodic evaluations: their cost, their lack of inclusiveness, and their tendency of not being timely for required decisions on either funding priorities or changes in program delivery. Programs have a habit of changing; readers of an evaluation may be perusing a report on a program that no longer exists. The (relevant) modified program has in effect just missed an evaluation, which may not be scheduled to recur for some years.

An alternative is to implement ongoing measurement systems that can be integrated with program delivery and normal requirements for administrative records (see, for example, Hatry et al., 1981). For example, background information and baseline data on factors the program aims to change can be collected as part of accepting referrals and doing intake. Data on the services provided to the clients can be collected on an ongoing basis. Measurement of the changes the program aims to effect can be taken at specified times during the treatments, or termination, or during a follow-up period. In other words, the basic data requirements can often be met through an ongoing measurement system. From time to time, a study could be mounted, rolling up the data on hand, supplementing them when necessary with additional data, or complementing the procedure with additional research methods (e.g., setting up a control group).

USE OF PROGRAM EVALUATION FOR DECISION MAKING

The program manager should expect program evaluation to be a useful tool for decisions on the program. He or she should take steps to ensure that it works out this way. Havens suggested that useful results can come from even imperfect evaluations, but the rule still holds:

> The utility of the findings, however, is directly related to the ability of the evaluator to provide information (however qualified it must be) which is relevant to the decision which must be made [Havens, 1981].

Once again, we see that the purposes of the evaluation are paramount. What key questions will it answer for the manager? What, if anything, will it provide for external audiences such as the legislature or the board of directors? The activities of an evaluation all have to be dedicated to a set of managerially defined purposes.

PROGRAM EVALUATION PROCESS

Each chapter of this book is designed to deal with a particular stage of the program evaluation process. This section aims to provide an overview of these stages and to undertake the linkages among them. In Chapter 7, Ross Conner provides a case study to illustrate the manner in which these steps are carried out.

DEFINING THE CLIENT

There are inevitably numerous parties having an interest in the evaluation—legislators, client groups, interest groups, and the general public. An all-purpose evaluation that meets the information needs of these various parties is rarely possible. A study should be designed to address the information needs of a primary client. Therefore, the first step in planning an evaluation is to determine who is the primary client for the evaluation.

DETERMINING THE PURPOSE OF THE EVALUATION

The evaluator should be clear about the overt as well as possible covert purposes of the evaluation. Three broad purposes for evaluation are discussed below: (1) meaningful accountability, (2) improved program delivery, and (3) adding to the knowledge of the social sciences (Chelimsky, 1978). In addition, the covert purposes are discussed briefly.

Accountability. The demand for accountability (to funding bodies, legislative groups, and to some extent the public) has been the major impetus for program evaluation in the past few years. Fiscal constraints have increased the competition of public agencies for available dollars and raised questions of "value for money" from their activities. The accountability perspective on evaluation holds that the worth of the program must be reported and thereby demonstrated if it is to receive continued legislative, financial, and public support.

There are also internal dimensions of bureaucratic accountability in day-to-day program management. From the outsider's perspective, however, relevant questions are these: Is the program being implemented as it was originally authorized and funded? Is it achieving its objectives? Are the clients and public satisfied with the program? How does the program compare with other alternative means of pursuing the same objectives? Is the program achieving its objectives in the most efficient manner? What are its unintended effects—particularly negative ones?

Numerous reasons help explain this important linkage between program evaluation and accountability. The public is obviously concerned about the levels of government expenditure in the United States and Canada, as well as in other countries. Taxpayer revolts are one manifestation. Public concern over the inflationary impact of federal deficits is another. Budgetary restraint has attained a high priority. Thus program evaluation comes to be viewed as a responsible means of arriving at difficult decisions on the reallocation of resources. We are also witnessing negative attitudes toward many government programs—especially social programs whose objectives are often difficult to specify. The conservative trend is strengthened by accumulating evidence from evaluations showing disappointing results from many social programs.

Management. The management perspective on program evaluation sees it as a tool for making improved decisions about the design of programs and their delivery and about the type and amount of resources that should be devoted to the program. In this case, the line manager is the client of the evaluation study. He or she views it as a source of improved management control—that is, a source of information for managerial action.

Program evaluation can address several information needs of line managers: How is the program being implemented? Is it being carried out in the prescribed manner? What is the nature of the impediments to program implementation? What appear to be the outcomes or consequences of the program? Are the objectives being achieved? To what extent does the program produce unintended effects? How does the manner in which the program is being implemented affect its outcomes? What types of factors impede or facilitate achievement of its objectives? What types of clients appear to gain the most benefit from the program? Is a new type of service or a different way of delivering an existing service worth introducing as a pilot experiment? On a large scale?

The primary use of information here is to modify services and delivery mechanisms in order to increase their effectiveness. The key question raised by the previously mentioned accountability perspective was this: "Is the program any good?" This is a central question from the management perspective: "How can the program be made better?"

However, as we indicated earlier, evaluations that are primarily meant to serve program management can also be useful for accountability purposes. Answers to the questions in the preceding paragraph are also somewhat relevant to the accountability question. But the main emphasis is on improved program delivery.

Knowledge. Program evaluation can also be used to produce knowledge that may or may not be of immediate use to decision makers (either program managers or the people to whom they are accountable). It contributes, in this perspective, to potentially important additions to the state-of-the-art in different fields of practice. Such research may indeed by devoid of practical impact in the immediate future. On the other hand, it may lay the foundation for far-reaching program innovations in the longer term.

Examples abound of evaluations carried out by professionals or private foundations where the primary purpose is to develop knowledge about particular interventions and the theories underlying them. Fairweather (et al., 1975) spent more than 20 years conducting research on the problems of mental patients released from hospitals, examining the effectiveness of interventions that existed at the time and developing and testing new interventions in terms of their effectiveness.

These three different perspectives of program evaluation—accountability, management, and scientific curiosity—are not mutually exclusive. A study from the management perspective can at the same time meet at least some of the requirements of accountability. It may have by-products for the knowledge base of various disciplines. However, a primary commitment to one perspective as opposed to another is likely to have major consequences for the organizational arrangements for program evaluation and for the design and execution of evaluation studies.

Covert purposes. Finally, a word of caution on the dangers of hidden, or covert, purposes for the evaluation (Suchman, 1967). Evaluations may be undertaken to whitewash a program—to make it look good. The type of methodology that can accomplish this end is therefore invoked (e.g., asking questions only about client satisfaction with services). Another covert purpose may be to destroy the program. Again, evaluations can be used to avoid action or postpone it where a more honest, objective review would point clearly to needed changes (e.g., in the nature of services, the level of funding, number and quality of staff, location and kind of faciltiies). The evaluation might also be carried out as a token response to some requirement and have little, if any, practical significance.

The evaluator may not be in a position to do much about these covert purposes. However, recognizing them is important in understanding the context for the study and decisions about various aspects of the evaluation—funding, timetable, questions to be addressed, methodology, and reporting of findings.

PLANNING THE EVALUATION: EVALUABILITY ASSESSMENT

Program evaluations require careful planning to ensure that the study will be relevant and credible. An evaluability assessment is the front-end analysis that can be used to determine the manner and extent to which a program can be evaluated. The next chapter discusses the rationale for an evaluability assessment and the approach to conducting it. Other publications provide an extensive discussion on this topic (Rutman, 1980; Wholey, 1979).

The evaluability assessment focuses on program structure and examines the following questions: Is the program well defined? Is it implemented in the prescribed manner? Are the objectives and effects clearly defined? Are they plausible (i.e., within reach of the program)?

The answers to these questions indicate the extent to which it would be appropriate to undertake an evaluation of the program's effectiveness. Problems with program structure could point to the types of management action or progress research needed to address the identified shortcomings.

There is a second set of considerations in planning an evaluation: the type of methodology that is most feasible to achieve the purposes of the evaluation. This requires identification of the methodology that is best suited to the study's purpose. The feasibility of implementing the required methodology is then assessed, considering funds, available time frame, availability of data, and the variety of constraints that commonly arise: legal, political, ethical and administrative.

The completion of an evaluability assessment should result in terms of reference that include the objectives of the evaluation, focus (i.e., issues and questions to be addressed), information to be collected, source of the data, research design, time frame, and resources.

DEVELOPING AN ADMINISTRATIVE AGREEMENT

There is considerable merit in drawing up a working agreement between the evaluator and manager before launching the study. This agreement clarifies the critical issues of the study requirements and outlines the respective responsibilities of the evaluator and manager. Development of such an agreement identifies issues in advance, forestalls misunderstandings, and enables those that arise to be dealt with more readily. An agreement could cover such areas as these:

- breakdown of expenditures
- scope of the evaluation
- details about the data collection procedures and research design
- responsibilities of the program staff in carrying out evaluation tasks
- management consulting regarding program delivery
- controls to ensure adherence to the evaluation plan
- the consultative process to be followed
- publicity of the report

CONDUCTING PROGRAM EVALUATION

Conducting program evaluation entails three major tasks: (1) measurement; (2) the use of particular research designs, and (3) data analysis. Each of these topics is covered in separate chapters of this book. This section will introduce the important considerations that receive detailed discussion in the respective chapters.

Measurement

The first consideration in measurement is deciding on the amount and type of information required to address the evaluation questions. An evaluation can obtain four categories of information: (1) program, (2) objectives and effects, (3) antecedent conditions, and (4) intervening conditions. The relative emphasis placed on any of these categories would depend on the purpose of the study.

Program: Information should be collected on program process. The amount of detail can vary from simply documenting the type and volume of service provided to specific attributes of the process—for example, the focus of counseling sessions and the type of interaction between the therapist and client. Information on program process can be used to answer one or more of the following questions:

- How was the program implemented?
- Was it implemented in the prescribed manner?
- How does the manner in which it was implemented affect the results?
- What is the most cost-effective way of operating the program?

Objectives and effects: Program evaluation can uncover the effects of a program and/or determine the extent to which the program achieved its objectives or produced particular effects. In either case, the measurement of objectives and effects is central to an evaluation.

Antecedent conditions: Antecedent conditions refer to the context within which the program operates, characteristics of the client served, and background of practitioners. Information on antecedent conditions can help interpret the findings, making possible analysis to establish what clients benefit most, what types of practitioners produce the best results, and what type of context is most conducive to achieving the program's objectives.

Intervening conditions: Events or circumstances often arise while the program is being delivered that have an important influence on its performance. For example, clients of the program may be receiving services from other agencies. Staff turnover or changing organizational conditions can also affect the ability of the program to achieve its objectives. Measuring intervening conditions helps to illuminate evaluation findings by identifying the linking or bridging factors between the program and its outcomes.

The next major consideration is determining the methods of obtaining the required information. The starting point in making this determination is the purpose of the study. Other important considerations are available methodology, cost, confidentiality requirements, access to information, and the technical issues of validity and reliability.

The types of data collection procedures or data sources commonly used include the following:

- questionnaires (structured or unstructured, self-administered or through interviews)
- observations and ratings
- organizational records and files
- available government statistics

There are two key technical considerations for management procedures—validity and reliability (see Nunnally and Durham, 1975). Validity is the degree to which a procedure succeeds in measuring what it purports to measure. The validity issue appears in several forms, including the following:

- *Face validity:* It is obvious, on the face of it, that the proposed procedure is the best way of measuring the phenomenon of interest.
- *Content validity:* A test of the data collection instrument indicates that it will produce a reasonable sample of all possible responses, attitudes, behaviors, and so on.
- *Construct validity:* This is concerned with the extent to which scores on a proposed measure permit inferences about underlying traits, attitudes, behaviors, and the like.
- *Predictive validity:* The measure, if applied, can accurately predict something that will take place in the future.

Reliability is concerned with the stability and consistency of the measurement(s). Inconsistent and unstable measurement can be the result of different causes: poorly worded questionnaires, variations in the way they are administered, or missing information. A well-designed and well-executed evaluation aims to minimize such measurement problems.

Research Design

Research designs address two central concerns. To what extent did the program produce the measured results (i.e., *attribution*)? To what extent are the results of the evaluation relevant for situations (i.e., places, clients, and circumstances) other than those that existed for the evaluation (i.e., *generalizability*)? The importance of attribution and generalizability depends on the purpose of the evaluation and the questions that interest the decision maker (see Cook and Campbell, 1976).

Research designs concerned with attribution attempt to rule out nonprogram factors as explanations for the plausible cause. Such designs can include such features as the use of multiple measurement (including before and after measures), comparison or control groups, and a random assignment or other procedure to establish the control groups.

Generalizability is enhanced if the evaluation is conducted in a manner that involves a broad representation of clients, locations, and situations. In addition, the program should be designed and implemented in a manner that resembles the way it would typically operate.

Chapter 4 provides a detailed discussion of the rationale for using research designs to strengthen the study in regard to attribution and generalizability. It also describes the range of possible research designs that can be used for program evaluation.

Data Analysis

The lines of data analysis and the statistical methods employed are critical to drawing appropriate inferences about the program's performance. Data analysis requirements vary greatly among studies and are greatly influenced by the measures and research designs used in the study.

Inadequate attention to data analysis considerations can lead to misleading and erroneous conclusions about a program. Chapter 5 provides an extensive discussion of the issues.

UTILIZING PROGRAM EVALUATION

The definition of program evaluation refers to its use for decision-making. The ultimate aim is for decision makers to give serious attention to evaluation findings when considering policy options, making resource allocation decisions, or modifying the design and delivery of the program.

The issue of utilization should be addressed in the initial stages of planning the study to ensure that it is relevant to decision makers and that they are sufficiently involved in the evaluation process to develop some commitment to using the findings. There are all kinds of explanations for the lack of utilization, and the literature includes extensive discussion of this problem. However, the need is for experienced evaluators to provide direction for increasing utilization. Carol Weiss addresses this challenge in Chapter 6.

CONCLUSION

Program evaluation aims to produce credible information on the performance of a program to guide decision-making. This book has been structured to provide the reader with direction on how to plan and implement successful evaluations. We place heavy emphasis on a formal planning phase—the evaluability assessment. This helps ensure that adequate attention is paid to the evaluation issues of relevance to decision makers; program structure; and technical feasibility of implementing the required methodology, considering the variety of constraints that typically arise in an evaluation study. We present direction for doing program evaluation through separate chapters that focus on measurement, research designs, and data analysis. These chapters raise the major issues and provide practical advice on how to address them. Utilization of findings is a fundamental concern of program evaluation, and a chapter is devoted to this topic. Case studies are useful for providing concrete illustrations of how prescribed approaches are applied; Chapter 7 was designed with this purpose in mind. The reader can follow the case through the various stages of the evaluation process. A chapter on auditing program evaluation is included to demonstrate the methods of reviewing program evaluations to provide some assurance to outside parties about the adequacy of an evaluation.

REFERENCES

CHELIMSKY, ELEANOR (1978) "Differing perspectives of evaluation." New Directions for Program Evaluation 2 (Summer): 1-18.

COOK, THOMAS D. and DONALD T. CAMPBELL (1976) "The design and conduct of quasi-experiments in field settings," in Marvin M. Dunnette (ed.) Organizational Psychology. Chicago: Rand McNally.

FAIRWEATHER, GEORGE W., DAVID H. SANDERS, and LOUIS G. TORNAT-ZKY (1975) Creating Change in Mental Health Organizations. Elmsford, NY: Pergamon.

HATRY, HARRY, RICHARD E. WINNIE, and DONALD M. FISK, (1981) Practical Program Evaluation of State and Local Governments. Washington, DC: The Urban Institute.

HAVENS, HARRY S. (1981) "Program evaluation and program management." Public Administration Review (July/August): 382.

NUNNALLY, JIM C. and ROBERT L. DURHAM (1975) "Validity, reliability and special problems in measurement of evaluation research," in Elmer L. Struening and Marcia Guttentag (eds.) Handbook of Evaluation Research. Beverly Hills, CA: Sage.

RUTMAN, LEONARD (1980) Planning Useful Evaluations: Evaluability Assessment. Beverly Hills, CA: Sage.

SUCHMAN, EDWARD (1967) Evaluation Research. New York: Russell Sage.

WHOLEY, JOSEPH S. (1979) Evaluation: Promise and Performance. Washington, DC: The Urban Institute.

2

EVALUABILITY ASSESSMENT

Leonard Rutman

An attempt should be made to determine the extent to which a relevant and credible evaluation can be implemented before committing resources to any serious study. An evaluability assessment helps to establish the probability of a subsequent evaluation being successful. This chapter identifies the rationale for an evaluability assessment and outlines the steps for carrying it out.

RATIONALE FOR CONDUCTING AN EVALUABILITY ASSESSMENT

Evaluability assessments aim to ensure *credible* and *useful* evaluations for the client of the study. Many shortcomings of evaluations conducted to date could have been avoided had sufficient attention been paid to this important preevaluation work. Its key question is this: To what extent could the purposes of the intended evaluation be met, considering such factors as the program's characteristics, the

AUTHOR'S NOTE: This chapter is a modified version of Chapter 4 in Leonard Rutman and George Mowbray, *Understanding Program Evaluation*. Beverly Hills: Sage Publications, 1983.

available research methodology, cost, and constraints on the use of the desired research methods?

The evaluability assessment addresses two major concerns: (1) program structure and (2) the technical feasibility of implementing the desired methodology. The focus of this chapter is on program structure because issues pertaining to the design and delivery of programs generally receive less emphasis in the evaluation literature than does methodology. Moreover, the remainder of this book deals with the methodological issues that an evaluability assessment would address.

Weiss (1973: 54) emphasized why we should pay attention to program design and implementation in planning an evaluation study:

> The sins of the program are often visited on the evaluation. When programs are well-conceptualized and developed, with clearly defined goals and consistent methods of work, the lot of evaluation is relatively easy. But when programs are disorganized, beset with disruptions, ineffectively designed, or poorly managed, the evaluation falls heir to the problems of the setting.

An evaluability assessment establishes the extent to which the program is sufficiently well defined to consider evaluating it. Many program labels are vague. They may comprehend a variety of different approaches, conveying no coherent message as to the nature of the program. At the very least, we must have a proper description of the program so that the type of intervention supposedly being implemented (and assessed) is known in advance. Otherwise, we end up with a "black box" evaluation that draws conclusions about some undefined intervention (such as whether or not casework is effective). From such studies, evaluation findings cannot be related meaningfully to a particular form of intervention, so that it might be encouraged and replicated if the evaluation were positive, or modified and possibly stopped if the evaluation were negative.

Even complex interventions can yield to efforts at definition. For the evaluation conducted by Sloane and colleagues (1975), for example, several different dimensions were described for the interventions, the behavior therapy and psychotherapy: the formal characteristics of the patient-therapist interaction in both situations, the nature of the patient-therapist relationship, and the specific clinical techniques used in treatment.

An evaluability assessment is also used to describe how the program is being implemented as a prelude to decisions about the details of the intended evaluation. If the purpose of the planned evaluation is to determine what particular type of program component is effective, for example, the evaluator must be assured that the program will continue to be implemented in a representative way. Otherwise, the evaluator may wind up assessing something other than what was supposed to be studied.

A considerable body of literature has grown up about the failures of program implementation—that is, programs not being put into place in the field according to the intent of the program designers (see Williams and Elmore, 1976). Failure to recognize problems of program implementation may result in an evaluation that tests the effectiveness of the program but that cannot draw a distinction between its poor administration or apparent lack of effectiveness. The evaluability assessment can point out some of these problems of program design and delivery, leading to a possible decision that program evaluation should focus on understanding program implementation issues rather than measuring program effectiveness.

In many studies, vague program objectives were assessed without any assurances that the chosen measures were valid for what the program was trying to achieve. We are all aware of the types of objectives that are vague or nebulous—for example, "improve the quality of life," "strengthen leadership resources," "fulfill individual capacities," or "enhance social functioning."

Vague objectives are typically the consensus of promotional factions in the discussions leading up to the establishment of new programs. Moreover, vague objectives are popular with some program managers; such objectives provide them with flexibility for changing program activities as future circumstances suggest. In addition, programs cannot be held accountable in specific terms for unspecified objectives open to wide interpretation.

When it comes to program evaluation, the result of having vague objectives may be that the evaluator winds up defining them through the selection of measures for the study. This is risky: The evaluation may not be measuring the attainment of objectives that the manager feels he or she is working toward. I have emphasized the importance of specific objectives for the completion of successful evaluations. However, the problem is a deeper one. How could anyone *manage* a program in the absence of clarified goals? A program manager would be very short of criteria for mobilizing and directing program resources under such circumstances.

Numerous examples exist of evaluations that measure program effectiveness against the obviously unrealistic or overly ambitious initial objectives that were enunciated to support the launching of the program (and for general public consumption)—but not to serve as criteria for later accountability. For example, group counseling by prison guards may influence inmate behavior in a penitentiary, but it is not likely to affect future crime and reincarceration. A manpower training program may increase the employability of individuals who are trained in it, but it cannot be expected to reduce the unemployment rate because the causes of unemployment are not primarily a lack of training but more general political and economic conditions. Evaluations that attempt to determine the effectiveness of programs whose goals are not realistic predictably produce negative results. Many of the disappointing findings about the effectiveness of social interventions could be traced back to this problem—that is, evaluation of the attainment of objectives that were really meant to gain support for the program but that were used instead to hold it accountable in actual operation.

Analysis of the above-mentioned issues of program design and delivery can lead to decisions about the major thrust of subsequent, realistic evaluations—in collecting data to gain an understanding of program delivery and to permit justifiable program modifications. In short, evaluability assessment can often be as useful as the subsequent evaluation in providing directions for change to the manager. Attention paid to these issues can also enhance the manageability of a program by spotlighting areas for managerial action:

- Poorly defined programs that require elaboration to facilitate their implementation in the field.

- Failure of management to implement programs in the prescribed manner.

- Vague objectives that provide little basis for accountability and insufficient direction for the program manager.

- Unrealistic objectives that are beyond the reach of the program and for which its manager should not be held accountable.

- Unintended effects, negative or positive, that the program is likely to produce.

- Varying perceptions among managers and program staff about the meaning and priority of objectives.

- Competing or conflicting objectives.

Once the program design and implementation issues have been examined, attention needs to be paid to the feasibility of the type of evaluation that would achieve the desired results. Many of the pitfalls in evaluation can be identified in the preevaluation stage. This helps prevent the needless waste of resources in carrying out evaluations that have little chance of meeting managers' information needs.

The starting point for determining feasibility is to establish the manager's purpose(s) for doing the evaluation. This provides the basis for identification of required methodology. The methodological considerations that are the focus of the evaluation include types of data collection procedures, sampling, timing of measurement, use of control or comparison groups, and types of data analysis. The evaluability assessment attempts to establish the extent to which the methodological requirements can be applied within the available budget and in view of constraints such as those of a political, legal, ethical, and administrative nature.

There are inevitably compromises in the ideal methodology that would best meet the purpose(s) of the evaluation. Recognizing these compromises at the planning stage can result in modifications to the purpose(s) of the evaluation or removing constraints before conducting the evaluation study.

STEPS IN ASSESSING THE EVALUABILITY OF PROGRAMS

In this section, we present a step-by-step guide to evaluators for carrying out an evaluability assessment. (For detailed discussion, see Rutman, 1980.)

PREPARE A DOCUMENT MODEL OF THE PROGRAM

The evaluator begins by preparing a description of the program (components) as it is supposed to be according to such available documents as legislation, funding proposals, published brochures, annual reports, minutes of policymaking groups, and administrative manuals. Program documents reflect the formal commitments made through the program, to legislators who voted the money, to clients being served, and to the public. The Documents Model is the first step for the evaluator in understanding the purposes of the program, its components and outputs, and how these are all (ostensibly) connected. It also serves as the basis for interviews of program staff by the evaluator to obtain their views and perceptions about the basic nature of the program.

The process of developing the Documents Model begins with the evaluator listing all program components, outputs, objectives, and effects. Program components are the elements of a program that constitute a suitable focus for an evaluation. For example, a child welfare program would include such components as protection services (i.e., social work to families whose children live at home), foster home services, institutional care, or educational sessions.

Program outputs refer to the type of services delivered by the program, such as counseling sessions, referrals, or placements in an institution. The quantification of outputs makes possible the calculation of workloads and the level of efficiency.

Program objectives are the formally stated ends to whose achievement the program's resources are directed. For child welfare, objectives could include reduced neglect and improved family functioning.

Effects are unintended consequences of the program, desirable or undesirable. For example, programs can produce such unintended effects as stigma or dependency on the services.

Once the evaluator has identified all the elements that make up the Documents Model, he or she is in a position to construct this model. The exhibit in Figure 2.1 presents an example of such a model for an employment training program. It has three components:

(a) *On-the-job training*—providing employers with wage reimbursement for providing training to employees covered by the program.

(b) *Training courses*—classroom instruction for helping the program's clients develop basic skills.

(c) *Training allowance*—basic support payments to enrollees, plus reimbursement for expenses incurred while taking training.

I have also identified the relevant outputs for each program component. For example, the output of the training courses is the number of persons trained. Finally, I present the hierarchy of objectives and effects. The logic of the diagram is that if one achieves the immediate objective, the achievement contributes toward the intermediate and ultimate objectives. Therefore, in this example the development of skills is expected to increase the employability of the people enrolled in the program; this in turn is expected to increase their earnings and reduce unemployment in the community. In the case of on-the-job

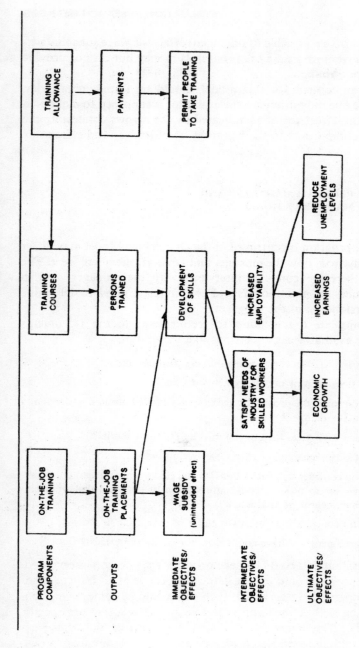

SOURCE: Audit Guide: Auditing of Procedures for Effectiveness (Ottawa: Office of the Auditor General of Canada, 1981), p. 14.

Figure 2.1 Documents Model of an Employment Training Program

training, we have a possible (unintended) effect—a wage subsidy earned by employers who take the program's money but do not provide the requisite training.

All of the content for this model should be found in program documents. The only inference the evaluator is supposed to make is in the cause-and-effect relations indicated by the arrows connecting the program's components to the hierarchy of objectives and effects.

INTERVIEW PROGRAM MANAGERS AND DEVELOP A MANAGER'S MODEL

How the program is portrayed in the Documents Model may differ substantially from how the manager and key staff members see it. The evaluator therefore conducts interviews with the manager, and in some instances the practitioners and key interest groups, to determine their understanding of the program.

In probing the organization for refinements to the Documents Model, the evaluator asks questions like these:

(a) Are any program components missing from the model?

(b) How does each of the components operate?

(c) Do you think the program's activities are carried out in a uniform and systematic manner?

(d) Are any objectives (or effects) missing from the model?

(e) What is the meaning of each objective and effect?

(f) Do you consider that each objective and effect is precise enough to permit measurement (i.e., could information be collected that would indicate its degree of attainment?)

(g) Do you consider the objectives and effects realistic?

(h) Does the program have conflicting objectives and effects?

Managers' models could be developed for each person interviewed. Such an approach would set out in the perspective of each manager or program supervisor interviewed. Included would be components considered to be well defined and objective and effects that are specific and realistic. The interview results, in the form of the Manager's Model, should be sent to each respondent for final comment, to ensure that it fairly represents the views of each.

The evaluator then reconciles the differences between the Documents Model and the Manager's Model. This may shed new light on the degrees of difference between the formal objectives and activities and the operationally defined objectives and activities as perceived by program staff. The differences help the evaluator design the fieldwork that provides direct observational confirmation (or disconfirmation) of the Manager's Model.

GO INTO THE FIELD TO FIND OUT WHAT IS REALLY HAPPENING

For most social programs, evaluators have to do fieldwork to find out what is actually going on in the program as a prelude to helping the manager decide how it should be evaluated. The Documents Model and the Manager's Model are not usually enough to yield a real understanding of the program's complex activities and the types of impact they may be producing. Fieldwork on the program's activities and processes is also useful for verifying the Program Model as developed as a result of this work. The evaluator is particularly sensitive to possible unintended effects not mentioned thus far by the people interviewed in the program.

Through fieldwork the evaluator tries to understand, in detail, the manner in which the program is being implemented. He or she compares actual operations with published guidelines. In particular, where the managers have had trouble explaining the nature of their interventions, the evaluator can check to see if, in fact, a systematic intervention of any kind is being effected. The evaluator can also try to find out what groups are being served by the program, especially in relation to any target population. He or she also collects information on the nature and seriousness of clients' problems. For example, attempts might be made to understand the alcohol and drug problems of clients coming to the agency. The evaluator can also search for latent goals of the program as well as potential unintended adverse effects. For example, in an observational study of welfare intake units, the researcher identified several unintended effects of the program on the applicants: embarrassment, misunderstanding, worry, suspicion and distress (Pesso, 1978).

Collecting information about a program's activities and effects need not be expensive and time-consuming. It is not the equivalent of formal research; the data collection procedures are not expected to measure up to scientific standards. The aim is to inform the evaluator (and hence the program manager) better about the program, not to draw conclusions about the nature and amount of its effects. This can be accomplished in various ways: reading actual client files, observing services in the course of their delivery, and interviewing field staff and clients.

PREPARE AN EVALUABLE PROGRAM MODEL

With the Documents Models, the Manager's Model, and the fieldwork results, the evaluator should now be in a position to identify which program components and which objectives and effects could be considered seriously for inclusion in an evaluation study. The criteria can be summed up as follows:

(a) Program components are well defined and can be implemented in a prescribed manner.

(b) Objectives and effects are specified clearly.

(c) Causal linkages between the program activities and its stated objectives are plausible.

These are preconditions for useful evaluations of program effectiveness. The Evaluable Program Model reflects them and sets the stage for a technical *feasibility* analysis of the proposed evaluation. Thus at this stage, the evaluation is at least pointed in the right direction. The Evaluable Program Model thus determines the *possibility* of certain kinds of evaluation. In other words, an evaluation along these lines would be appropriate if suitable methodology could be found and applied at reasonable cost. (Feasibility addresses this issue of cost, in relation to expected benefits from the evaluation.)

As already mentioned, besides providing direction for doing evaluations, evaluability assessment in many cases brings secondary benefits. It can lead to the program manager giving attention to shortcomings in program design and delivery, to the restatement of objectives in a clearer fashion, and to more realistic objectives.

DECIDE KEY QUESTIONS AND THE INFORMATION NEEDED
TO ANSWER THEM

The results of the evaluability assessment enable the manager to decide what key questions should be answered in the forthcoming evaluation, or in a process of continuing evaluation to be launched. These questions come out of clarification of the purpose for doing the evaluation—that is, the types of decisions that the evaluation is expected to inform. The managerial perspective on evaluation should elicit questions and information requirements that imply subsequent possible decisions on ways to improve the delivery of program services: "What will happen if we get the answer?"

The manager and other principal program people should be able to nominate corresponding key indicators for program processes as well as outcomes and effects. They can also suggest appropriate forms of measurement—not in detail, but in ways that will enable research methods and measurement tools to be designed and tested. Some indicators may be simple and quantitative, such as the number of clients seen or counseling sessions conducted. Others may be more complicated, such as how to measure the changes in clients' anxiety.

DETERMINE THE FEASIBILITY OF EVALUATION PROCEDURES

Feasibility of evaluation procedures means considering what we might do and the cost of doing it. The program manager's starting point for assessing the feasibility of implementing an evaluation study is weighing its expected benefits, the impact of its probable results.

The manager's perception of future decisions and external interests in the evaluation is based, in general, on the value of the information to be produced. This in turn poses a budgetary question: How much should the manager be willing to pay for getting it?

The evaluability assessment step in the evaluation process sets the stage for decisions on measurement and research design. These obviously have a bearing on the final view of the feasibility of any given plan for an evaluation. Is the required information accessible or available? Can the specified data collection procedures be implemented? Would the source of data and the means of collection produce reliable and valid information? Is there a need for sampling participants in the program, on some aspect of its implementation? How could this be done? Is there a need for a control or comparison group? How could this be established? Randomly? At what periods would measurements be taken—before clients' involvement in the program, during it, at its end, somewhat later in time after it was over? What type of data analysis is needed to deal adequately with the manager's information needs? These issues are dealt with in the following chapters. Here, I simply make the point that the technical requirements should be identified and assessed before they are defined as being feasible in practical terms.

Finally, the feasibility of an evaluation is affected, like any other program action, by various constraints that the manager has to keep in mind: for example, shortages of funds, political restrictions, legal limitations on asking certain questions or looking for privileged data, ethical considerations such as might be involved in withholding certain services for the sake of research, and administrative disruptions from an evaluation that might be intolerable. The important thing is not that these constraints appear but determining what should be done about them.

In some cases, the manager may be able to persuade the legal custodians of information to release it. Or means may be at hand to reconcile clients to the withholding of certain services during the evaluation period. Perhaps extra funds can be found to finance the evaluation outside the usual program budget. Political problems may be overcome with suitable persuasion. Program staff may be open to conviction that the benefits of the evaluation will outweigh inconveniences and extra work it will entail for practitioners. On successful application of such remedies, the evaluation may be pursued in a more optimum way. But on the other hand, certain constraints may be intractable. To this extent, the evaluation will have to be modified; its environmental constraints are then reflected in research constraints that may limit the usefulness of its ultimate results. With suitable confrontations, the manager may be able to save the proposed evaluation and ensure that it maximizes the scope for practical decisions emanating from it.

CONCLUSIONS

We know from experience that evaluability assessments can increase the probability of achieving useful and credible evaluations. Through this preevaluation step, the evaluation determines the extent to which the initial purposes of an evaluation can be achieved. The evaluability assessment improves the terms of reference for the evaluation. It can also lead to many incidental benefits to the manager, facilitating desirable changes in program delivery prior to formal evaluation.

REFERENCES

PESSO, TANA (1978) "Local welfare office: managing the intake process." Public Policy 26: 305-330.

RUTMAN, LEONARD (1980) Planning Useful Evaluations: Evaluability Assessment. Beverly Hills, CA: Sage.

SLOANE, R. BRUCE (1975) Psychotherapy vs. Behavioral Therapy. Cambridge: Harvard University Press.

WEISS, CAROL H. (1973) "Between the cup and the lip." Evaluation 1 (2).

WILLIAMS, WALTER and RICHARD F. ELMORE [eds.] (1976) Social Program Implementation. New York: Academic Press.

3

DATA COLLECTION:
OPTIONS, STRATEGIES, AND CAUTIONS

Michael Quinn Patton

The focus of this chapter is the information collected in an evaluation. Information comes from the measurements made of program processes and outcomes, from narrative descriptions, observations, interviews, questionnaires, tests, documents, routine statistics, social indicators, management information systems, program records, and group discussions. The currency of evaluation is information. That currency can be used to manage program processes, to improve effectiveness, and to make decisions about future program directions and funding.

Data collections options and strategies for any particular evaluation depend on answers to several questions:

(1) *Who* is the information for, and *who* will use the findings of the evaluation?
(2) *What* kinds of information are needed?
(3) *How* is the information to be used? For what purposes?
(4) *When* is the information needed?
(5) *What* resources are available to conduct the evaluation?

Answers to these questions will determine the kinds of data that are appropriate in a particular evaluation. The challenge in evaluation is getting the best possible information to the people who need it—and then *getting those people to use the information in decision-making*. The challenge of producing useful information makes evaluation different from traditional research in important ways. In recent years, evaluators have been working at identifying the unique and critical elements of effective, high-quality evaluations. That work has culminated in the publication of new standards for evaluation. This chapter will begin by reviewing some of the standards that distinguish data collection issues in evaluation, then specific data collection and measurement options will be discussed.

EVALUATION STANDARDS: QUALITY CRITERIA

Evaluation as a special field of professional practice emerged in the 1960s as federal human service and education programs multiplied. During this seminal period, concerns about data validity and reliability dominated the meetings and writings of professional evaluators. By the mid-1970s, however, it had become clear that methodological rigor was not enough. Evaluators became concerned that their work was having little impact on programs. Studies of high methodological quality were being ignored. Program funders, administrators, and staff were openly complaining that evaluations were too costly, too often irrelevant, and too academic. Yet standards for judging evaluations remained tied to traditional academic research, with its emphasis on scientific methods and measurement.

In 1981, with the official publication of new standards of excellence, evaluation could be separated more distinctly from basic scientific research and judged by different criteria. In the past an evaluation was considered good if the measuring instruments were constructed carefully, if samples were drawn randomly, if experimental designs were used, and if results were analyzed statistically. Under the new standards, evaluations must also be useful, understandable, relevant, and practical.

FOUR MAJOR CRITERIA

The most comprehensive effort at developing standards took place over five years by a 17-member committee appointed by 12 professional organizations with input from hundreds of practicing evaluation professionals. The standards published by the Joint Committee on Standards for Educational Evaluation (Evaluation Standards Committee, 1981) dramatically reflect the ways in which the practice of evaluation has developed and changed during the last decade. Just prior to publication, Dan Stufflebeam, chair of the committee, summarized the committee's work as follows:

> The standards that will be published essentially call for evaluations that have four features. These are *utility, feasibility, propriety,* and *accuracy.* And I think it is interesting that the Joint Committee decided on that particular order. Their rationale is that an evaluation should not be done at all if there is no prospect for its being useful to some audience. Second, it should not be done if it is not feasible to conduct it in political terms, or practicality terms, or cost effectiveness terms. Third, they do not think it should be done if we cannot demonstrate that it will be conducted fairly and ethically. Finally if we can demonstrate that evaluation will have utility, will be feasible and will be proper in its conduct then they said we would turn to the difficult matters of the technical adequacy of the evaluation, and they have included an extensive set of standards in this area [Stufflebeam, 1980: 90].

For each of these four basic concerns the Joint Committee articulated specific standards. Eight *utility standards* are identified to ensure that evaluations will serve the practical information needs of given audiences. These standards call for clear identification of audiences, clear and understandable reports, getting evaluations done on time, stating evaluator qualifications and biases, and taking responsibility for how an evaluation is used. Three *feasibility standards* are identified mandating that an evaluation should be realistic, diplomatic, and frugal. Eight *propriety standards* are intended to ensure that an evaluation will be conducted legally, ethically, and with due regard for the welfare of those involved in the evaluation, as well as those affected by its results. Finally, eleven *accuracy standards* deal with such issues as the technical adequacy of evaluative information, sources of data, validity, reliability, data control, use of statistics, analysis of qualitative information, drawing conclusions, and objectivity. A parallel set of standards has been developed by the Evaluation Research Society. Both sets of standards place emphasis on doing evaluations that are useful, practical, ethical, and accurate. Several of the standards that bear most directly on measurement and data collection are produced below.

Utility Standard on Information Scope and Selection: Information collected should be of such scope and selected in such ways as to address pertinent questions about the object of the evaluation and be responsive to the needs and interests of specified audiences.

Feasibility Standard on Practical Procedures: The evaluation procedure should be practical, so that disruption is kept to a minimum and so that needed information can be obtained.

Propriety Standard on Rights of Human Subjects: Evaluations should be designed and conducted so that the rights and welfare of the human subjects are respected and protected.

Propriety Standard on Balanced Reporting: The evaluation should be complete and fair in its presentation of strengths and weaknesses of the object under investigation, so that strengths can be built upon and problem areas addressed.

Accuracy Standard on Defensible Information Sources: The sources of information should be described in enough detail so that the adequecy of the information can be assessed.

Valid Measurement: The information-gathering instruments and procedures should be chosen or developed and then implemented in ways that will assure that the interpretation arrived at is valid for the given use.

Reliable Measurement: The information-gathering instruments and procedures should be chosen or developed and then implemented in ways that will assure that the information obtained is sufficiently reliable for the intended use.

ACCURACY STANDARDS:
ISSUES AND EXAMPLES

Accuracy standards focus on the technical quality of evaluation data. For information to be useful and to merit utilization, it should be as accurate as possible. Limitations on the degree of accuracy should be stated clearly. Research by Weiss and Bucuvalas (1980) found that decision makers apply "truth tests" (whether data are believable and accurate) and "utility tests" (whether data are relevant) in deciding how seriously to pay attention to research and evaluation findings. Decision makers want highly accurate and trustworthy data. This means they want data that are valid and reliable.

VALIDITY

A measure is valid to the extent that it captures or measures the concept (or thing) it is intended to measure. Validity is often difficult to establish, particularly for new instruments. Over time scientists develop a consensus about the relative validity of often-used instruments like major norm-referenced standardized educational tests. Rossi et al. (1979) discuss three common criteria for validity of quantitative instruments.

(1) *Consistency with usage:* A valid measurement of a concept must be consistent with past work that used that concept. Hence, a measure of adoption must not be in contradiction to the usual ways in which that term has been used in previous evaluations of interventions.

(2) *Consistency with alternative measures:* A valid measure must be consistent with alternative measures that have been used effectively by other evaluators. Thus a measure must produce roughly the same results as other measures that have been proposed, or, if different, have sound conceptual reasons for being different.

(3) *Internal consistency:* A valid measure must be internally consistent. That is, if several questions are used to measure adoption, the answers to those questions should be related to each other as if they were alternative measures of the same thing [Rossi et al., 1979: 170-171].

Qualitative data collection (i.e., such techniques as participant observation and in-depth, open-ended interviewing), pose different validity problems. In qualitative methods validity hinges to a greater extent on the skill, competence, and rigor of the researcher because the observer or interviewer *is* the instrument. Guba and Lincoln (1981: 113) comment on this validity problem as follows:

Since as often as not the naturalistic inquirer is himself the instrument, changes resulting from fatigue, shifts in knowledge, and cooptation, as well as variations, resulting from differences in training, skill, experience among different "instruments," easily occur. But this loss in rigor is more than offset by the flexibility, insight, and ability to build on tacit knowledge that is the peculiar province of the human instrument.

The relative strengths and weaknesses of qualitative and quantitative methods are discussed at greater length later in this chapter.

Validity is also a concern in using official statistics. Evaluators frequently use government statistics as social indicators to measure changes in phenomena of interest, such as health or crime statistics. Hudson (1977) discussed at length the validity problems of crime statistics.

A major validity problem associated with the use of common measures of program outcomes in criminal justice programs is that they are based upon information collected and reported by the criminal justice agencies themselves, usually as a routine part of their everyday activities.... This feature of the measures used in criminal justice evaluation poses several problems. First, officially collected information used as measures of program outcomes are, by their very nature, indirect measures of behavior. For example, we have no practical or direct way of measuring the actual extent to which graduates of correctional programs commit new crimes. Second, the measurements provided are commonly open to serious problems. For example, the number of crimes known to authorities in most situations is only a fraction of the number of crimes committed, although that fraction varies from crime to crime. This problem is compounded by the fact that the relationship between reported and unreported crime is not constant but variable over time. Thus, changes in policy and public attitudes can result in changes in the proportions of reported crime between both different geographical jurisdictions, different times, and different types of reported crime. The growing willingness of victims of sexual assault to report their crimes to the police and actively cooperate in prosecution is an example of the manner in which public attitudes can affect officially recorded rates of crime.

Of the various criteria used to measure recidivism, that of arrest appears to be especially problematic. The use of arrest as a measure of recidivism seems to fly in the face of the principle that an individual is presumed innocent until proven guilty. Recidivism rates based on arrest do not tell us whether those arrested have, in fact, returned to criminal behavior but only that they are presumed to have done so. At the same time, however, one might suggest that arrests may be the most accurate measure of return to criminal behavior on the grounds that it is the institutional response closest to the individual's behavior. In other words, it is argued that the further one is processed through the criminal justice system, the more likely it is that the institutional response will not be descriptive of the individual's behavior. For example, an individual convicted of trespassing may have been arrested in the act of committing a burglary and plea bargained the offense down.

The widespread discretion exercised by the police to arrest is a further source of invalidity. For example, it is probably reasonable to expect that the number of individuals arrested for a particular type of crime within a jurisdiction is to some extent a direct reflection of changing police policies and not totally the function of changing patterns of law-violating behavior. In addition to the power of deciding when to arrest, police also have discretionary authority to determine which of a number of crimes an individual will be arrested for in a particular situation. Thus, if policy emphasis is placed upon combating burglary, this may affect the decisions as to whether an arrestee is to be arrested for burglary, simple larceny, or criminal damage to property. In short, the discretion of the police to control both the number and type of arrests raises serious validity problems in evaluations which attempt to use this measure of program outcome [Hudson, 1977: 88-89].

In summary, then, validity problems are of concern for all kinds if data collection—quantitative measures, questionnaires, qualitative observations, and social indicators. The precise nature of the validity problem varies from situation to situation, but the evaluator must always be concerned about the extent to which the data collected actually measure what is supposed to be measured. The next section examines a validity issue of special, though not unique, concern to evaluators: the issue of face validity.

THE BELIEVABILITY OF DATA: FACE VALIDITY IN UTILIZATION-FOCUSED MEASUREMENT

Involving identified decision makers and information users in measurement and design decisions is based on the assumption that utilization is enhanced if users believe in and have a stake in the data. Belief in the data is increased by understanding it; understanding is enhanced by involvement in the painstaking process of making decisions about what data to collect, how to collect it, and how to analyze it. Decision makers who acquiesce to the expertise of the evaluator may later find that they neither understand nor believe in the evaluation data. By the same token, evaluators can expect low utilization if they rely on the mysticism of their scientific priesthood to establish the credibility of data rather than on the understanding of decision makers directly involved with it.

One of the best ways to facilitate decision maker understanding of and belief in evaluation data is to place a high value on *face validity* of research instruments. Face validity concerns "the extent to which an instrument looks as if it measures what it is intended to measure" (Nunnally, 1970: 149). An instrument has face validity if decision makers and information users can look at the items and understand what is being measured. Face validity, however, is generally held in low regard by measurement experts. Predictive validity, concurrent validity, construct validity—these technical approaches are much preferred by psychometricians. Nunnally (1970: 149) considers face validity to have occasional public relations value when data are gathered for the general public: "Less logical is the reluctance of some administrators in applied settings, e.g., industry, to permit the use of predictor instruments which lack face validity." Yet from a utilization perspective, it is perfectly logical for decision makers to want to understand and believe in data they are expected to use. Nunnally (1970: 150) disagrees: "Although one could make a case for the involvement of face validity in the measurement of constructs, to do so would probably serve only to confuse the issues." It is little wonder that evaluators, most of whom cut their measurement teeth on Nunnally's textbooks, have little sympathy for the face validity needs of decision makers. Nor is it surprising that such evaluators complain that their findings are not used. Consider the following case.

The board of directors of a major industrial firm decided to decentralize organizational decision making in hopes of raising worker morale. The president of the company hired an organizational consultant to monitor and evaluate the decentralization program and its effects. From the literature on the sociology of organizations, the evaluator selected a set of research instruments designed to measure decentralization, worker autonomy, communication rates and patterns, worker satisfaction, and related organizational dimensions. The scales had been generated empirically and used by sociologists to measure organizational change in a number of different settings. The factorial composition of the scales had been established. The instruments had high predictive validity and construct validity, but they had low face validity.

The evaluator selected a simple pretest and posttest design with nine months separating pre- and postadministration of the instruments. Data analysis showed no statistically significant changes between pretest and posttest. The evaluator reported that the decentralization program had not been implemented successfully and that worker morale remained low. These negative findings were reported for the first time at a meeting of the board. The president of the company had a considerable stake in the success of the program; he did not have a stake in the evaluation data. He did what decision makers frequently do in such cases—he began to attack the data.

PRESIDENT: "How can you be so sure that the program has not been implemented? How did you determine that the program is inefficient?"

EVALUATOR: "We collected data using the best instruments available. I won't go into all the technical and statistical details of factor analysis and Cronbach's Alpha. Let me just say that these scales have been shown to be highly valid and reliable."

"Take this scale on 'individual autonomy.' It's made up of ten items. Each item is an indicator of 'autonomy.' For example, the best predictor item in this particular scale asks respondents: (a) 'Do you take coffee breaks on a fixed schedule?' or (b) 'Do you go to get coffee whenever you want to?' "

PRESIDENT: (visibly reddening and speaking in an angry tone) "Am I to understand that your entire evaluation is based on some kind of questionnaire that asks people how often they get coffee, that you never personally talked to any workers or managers, that you never even visited our operations?"

"Am I to understand that we paid you $20,000 to find out how people get their coffee?"

EVALUATOR: "Well there's a lot more to it than that, you see..."

PRESIDENT: "That's it! We don't have any more time for this nonsense. Our lawyers will be in touch with you about whether we want to press fraud and malpractice charges!"

Clearly the president was predisposed to dismiss any negative findings. But suppose the evaluator had gone over the measurement and design decisions with the president before gathering data. Suppose the evaluator had shown him the items, explained what they were supposed to indicate, and then asked: "Now, if we administer these questionnaires with these items measuring these factors, will they tell you what you want to know? Does this kind of evaluation make sense to you? Are you prepared to act on this kind of data? Would you believe the results if they came out negative?"

Such an exchange might not have made a difference. It is not easy to get decision makers to look carefully at instrumentation in advance, nor do evaluators want to waste time explaining their trade. Decision makers are just as happy not being bothered with technical decisions

—after all, that is why they hired an evaluator in the first place, to design and conduct the evaluation! But the costs of such attitudes to utilization can be high. Utilization-focused evaluation makes the face validity of instrumentation—determined before data are collected —a major criterion in evaluation measurement. Data analysis, data interpretation, and data utilization are all facilitated by attention to face validity criteria.

RELIABILITY

Validity focuses on the meaning and meaningfulness of data; reliability focuses on consistency. A measure is reliable to the extent that essentially the same results are produced in the same situation, and that these results can be reproduced repeatedly as long as the situation does not change. For example, in measuring the height of an adult person, one should get essentially the same results over time. Measuring attitudes, however, is more difficult because one can never be sure if a measured change means the attitude has changed or if the data collection is unreliable.

In essence, reliability concerns the problem of error in data collection. Evaluation measures can be seductive in their apparent precision. To say, for example, that a student has scored at the seventieth percentile on a standardized achievement test sounds terribly precise and scientific. It is easy to forget that the numbers are merely probabilistic indicators of real things; the numbers are not the thing. Eminent psychologist Ann Anastasi commented on this kind of confusion with regard to IQ scores: "One still hears the term 'IQ' used as though it referred, not to a test score, but to a property of the organism" (Anastasi, 1973: XI). In other words, the numbers that come out of standardized tests or other evaluation instruments are not embedded in the genes or on the foreheads of students or clients. They are only rough approximations of some characteristic at a specific point in the time under particular conditions. Test results or questionnaire responses are only one piece of information about a person or a group —a piece of information that must be interpreted in connection with other information we have about that person or group. Test scores, then, are neither good nor bad. They are pieces of information that are subject to considerable error—and that are more or less useful depending on how they are gathered, interpreted, applied, or abused and used.

All kinds of statistical information are subject to error and unreliability. I have chosen to focus on standardized tests as an example in this section on errors because nonscientists seem particularly subject to a belief in the absolute accuracy of such evaluation instruments. The importance of looking for potential sources of error in any measurements is, however, a principle that applies generally. For many reasons, all tests and other evaluation instruments are subject to some measurement error. Henry Dyer, a president of the highly respected Educational Testing Service (ETS), tells of trying to explain to a government official that test scores, even on the most reliable tests, have enough measurement error that they must be used with extreme caution. The government official, who happened to be an enthusiastic proponent of performance contracting, responded that test makers should "get on the ball" and start producing tests that "are 100% reliable under all conditions."

Dyer's comments on this conversation are particularly relevant to an understanding of error in evaluation instruments. He asks:

> How does one get across the shocking truth that 100% reliability in a test is a fiction that, in the nature of the case, is unrealizable? How does one convey the notion that the test reliability problem is not one of reducing measurement error to absolute zero, but of minimizing it as far as practicable and doing one's best to estimate whatever amount of error remains, so that one may act cautiously and wisely in a world where all knowledge is approximate and not even death and taxes are any longer certain? [Dyer, 1973: 87]

Sources of error are many. For example, continuing with the problems of errors in test scores, there are myriad reasons why a particular student's score may be subject to error. The health of the child on the day the test is given can affect the score. Whether or not the pupil had breakfast can make a difference. Noise in the classroom, a sudden fire drill, whether or not the teacher or a stranger gives the test, a broken pencil, and any number of similar disturbances can change a test score. The mental state of the child—depression, boredom, elation, a conflict at home, a fight with another student, anxiety about the test, a low self-concept—can affect how well the student performs. Simple mechanical errors such as marking the wrong box on the test sheet by accident, accidentally skipping a question, or missing a word while reading are common problems for all of us. Students who have trouble reading will perform poorly on reading tests; but they are also likely to perform poorly on social studies, science, and arithmetic tests because all of these tests require reading. Thus the test may considerably underestimate the real knowledge of the child.

Some children perform better on tests because they have been taught how to take written tests. Some children are simply better test-takers than other children because of their background or personality or how seriously they treat the idea of the test. Some schools make children sit all day long taking test after test, sometimes for an entire week. Other schools give the test for only a half-day or two hours a day to minimize fatigue and boredom. Some children like to take tests; some do not. Some teachers help children with difficult words, or even read the tests along with the children; others do not. Some schools devote their curriculum, or at least some school time, to teaching students what is in the tests. Other schools, notably alternative schools (open classrooms, free schools, street academies), place little emphasis on test-taking and paper-and-pencil skills, thus giving students less experience in the rigor and tricks of taking tests.

All these sources of error—and I have scarcely scratched the surface of such possibilities—can seriously affect an individual child's score. Moreover, they have virtually nothing to do with how good the test is, how carefully it was prepared, and how valid its content is for a given child or group. Intrinsic to the nature of standardized testing, these errors are always present to some extent and are largely uncontrollable. They are the reason that statisticians can never develop a test that is 100% reliable.

The errors are more or less serious depending on how a test is used. When looking at test scores for large groups, we can expect that because of such errors some students will perform above their true level and other students will perform below their true score. For most groups, statisticians believe that these errors cancel each other. The overly high scores of some students compensate for the overly low scores of others, so that the group result is relatively accurate. The larger the group tested, the more likely this is to be true.

However, for a specific individual, no other scores are available to make up for the error in his or her score. The only hope is that the questions the student answered wrong because of error will be compensated for by the questions he or she got right either accidentally or by guessing. This type of error compensation is much less reliable in correcting for error than the situation described for large groups. The least reliable result is one individual's answer on a single question. Nothing can compensate for error in this case. Thus one must be extremely cautious about making too much of results for individuals, particularly on single, specific test questions and short tests.

Different evaluation instruments are subject to different kinds of errors. Measurement error can also result from the sampling procedures employed, the way instruments are administered, and other design problems. Whether the evaluation includes data from tests, questionnaires, management information systems, government statistics, or whatever, the analysis should include attention to potential sources of error. Statistical procedures are available for computing the relative size of various kinds of error.

The point is that evaluators do their clients a disservice when they treat lightly the problem of errors in evaluation data. Evaluators need not be defensive about errors. Decision makers and information users can be helpful in identifying potential sources of error. In my experience, their overall confidence in their ability to use evaluation data correctly and appropriately is increased when there has been frank and full discussion of the data's strengths *and* weaknesses. In this way, evaluators are helping to make evaluation clients more knowledgeable so they will understand what Dyer's government official did not:

> The problem is not one of reducing measurement error to absolute zero, but of minimizing it as far as practicable and doing one's best to estimate whatever amount of error remains, so that one may act cautiously and wisely in a world where all knowledge is approximate and not even death and taxes are any longer certain.

MAKING DATA COLLECTION DECISIONS

There are no rigid rules that can be provided for making data collection and methods decisions in evaluation. Cronbach observed that designing an evaluation is as much art as science: "Developing an evaluation is an exercise of the dramatic imagination" (Cronbach, 1982: 239). The art of evaluation involves creating a design and gathering information that is appropriate for a specific situation and particular policy-making context. In art there is no single, ideal standard. Beauty is in the eye of the beholder, and the evaluation beholders include decision makers, policymakers, program managers, and the general public. Thus for Cronbach there are no preferred measures, nor ideal measures, not even in a particular situation. Any given design is necessarily an interplay of resources, possibilities, creativity, and personal judgments by the people involved.

> There is no single best plan for an evaluation, not even for an inquiry into a particular program, at a particular time, with a particular budget [Cronbach, 1982: 231].

BREADTH VERSUS DEPTH TRADE-OFF

Deciding what information and how much data to gather in an evaluation involves difficult decisions about trade-offs. Getting more data usually takes longer and costs more, but getting fewer data usually reduces confidence in the findings. Studying a narrow question or very specific problem in great depth may produce clear results but leave other important issues and problems unexamined. On the other hand, gathering information on a large variety of issues and problems may leave the evaluation unfocused and may result in knowing a little about a lot of things but not knowing a lot about anything.

Thus in the early part of the evaluation some boundaries must be set on data collection. Should all parts of the program be studied, or only certain parts? Should all clients be studied, or only some subset of clients? Should the evaluator aim at describing all program processes, or is there reason to examine only certain selected processes in depth? Should all outcomes be examined, or should the evaluation focus on the attainment of only certain outcomes of particular interest at this time?

In my own experience the problem of establishing focus and priorities is more difficult than the problem of generating potential questions at the beginning of the evaluation. Once a group of decision makers and information users begins to take seriously the notion that they can learn from the collection and analysis of evaluative information, they soon find that there are lots of things they would like to find out. The evaluator's role is to help decision makers and information users move from a rather extensive list of potential questions to a much shorter list of realistic questions, and finally to a focused list of essential and necessary questions.

An example of variations in measurement focus may help illustrate the kinds of trade-offs involved. Suppose that a group of educators is interested in studying how a school program affects the social development of children of school age. They want to know if the interaction of children with others in the school setting contributes to the development of social skills. They believe that those social skills will be different for different children, and they are not sure of the range of social interactions that may occur, so they are interested in a descriptive evaluation that will capture variations in experience and individualized outcomes. Still, there are trade-offs in determining the final focus. It is clear that any given child has social interactions with a great many people. The problem in focusing our evaluation research endeavor is to determine how much of the social reality experienced by children we should attempt to describe. In a narrowly focused evaluation we might select one particular set of interactions between teacher and children. Broadening the scope somewhat, we might decide to look at only those interactions that occur in the classroom, thereby increasing the scope of the study to include interactions not only between teacher and child but also among peers in the classroom and between any volunteers and visitors to the classroom and the children. Broadening the scope of the study still more, we might decide to look at all of the social relationships that children experience in schools; in this case we would move beyond the classroom to look at interactions with other teaching personnel in the school—for example, the librarian, school counselors, special subject teachers, the custodian, and/or school administration staff. Broadening the scope of the study still further, the educators might decide that it is important to look at the social relationships children experience in home and in school in order to understand how children experience those settings differently, and therefore to understand better the unique effects of the school. In this case we would include in our design interactions with parents, siblings, and other people in the home. Finally, one might look at the social relationships experienced throughout the full range of societal contacts that children have, including church, clubs, and even mass media contacts.

All of these are potentially important evaluation research questions. Suppose now that we have a set amount of resources—for example, $25,000—to conduct the study. At some level, any of these research endeavors could be undertaken for $25,000. It is immediately clear, however, that there is a trade-off between breadth and depth. A highly focused question like the interactions between teacher and child could consume the entire amount of our resources and allow us to investigate the problem in great depth. On the other hand, we might attempt to look at all social relationships that children experience, but to look at each of them in a relatively cursory way in order, perhaps, to explore which of those relationships is primary. (If school relationships have very little impact on social development in comparison to relationships outside the school, decision makers could use that information to decide whether or not the school program ought to be redesigned to have greater impact on social development or if the school should forget about trying to affect social development directly at all.) The trade-offs involved are the classic trade-offs between breadth and depth.

QUALITATIVE AND QUANTITATIVE DATA CHOICES

Considering trade-offs between breadth and depth often leads to consideration of the relative strengths and weaknesses of qualitative and quantitative data. Qualitative methods permit the evaluator to study selected issues in depth and detail; the fact that data collection is not constrained by predetermined categories of analysis contributes to the depth and detail of qualitative data. Quantitative methods, on the other hand, require the use of a standardized stimulus so that all experiences of people are limited to certain response categories. The advantage of the quantitative approach is that it is possible to measure the reactions of many subjects to a limited set of questions, thus facilitating comparison and statistical aggregation of the data. By contrast, qualitative methods typically produce a wealth of detailed data about a much smaller number of people and cases.

Quantitative data permit the complexities of the world to be broken into parts and assigned numerical values. Quantitative data come from questionnaries, tests, standardized observation instruments, and program records. To obtain quantitative data, it is necessary to be able to categorize the object of interest in ways that permit counting. Quantitative data are parsimonious, easily computerized, and amenable to statistical analysis. Statistical techniques make it possible to analyze a great deal of data systematically according to accepted operational procedures.

Qualitative data consist of detailed descriptions of situations, events, people, interactions, and observed behaviors; direct quotations from people about their experiences, attitudes, beliefs, and thoughts; and excerpts or entire passages from documents, correspondence, records, and case histories. The detailed descriptions, direct quotations, and case documentation of qualitative methods are raw data from the empirical world. The data are collected as open-ended narrative without attempting to fit institutional activities or peoples' experiences into predetermined, standardized categories such as the response choices that comprise typical questionnaires or tests.

Quantitative measurement relies on the use of instruments that provide a standardized framework in order to limit data collection to certain predetermined response or analysis categories. The experiences of people in programs and the important variables that describe program outcomes are fit into these standardized categories to which numerical values are then attached. By contrast, the evaluator using a qualitative approach seeks to capture what people's lives, experiences, and interactions mean to them in their own terms and in their natural settings. Qualitative data provide depth and detail. Depth and detail emerge through direct quotation and careful description. The extent of depth and detail will vary depending on the nature and purpose of a particular study.

Sociologist John Lofland suggested that there are four elements in collecting qualitative data. First, the qualitative evaluator must get close enough to the people and situation being studied to be able to understand the depth and details of what goes on. Second, the qualitative evaluator must aim at capturing what actually takes place and what people actually say: the perceived facts. Third, qualitative data consist of a great deal of pure description of people, activities, and interactions. Fourth, qualitative data consist of direct quotations from people, both what they speak and what they write down.

> The commitment to get close, to be factual, descriptive and quotive, constitutes a significant commitment to represent the participants in their own terms. This does not mean that one becomes an apologist for them, but rather that one faithfully depicts what goes on in their lives and what life is like for them, in such a way that one's audience is at least partially able to project themselves into the point of view of the people depicted. They can "take the role of the other" because the reporter has given them a living sense of day-to-day talk, day-to-day activities, day-to-day concerns and problems....
>
> A major methodological consequence of these commitments is that the qualitative study of people in situ is a process of discovery. It is of necessity a process of learning what is happening. Since a major part of what is happening is provided by people in their own terms, one must find out about those terms rather than impose upon them a preconceived or out-

sider's scheme of what they are about. It is the observer's task to find out what is fundamental or central to the people or world under observation [Lofland, 1971: 4].

The relative strengths and weaknesses of qualitative and quantitative data have been the subject of much debate in evaluation (e.g., Cook and Reichardt, 1979; Cronbach, 1975; Guba, 1978; Patton, 1978, 1980). Quantitative information tends to be viewed as "hard" data, whereas qualitative data tend to be viewed as "soft." Statistical presentations tend to have more credibility, to seem more like "science," whereas qualitative narratives tend to be associated with journalism.

The emergent consensus in evaluation, however, seems to be moving toward a position where *both* qualitative and quantitative data are valued and recognized as legitimate. There is widespread recognition that evaluators must be able to use a variety of methods in evaluating programs. Evaluators are encouraged to be sophisticated and flexible in matching research methods to the nuances of particular evaluation questions and the idiosyncracies of specific decision maker needs (Patton, 1982). There are no logical reasons why qualitative and quantitative methods cannot be used together. *Qualitative Evaluation Methods* (Patton, 1980) describes conditions under which qualitative methods are particularly appropriate in evaluation research. Sometimes quantitative methods alone are most appropriate. But in many cases both qualitative and quantitative methods should be used together.

Wherever possible, multiple methods should be used. Where multiple methods are used, the contributions of each kind of data should be fairly assessed. In many cases this means that evaluators working in teams will need to work hard to overcome their tendency to dismiss certain kinds of data without first considering seriously and fairly the merits of those data.

NO RULES OF THUMB

There are no rules that tell evaluators what data mix is best. The breadth versus depth trade-off is applicable not just in comparing quantitative and qualitative methods; the same trade-off applies within either quantitative or qualitative methods. The human relations specialists tell us that we can never fully understand the experience of

another person. The research question asks how much time and effort
we are willing to invest in trying to increase our understanding about
any single person's experience. Again, under conditions of limited resources, we can look at a narrow range of experiences for a smaller
number of people.

Take the case of interviews. Interviewing with an instrument that
provides a respondent with a largely open-ended stimulus typically
takes a great deal of time. In North Dakota when I was studying various aspects of open education, we developed an open-ended interview
consisting of 20 questions that were asked of children in grades one to
eight in various open classrooms. Those questions consisted of items
such as, "What do you like most about school?" and 'What don't you
like about school?'' These interviews took between half an hour and
two hours depending on how articulate students were and how old
they were. It would certainly have been possible to have longer interviews. Indeed, I have conducted in-depth interviews with people that
ran six to eight hours over a period of a couple of days. On the other
hand, it would have been possible to ask fewer questions, to make the
interviews shorter, and to obtain less depth.

To illustrate this trade-off between breadth and depth in sampling
human behavior, let us consider the full range of possibilities. It is
possible (and indeed it has been done) to study a single individual over
an extended period—for example the study, in depth, of one day in
the life of one child. This necessitates gathering detailed information
about every occurrence in that child's life and every interaction involving that child during some period. With a more limited research question we might study several children during a more limited period.
With still a more limited research question, or an interview of a half-
hour, we could interview yet a larger number of children on a smaller
number of issues. The extreme case would be to spend all of our resources and time asking a single question of as many children as we
could interview given the resource constraints.

There is no rule of thumb that tells an evaluator precisely how to
focus an evaluation question. The extent to which a research question
is broad or narrow depends on the resources available, the time available, and the needs of decision makers. In brief, these are choices not
between good and bad but among alternatives, all of which have
merit.

It's relatively easy to generate a great deal of information with
sophisticated evaluations made possible by fairly ample resources. It's

also relatively easy to design an extremely simple evaluation with limited resources, one that generates a certain minimum amount of acceptable information. What is more difficult is to generate a great deal of really useful information with extremely scarce resources. The latter challenge seems also to be the most typical.

BE CLEAR ABOUT DEFINITIONS

A frequent source of misunderstanding in evalution is confusion about what was actually measured or studied. In workshops on measurement I give the participants statistics on farmers, on families, and on recidivism. In small groups the participants are asked to discuss the meaning of the different sets of data. Almost invariably they jump right into making interpretations without asking how "farmer" was defined in the data collection, how "family" was defined, or what "recidivism" actually represents in the data at hand. A simple term such as "farmer" turns out to vary enormously in its use and definition. When does the weekend gardener become a farmer, and when does the large commercial farmer become an "agribusinessperson"? There is a whole division of the Census Bureau that wrestles with this problem.

Defining "family" is no less complex. There was a time, not so long ago, when our society may have shared a common definition about family. Now there is a real question about who has to be doing what to whom under what conditions before we call it a family. Before interpreting any statistics on families, it would be crucial to know how "family" was defined.

Recidivism is by no means unusual as a concept in evaluation research. But the term offers a variety of different definitions and measures. Recidivism may mean (1) a new arrest, (2) a new appearance in court, (3) a new conviction, (4) a new sentence, or (5) actually committing a new crime regardless of whether the offender was apprehended. The statistics will vary considerably depending on which definition of recidivism is being used.

A study published by the National Federation of Decency attacked the decadent content of Phil Donahue television shows. One of the categories of analysis in the study reported on Donahue programs that encouraged "abnormal sex." The author of the report later acknowledged that it was probably a bit excessive of the federation to have included breast-feeding in this category (Boulder *Daily Camera*, Sept. 30, 1981: 2). But then, definitions of "abnormal sex" do seem to vary somewhat. Any reader of a research report on the subject would be well advised to look with care at the definition used by the researcher. Of course, any savvy evaluator involved in such a study would certainly be careful to make sure that his or her own sexual practices, whatever they might be, were categorized as "normal."

In the 1972 presidential campaign Nixon gained considerable press attention for making a major budget shift from defense spending to spending for social services. One had to listen attentively and read carefully to learn that all that had happened was moving the Veterans Administration expenditures from the defense side of the ledger to the social services side of the ledger. The statistical changes in proportion of expenditures for different purposes was entirely an artifact of the change in definition of those services.

Such examples are not meant to make people cynical about social science measurement. Many distortions of this kind are inadvertent, due to sloppy thinking, unexamined assumptions, hurrying to complete a final report, or basic incompetence. But those are reasons, not excuses. The next section on comparisons discusses related issues.

MAKE COMPARISONS CAREFULLY AND APPROPRIATELY

Virtually all data analysis in evaluation ends up in some way being comparative. Numbers cited in isolation, standing alone, without a frame of reference or basis of comparison seldom make much sense. A recidivism rate of 40% is a meaningless statistic. Is that high or low? Does that represent improvement or deterioration? An error of $1 million in IRS audits is a meaningless number. Some basis of comparison or standard of judgment is needed in order to interpret such statistics. The problem comes in selecting the appropriate basis of comparison. In a study of the U.S. Internal Revenue Service, the General Accounting Office believed that the appropriate standard was an error of zero dollars, absolute perfection in auditing. The IRS considered such a basis of comparison completely unrealistic in both practice and theory, and they suggested a basis of comparison against the total amount of corrections made in all audits.

During the writing of this book, there has been considerable controversy about the profits of oil companies in the United States. The oil companies wanted to compare their profits to those of the television networks to show just how low their return on capital really is in comparison to an industry where profits are high. Those who are interested in showing oil profits to be exorbitant would prefer to choose as a basis of comparison the profits of the automobile industry, which was in depression from 1980-1982. There are a variety of ways of computing profits: return on sales, return on investment, profit in absolute dollars, percentage profit over a five-year period, profits this year compared to last year, actual profits compared to expected profits. All of these figures turn out to be quite different, the general result being that the public is confused and skeptical.

Similar skepticism can occur in evaluation analyses where the basis for comparison appears to be arbitrary and contrived. It is important to think carefully about what kind of comparisons are appropriate, preferably before data analysis, so that the evaluation question is focused carefully on information that will illuminate the situation and provide a clear basis for action and decision. This is no easy task, for the available choices are quite varied.

The outcomes of a program can be compared to the following:

(1) the outcomes of "similar" programs,
(2) the outcomes of the same program the previous year,
(3) the outcomes of model programs in the field,
(4) the outcomes of the programs known to be having difficulty,
(5) the stated goals of the program,
(6) external standards of desirability as developed by the profession,
(7) standards of minimum acceptability (e.g., basic licensing standards),
(8) ideals of program performance, or
(9) guesses made by staff or other decision makers about what the outcomes should be.

Consider the new jogger or running enthusiast. At the beginning runners are likely to use as a basis for comparison their previous sedentary lifestyle. By that standard, the initial half-mile or one-mile run appears to be pretty good. Then the runner discovers that there are a lot of other people running, many of them running three miles, four miles, five or ten miles a week. By that standard, they haven't done so well, so they push on. On days when they want to feel particularly good, they may compare themselves to all the people who don't run at all. On days when they need some incentive to push harder, they may compare themselves to people they know who run twice as much as they do. Some adopt the standards from medical people about the minimum amount of running needed for basic conditioning, something on the order of 30 minutes of sustained and intense exercise at least three times a week. Some measure their progress in miles, others in minutes and hours. Some compare themselves to friends; others get involved in official competitions and races.

In politics it is said that the conservatives compare the present to the past and see all the things that have been lost, whereas the liberals compare the present to what could be in the future and see all the things yet to be attained. None of these comparisons is right or wrong; all are simply different. Each basis of comparison provides a different perspective, a different way of looking at things, and different information. Evaluators must work carefully with decision makers to decide which comparisons are appropriate and relevant to give a full and balanced view of what is happening in the program.

One of the areas in which there is great confusion when making comparisons is the use of norms. Darrell Huff, the ingenious author of *How To Lie With Statistics*, commented on how easily people are beguiled by normative comparisons.

> Let a parent read, as many have done in such places as Sunday roto-gravure sections, that "a child" learns to sit erect at the age of so many months and he thinks at once of his own child. Let this child fail to sit by the specified age and the parent must conclude that this offspring is "retarded" or "subnormal" or something equally insidious. Since half the children are bound to fail to sit by the time mentioned, a good many parents are made unhappy. Of course, speaking mathematically, this unhappiness is balanced by the joy of the other fifty percent of parents in discovering that their children are "advanced." But harm can come of the efforts of unhappy parents to force their children to conform to the norms and thus be backward no longer....

> Hardly anyone is normal in any way.... Confusing "Normal" with "desirable" makes it all the worse [1945: 44-45].

Evaluators can work with decision makers and information users to help them avoid thinking that, for example, everyone should be above the norm. The norm is simply an average score, so for a general population norm, half of the population must, *by definition*, fall below the norm. Another way of helping the people with whom one is working become more sophisticated about comparisons is to be sure to include a discussion of potential sources of error in data analysis presentations. Thus validity and reliability concerns discussed earlier in this chapter should be part of an analysis discussion.

SUMMARY

This chapter has been concerned with data collection options, strategies, and cautions in conducting program evaluations. The chapter opened with a discussion of the challenge of getting the best possible information to the people who need it—and then getting those people to use information in decision-making. This led to a review of four evaluation standards: utility, feasibility, propriety, and accuracy. These four standards guide data collection efforts. They are standards of quality aimed at making evaluations more useful, practical, ethical, and accurate.

The chapter then focused on the accuracy issues of validity and reliability. Different kinds of data (social indicators, in-depth interviews, participant observations, tests, or questionnaires) introduce different kinds of validity and reliability concerns. But no data collection is perfect, for all data must be examined for errors. Making method decisions requires considering trade-offs between the strengths and weaknesses of different data collection strategies and options. Some of the options reviewed here include the trade-offs between breadth and depth in data collection; qualitative and quantitative data choices; and different ways of focusing evaluation questions. Data collection quality is improved by being clear about definitions and making comparisons carefully and appropriately.

In all of these evaluation issues there is an underlying concern with providing useful and accurate information for decision-making. The evaluator's data collection task has been poignantly summarized by Cronbach et al. (1980: 11):

> Those who shape policy should reach decisions with their eyes open. It is the evaluator's task to illuminate the situation, not to dictate the decision.

REFERENCES

ANASTASI, ANN (1973) "Preface," in Assessment in Plurastic Society. Proceedings of the 1972 Invitational Conference on Testing, Princeton, New Jersey.

COOK, T. D. and C. I REICHARDT (1979) Qualitative and Quantitative Methods in Evaluation Research. Beverly Hills, CA: Sage.

CRONBACH, L. J. (1982) Designing Evaluation of Educational and Social Programs. San Francisco: Jossey-Bass.

———(1975) "Beyond the two disciplines of scientific psychology." American Psychologist 30: 116-127.

——— et al. (1980) Toward Reform of Program Evaluation. San Francisco: Jossey-Bass.

DYER, HENRY S. (1973) "Recycling the problems in testing," in Assessment in a Pluralistic Society. Proceedings of the 1972 Invitational Conference on Testing, Princeton, New Jersey.

Evaluation Standards Committee [The Joint Committee on Standards for Educational Evaluation] (1981) Standards for Evaluations of Educational Programs, Projects, and Materials. New York: McGraw-Hill.

GUBA, EGON G. (1978) Toward a Methodology of Naturalistic Inquiry in Educational Evaluation. Monograph Series, No. 8. Los Angeles: UCLA Center for the Study of Evaluation.

GUBA, EGON G. and YVONNA S. LINCOLN (1981) Effective Evaluation: Improving the Usefulness of Evaluation Results Through Responsive and Naturalistic Approaches. San Francisco: Jossey-Bass.

HUDSON, JOE (1977) "Problems of measurement in criminal justice," pp. 73-100 in Len Rutman (ed.) Evaluation Research Methods. Beverly Hills, CA: Sage.

HUFF, DARRELL (1954) How to Lie with Statistics. New York: W. W. Norton.

LOFLAND, JOHN (1971) Analyzing Social Settings. Belmont, CA: Wadsworth.

NUNNALY, JAMES C., Jr. (1970) Introduction to Psychological Measurement. New York: McGraw-Hill.

PATTON, MICHAEL Q. (1982) Practical Evaluation. Beverly Hills, CA: Sage.

———(1980) Qualitative Evaluation Methods. Beverly Hills, CA: Sage.

———(1978) Utilization-Focused Evaluation. Beverly Hills, CA: Sage.

ROSSI, PETER H., HOWARD E. FREEMAN, and SONIA R. WRIGHT (1979) Evaluation: A Systematic Approach. Beverly Hills, CA: Sage.

STUFFLEBEAM, DANIEL (1980) "An interview with Daniel L. Stufflebeam." Educational Evaluation and Policy Analysis 2, 4.

WEISS, CAROL H. and MICHAEL BUCUVALAS (1980) "Truth test and utility test: decisionmakers' frames of reference for social sciences research." American Sociological Review (April): 302-313.

4

DESIGN OF RANDOMIZED EXPERIMENTS AND QUASI-EXPERIMENTS

Melvin M. Mark and Thomas D. Cook

Questions of causality frequently arise in discussions about social programs and policy changes. Examples abound. Does Head Start cause increased school performance? Which of two job training programs causes higher employment? Does an early release program for prisoners affect recidivism? In the present chapter we discuss the design of evaluations that are intended to answer such causal questions. Thus our focus is on summative rather than formative evaluations.

According to Scriven (1967), who introduced the often-used distinction, formative evaluations are conducted to provide information about how to improve a developing program or its management, whereas summative evaluations are conducted to assess a program's impact. The formative-summative distinction does not include all the types of research that evaluators conduct (e.g., process analysis and much descriptive research). Further, the distinction can be misleading because evaluations designed to assess a program's impact are used mostly in formative fashion, whereas formative research is often used as part of the background for estimating impact (Cook, 1981; Cron-

AUTHORS' NOTE: We thank Fay Lomax Cook for her helpful comments on an earlier draft of this chapter.

bach et al., 1980). Nevertheless, the terminology suffices to describe the primary focus of the present chapter, which is on the design of summative evaluations that seek to draw causal inferences about the effects of a program. However, to clarify our focus, we also discuss other kinds of questions an evaluation might address, and we critically analyze when rigorous summative evaluations might be scheduled in a broader program of evaluation.

Summative evaluations generally (but not invariably, as we shall see) require the use of an experimental framework. An experimental framework is implemented to estimate the impact of a possible causal agent, or *treatment*, on some potential effect, or *outcome*. Units to which the treatment is assigned must be observed, whether these are persons, classrooms, schools, neighborhoods, work groups, or other social aggregates. The effect of the treatment on the outcome is assessed by (a) the systematic scheduling of measurement and/or (b) the systematic observation either of units receiving no treatment (a control group), units receiving an alternative treatment, or both. Also crucial is (c) knowledge of how the units were assigned to treatments and (d) the critical appraisal of background knowledge from previous research, theory or practice, for such background knowledge can contribute to decisions about both causal impact and the generalizability of inferred impacts (Cook, 1983).

Experimental frameworks can be categorized into two major classes, depending on the way assignment to treatment occurs. In *randomized experiments,* the experimental units are assigned randomly to the treatment or control group, or to one treatment rather than to another. Consequently, the assignment process is completely known. In *quasi-experiments,* assignment to treatments occurs in nonrandom fashion, usually because individuals select for themselves the treatment they receive or are assigned to treatments by program personnel who believe that certain kinds of individuals should receive particular treatments. In later sections of this chapter we discuss the design of randomized experiments and quasi-experiments.

We must point out that research techniques other than randomized experiments and quasi-experiments are important in evaluation research. In particular, qualitative methodologies can be applied with great benefit. However, qualitative methods and their use are beyond the scope of the present chapter (but see Cook and Reichardt, 1979; Hendricks, 1981; Morgan, 1983; Patton, 1982). We must also point out that causal inference is not the only purpose of evaluation research. Other goals include development of a theory of the program; monitoring of treatment delivery, including description of who receives services; assessment of whether a program has been implemented as planned; description of the context in which the program operates; discovery of ways to improve the program; study of the process by which the program has its effects; and estimation of a cost-benefit or cost-effectiveness ratio (or some similar ratio). In fact, causal analysis of the program's effects is often meaningless unless it occurs in the context of some of these other activities. We return to this point in a later section.

To make that discussion and our discussion of randomized and quasi-experiments more meaningful, we first present a typology of types of validity. The typology is useful for illustrating how well randomized experiments and quasi-experiments achieve their goal of causal inference about treatments.

FOUR TYPES OF VALIDITY

The ability to make confident causal inferences is obviously critical when one wishes to evaluate the effect of a treatment on an outcome or set of outcomes. However, issues other than causal inference arise in research. Cook and Campbell (1976, 1979), expanding on Campbell and Stanley's (1963) classic work, presented a fourfold typology of validity issues in research. Other schemes exist for describing validity issues (e.g., Cronbach, 1982; Kruglanski and Kroy, 1975; Reichardt, 1983) and it is difficult to select one scheme over another on purely logical grounds; the Cook and Campbell scheme provides a highly useful heuristic for thinking about research.

Although drawing causal inferences is our central focus, a sophisticated philosophical discussion of the concept of cause is beyond the scope of this chapter. (For such a discussion, see Cook and Campbell, 1979). Suffice to say that cause can be understood as a concept imbued with manipulation (e.g., taking an aspirin causes my headache to go away) or as a concept imbued with explanatory power (e.g., aspirin alleviates headaches because it . . .). The aspirin example is a good one, for it illustrates that dependable inferences can be made about causal relations involving *manipulation* even in the absence of causal *explanation*. Scientists still cannot explain why aspirin is helpful, although we all know it is. In this chapter we will be concerned more with manipulatory causal relations; however, we believe that studies that have as their primary purpose examining manipulatory causes should also probe to explain why particular causal relationships hold. Inferences about manipulatory causes depend on showing that (a) a presumed cause and effect covary (i.e., are related); (b) change in the cause temporally precedes change in the effect; and (c) no plausible alternative explanation exists for the relation other than that the treatment as manipulated affected the outcome as measured.

Given these three requirements, it is important to make valid inferences about whether a treatment and possible effect are related at all, irrespective of whether the relation is causal. Inferential statistics are generally used for drawing conclusions about covariation, although they are not necessary for it. Unfortunately, such statistics can be used incorrectly, and even when used correctly they can lead to the wrong conclusion about the program under analysis. We shall use the term *statistical conclusion validity* to refer to the validity of conclusions about whether or not a presumed cause and a presumed effect are statistically associated.

To infer statistical association with a high degree of confidence does not logically permit inferring that the association is causal. Confident causal inference follows only after one has ruled out all competing explanations of why the treatment as implemented and the effect as measured are associated. One must demonstrate, for example, that the statistical association of treatment as implemented and effect as measured does not occur because some third variable caused them both. We shall use the term *internal validity* to refer to the validity of conclusions about whether an observed association between treatment as implemented and effect as measured is due to a causal relation between the two (or conversely, whether the lack of statistical association implies the absence of a causal relation).

Internal validity deals with the relation between variables *as they were manipulated or measured*. Researchers are rarely interested in drawing conclusions about a treatment *as implemented* or an outcome *as measured*. Instead, they would like to refer to more general, abstract constructs. For example, we would be more interested in a conclusion about the effect of Head Start on cognitive abilities than in a conclusion about the effect of Mrs. Jones's teaching activities on scores on test X. The problem is how to use particular, concrete research operations as a basis for drawing valid inferences about generalized, hypothetical, theory- or policy-relevant constructs. We shall refer to *construct validity* as the validity with which inferences about constructs are based on particular manipulations or measures. For simplicity's sake, we restrict our discussion to the construct validity of causes and effects, although it must be acknowledged that the problem of labeling is more general than this.

External validity also deals with the question of generalizability. Here the question is not one of generalizing from specific treatments and measures to more general constructs. Rather, the targets of our attempts to generalize are persons, settings, and historical times, and the validity issue is this: To what extent can a causal relation be generalized to or across persons, settings, or times? We mention generalizing both to and across because some research questions demand generalizing to specified populations of persons and times (e.g., "Does flextime work scheduling reduce turnover among the production line workers of the Widget Corp.?"), whereas other research questions are less specific and require generalizing across a variety of populations (e.g., "With which types of workers doing what sort of work in which types of companies does flextime reduce turnover?"). Further, even though a researcher may design a study to facilitate generalizing to a specific population, other researchers or policy makers may be more interested in other populations. For example, readers may say: "Granted that flextime reduces turnover among production line workers of the Widget Corp. and granted that was the original researcher's main research question, I would nevertheless like to know whether it will be effective with management, with office workers, with auto workers, etc." Thus, external validity is concerned with generalizing to both intended targets of inference and unplanned ones. It has to do with assessing the range of applicability of a causal relation, not just with assessing whether the relation holds with particular preordained populations of persons, settings, and times.

INCREASING VALIDITY

In this section we briefly present suggestions as to how to increase each of the four kinds of validity. In general, our suggestions are action oriented; that is, we describe specific steps that can be taken to increase validity. Our suggestions are presented without extensive discussion, and for many of the recommended actions references are provided to more complete treatments. (In addition, most of the topics in this section are discussed more fully in Cook and Campbell, 1979.) Unlike our treatment of the other three types of validity, our discussion of internal validity does not focus on specific recommendations, because later sections on randomized and quasi-experiments describe the design issues that increase internal validity.

INCREASING STATISTICAL CONCLUSION VALIDITY

Increasing statistical conclusion validity is accomplished, first, by increasing the power of statistical analyses, and second, by using inferential statistics in ways that do not violate important assumptions or capitalize on chance. The power of an evaluation to detect a treatment effect of a given size can be increased in several ways.

(1) Use "large" sample sizes. The desired size depends, of course, on the expected size of the effect relative to the expected variance (see Cohen, 1970).

(2) Decrease extraneous sources of error. For example, one might use a homogeneous sample of respondents and standardize the experimental setting.

(3) Standardize implementation of the treatment, preferably with a high level of exposure to the treatment, where this is possible and does not violate the purposes of the research.

(4) As an alternative, one might account for extraneous sources of variance in the statistical analysis. For example, respondent heterogeneity can be accounted for by measuring respondent characteristics and using them as covariates in an analysis of covariance or in a randomized block design (see Winer, 1971). Similarly, internal analyses can be conducted in which the units receiving a treatment are stratified by the extent to which they received it, thereby permitting analyses of the consequences of differential exposure (e.g., Boruch and Gomez, 1977); but see Mark (1983) concerning implications for internal validity.

(5) Increase the reliability of all measures, particularly outcome measures.

Further, the valid use of statistics requires that the imporant assumptions underlying a statistical test be met. For example, results from an analysis of variance can be misleading if the assumption of uncorrelated errors is violated. An analyst should be aware of such assumptions and know how robust a statistical test is with respect to violations of an assumption. Test should generally be conducted to determine whether important assumptions are violated and adjustments made as appropriate. (Standard statistical references can be consulted for further information about the assumptions underlying various statistical tests and the consequences of their violation.) The valid use of statistical tests also requires adjustments when multiple statistical tests are conducted in an evaluation. When multiple tests are conducted at a given α level, unless a correction is made, the probability of concluding falsely that covariation exists in at least one of the comparisons is greater than α (Ryan, 1959). Corrective adjustments include the use of multivariate analysis of variance prior to examining univariate F tests and the use of multiple comparison tests (e.g., Tukey or Newman-Keuls tests).

Although all these precautions may be taken, it is still possible to conclude that a treatment is related to an outcome when, in fact, it is not so related (Type I error), or that a treatment and outcome are not related when in fact they are (Type II error). The possibility of Type I and Type II errors can never be ruled out because inferences about covariation are ultimately probabilistic. Nonetheless, it is possible to increase statistical conclusion validity—that is, to increase the likelihood of drawing a correct inference about covariation—by employing the procedures we have outlined briefly.

INCREASING EXTERNAL VALIDITY

External validity deals with our ability to specify accurately whether a causal relation generalizes to and across populations of persons, settings, and times. External validity can be thought of as involving two issues: (1) the fit between the desired target population and the sample actually achieved at the end of an evaluation; and (2) whether the treatment effect is similar across various kinds of persons, settings, and times. Thus external validity is threatened, first, if the achieved sample is a poor representation of the target of interest and, second, if there exist interactions between the treatment and some category of persons, settings, or times not revealed by the evaluation.

In designing an evaluation, three major models can be followed to increase external validity. *Random sampling* from a designated universe allows us to generalize results to that universe. Consider, for example, an evaluation designed to assess the effects of a new educational program for junior high school students. The random sampling model could be applied by selecting a random sample of all U.S.

junior high students to use as participants. If implemented successfully, such random sampling would allow generalization to the target population of interest. In many instances it would be preferable to use a stratified random sample, to ensure that subpopulations of interest are represented in sufficient number for analysis. (For an introduction to random sampling techniques, see Kish, 1965.)

Although random sampling is desirable, its value for increasing external validity is limited because random selection for representativeness often will not be possible. Further, generalizability is based on the sample represented in an evaluation *when it ends*, and attrition may mean that the final achieved sample is not a random one. In addition, although it may sometimes be possible to sample *persons* randomly, typically it will not be possible to sample at random from a meaningful target population of *settings*, and it is obviously impossible to sample time randomly. (Note that we are speaking here of random sampling from a population to determine who will be in the experiment—an external validity concern—and not of assigning units randomly to treatment conditions—an internal validity concern. This distinction will be discussed in greater detail later.)

A more practical and often more useful model for extending external validity involves *deliberately sampling for heterogeneity*. That is, one deliberately attempts to include disparate types of persons, settings, or times in the evaluation. In the educational evaluation example, one might deliberately sample for variability in persons by ensuring that respondents included boys and girls of widely different backgrounds, achievement levels, and aptitudes. One could also select disparate sites—for example, good and bad schools, schools from exclusive suburbs, inner cities, and rural settings. Generalizability could then be tested by determining whether the treatment has a similar effect across the various subgroups of children and settings. Because reasonable conclusions are difficult if only two extreme instances are examined and the treatment does not have similar effects, it is desirable to include intermediate instances as well (e.g., it is desirable to include one or more typical schools as well as extremely good and bad schools). One could also sample for heterogeneity in implementation of the program to see how well the program works at different levels of implementation.

The *modal instance* model is another practical way to increase external validity. This model requires explicating the kinds of persons, settings, and times to which generalization is desired, and selecting instances that are impressionistically or demonstrably similar to the modal instance. For example, one might determine what schools are likely to adopt the new program if it proves successful and then select an experimental site (or sites) that represent(s) well the prospective user districts. This can be done by examining descriptive data on school size, per capita expenditures, achievement scores, and the like and selecting experimental schools that appear modal. One may also elicit the opinions of local experts about whether a particular school is typical. The modal instance model is best suited for applied research in which the desired range of generalizability is limited. If the target population is relatively heterogeneous, multiple "modal" instances will be required.

In addition to selecting the most appropriate of the three models, other steps can enhance external validity. The three models can sometimes be combined. In particular, one might sample randomly from a set of modal instances, or from members of heterogeneous groups. Another simple but important means of enhancing external validity is the clear, careful specification of the population to which generalization is desired. This may sound obvious, but some evaluations have suffered from not explicating in advance the target population of likely interest (Cronbach, 1982). The thoughtful use of substantive knowledge can also strengthen one's ability to generalize confidently from the results of an evaluation. Substantive knowledge of a research area is important in each of the models for increasing external validity. Substantive knowledge should influence the choices of variables for use in stratification, in seeking heterogeneity, or in defining the modal instance. Finally, the primary tool in gaining external validity is replication—replication across sites and subgroups within a study and replication across studies.

INCREASING CONSTRUCT VALIDITY

Conceptually there are two general ways to increase construct validity. The first involves carefully tailoring one's manipulations and measures to the rigorously defined constructs they are meant to represent. The second involves providing evidence of convergent and discriminant validity (Campbell and Fiske, 1959). Convergent validation derives from showing that measures or manipulations covary with other operationalizations of the *same* construct. For example, one might show that two independent measures of anxiety correlate highly and they provide a similar estimate of a therapy's effectiveness. Discriminant validation derives from showing that the measures or manipulations of *different* constructs do not covary strongly. For instance, one might show that a desired manipulation of communicator credibility does not inadvertently manipulate distinct but similar constructs such as communicator attractiveness or power. In practice, more attention is typically given to convergent than discriminant validity.

Practically, several steps can be taken to enhance construct validity.

(1) Carefully explicate the constructs of interest. This will probably involve discussion with policymakers and program staff, as well as the construction of a theory of the program (Chen and Rossi, 1983; Cook et al., 1983; Cronbach et al., 1981). Careful explication of the constructs is necessary for the thoughful selection and creation of measures, as well as for adequate monitoring of the treatment.

(2) Study the literature for extant validity evidence if existing measures are of potential use (even though it should not simply be assumed that a measure that was valid in one situation will be valid in another).

(3) If at all possible, use a pilot testing phase prior to the evaluation to obtain evidence of convergent and discriminant validity.

(4) Carefully monitor research operations, in particular the implementation of the treatment. In traditional, short-term social science experiments one uses a *manipulation check* to assess the "take" of the independent variable—that is, to determine whether the independent variable manipulated what it was intended to. In more complex evaluations, one should conduct an *implementation assessment* or empirical *program analysis* to obtain evidence about what the program actually consisted of. Such efforts may involve checklists for observers or program personnel, or the use of qualitative observers and interviews (see Schreirer and Rezmovic, 1983; McLaughlin, forthcoming). In addition, monitoring systems should be employed to ensure that treatment delivery does not break down (Boruch and Gomez, 1977; Mark, 1983).

(5) Use multiple operationalizations of constructs. This will be more feasible for effect constructs than for causal constructs. It is particularly desirable to have multiple operations that employ multiple methods (e.g., it is preferable to use one paper-and-pencil measure and one observational method than to use two paper-and-pencil measures of a construct). When multiple operations of constructs are employed, sophisticated analysis procedures can be used to aid in drawing inferences about the constructs (e.g., Jöreskog and Sörbom, 1979).

(6) Construct validity can be enhanced further by conducting a *process analysis*—that is, by examining the linkages through which the treatment affects the outcome. One strategy for studying mediation within a more quantitative research tradition is to collect measures of the process variables specified by the program theory; these are then included in a causal model to study mediation (Judd and Kenny, 1981). However, process analysis can also involve the use of qualitative methods that have the additional benefit of helping to uncover theoretical links that were not previously known or considered relevant (Cook and Reichardt, 1979). A process analysis enhances construct validity because it helps to locate the constructs in an "nomological net" (Cronbach and Meehl, 1955)—that is, it tests theoretical predictions about interrelations between constructs.

(7) After the evaluation is completed, do the detective work of seeing whether a pattern of results emerges that suggests revisions of one's initial constructs. Sophisticated statistical analyses are extremely useful, but they cannot substitute for thoughtful consideration of the patterns of results that emerge in a study. (For example, see Cook and Campbell's [1979] discussion of Feldman's [1968] cross-cultural study of helping.)

Ultimately, construct validity accumulates over many studies, as evidence grows about the pattern of relations among numerous research operations. Nevertheless, by following the suggestions we have outlined, it is possible to enhance greatly the construct validity associated with a particular evaluation.

INCREASING INTERNAL VALIDITY

Internal validity is concerned with the accuracy of inferences about whether the treatment as manipulated caused any change in the outcome as measured. Essentially this involves ruling out or, more accurately, rendering implausible various threats to internal validity. The threats to validity we list are taken from Cook and Campbell's (1976, 1979) slightly larger list, which derives from the work of Campbell and Stanley (1963). These threats represent a typology of possible alternative explanations for an observed treatment effect (or absence of a treatment effect). If all the threats to internal validity are rendered implausible, confident causal inferences are warranted. To the extent that one or more internal validity threats remains plausible, it is tenuous to infer that any observed effect is due to the treatment. Definitions of specific threats follow:

History. History is a threat when an observed effect might be due to some event, other than the treatment, that occurred between the pretest and the posttest.

Maturation. Maturation is a threat when an observed effect might be due not to the treatment, but to participants growing older, wiser, more tired, and so on, between the pretest and the posttest.

Selection. Selection is a threat when an observed effect may be due to differences in the kinds of people in the different experimental groups, rather than to the treatment.

Instrumentation. This threat refers to the possibility that the observed effect is attributable to a change in the measuring instrument between pretest and posttest.

Attrition. Attrition, or mortality, is a threat when an apparent effect may arise because experimental participants drop out of the experiment.

Statistical Regression. This is a threat when unreliable, extreme pretest scores (or other unreliable pretreatment measures) determine assignment to, or the onset of, the treatment; the observed effect may be due to the predictable failure of the posttest to reproduce the extreme value of the unreliable pretest. Statistical regression is a difficult concept to grasp, and a concrete example may help. Imagine that after a night of excessive eating and drinking, you cast a single blurry-eyed glance at your scale and observe that you have gained 10 pounds. If this leads you to begin a diet immediately, statistical regression will almost certainly guarantee a spurious treatment effect, because subsequent posttest measures will not be so affected by the factors that led to your extremely high pretest weight measurement.

Interactions with Selection. Many internal validity threats can interact with selection to create spurious effects. Perhaps the most common is a "selection-maturation" interaction, in which experimental groups are composed of different kinds of persons who are maturing at different rates. Another can be called "selection-history," or local history. It is involved when the different experimental groups experience different events between the pretest and posttest, and the dissimilar historical events might differentially affect posttest scores.

Each of the preceding threats is rendered implausible by the successful completion of a randomized experiment in which experiment units are assigned to treatments randomly. Thus a generally useful means of increasing internal validity is to assign units to treatments randomly.[1] However, it is difficult for random assignment to be completed successfully in field settings, and there are additional internal validity threats that random assignment does not rule out. We return to these important limitations of randomized experiments in a later section, in which we discuss in greater detail the conduct of randomized experiments.

In contrast to randomized experiments, in quasi-experiments the preceding threats to internal validity must be ruled out individually. This can be accomplished in three ways, listed in order of general value: (1) by the wise design of the quasi-experiment; (2) by examining additional data that might indicate whether the threat is plausible (for an example, see Ross, 1973); and (3) by assuming, because of theory or common sense, that a particular threat is not plausible in the particular evaluation under discussion. The design of quasi-experiments is discussed in greater detail in a later section.

RELATIONSHIPS AMONG THE FOUR TYPES OF VALIDITY

The four types of validity are not independent. Statistical conclusion validity could be considered a subcategory of internal validity because association is a necessary condition for causal inference. Further, construct validity and external validity both have to do with making generalizations—to abstract constructs in the one case and to populations of persons, settings, and times in the other. Further, some ways of increasing one kind of validity will tend to decrease another type of validity. For example, statistical conclusion validity can be increased by applying rigidly standardized treatments to a homogeneous sample, but this could reduce construct and external validity. These and other trade-offs among validity types must be considered in light of the goals of a study. Further, in some cases trade-offs can be avoided, especially by conducting a *program* of research rather than a single study.

THE RELATIVE PRIORITY OF
THE FOUR VALIDITY TYPES
IN EVALUATION RESEARCH

This chapter, like its intellectual predecessors (e.g., Campbell and Stanley, 1963; Cook and Campbell, 1976, 1979), focuses primarily on internal validity issues. In fact, our predecessors have argued explicity for the primacy of internal validity (e.g., Campbell and Stanley, 1966: 5). Critics, most notably Cronbach and his associates (Cronbach, 1982; Cronbach et al., 1980), have argued against the primacy of internal validity, contending instead that in evaluation research external validity is more important than internal validity. It is illuminating to examine these criticisms, and in doing so we will clarify our own position about the role of internal validity and randomized experimentation in evaluation.

According to our reading, Cronbach (1982, Cronbach et al., 1980) makes three distinct arguments against Campbell and Stanley's (1963) and Cook and Campbell's (1976, 1979) emphasis on internal validity and randomized experiments. Our responses to the first two arguments overlap, and so we will consider these two in conjunction. Cronbach's first argument is that in evaluation valid causal inference is less important than relevance. Relevance, to Cronbach, essentially means providing information that policy makers and others can use to make judgments about treatments, persons, outcomes, and settings beyond those examined in the particular evaluation. As Cronbach notes, evaluation is a form of historical inquiry, in that an evaluation describes the effect of a particular implementation of a treatment on particular outcomes, as assessed by particular measures, in a particular sample of units in a particular setting; and the effects thus observed are historical (i.e., they are past). Yet policymakers need to base decisions about the future and probably about somewhat different treatments, outcomes, units, and settings than were observed in the evaluation. According to Cronbach, such decisions are facilitated when evaluations take external (and construct) validity, rather than internal validity, as primary.

Cronbach's (1980; Cronbach et al., 1982) second argument against the primacy of internal validity and experimentation is that programs pass through different stages and that different kinds of research goals are appropriate at different program stages. Cronbach sees randomized experiments and internal validity as less important than external and construct validity at most stages of program development. In addition, Cronbach and his colleagues (Cronbach, 1982; Cronbach et al., 1980) argue that overemphasis on causal inference often leads to the premature use of randomized experiments. As Cronbach notes, substantial work should generally precede a summative evaluation.

We are in agreement with much of what Cronbach and his associates say. As Cronbach notes, some of the apparent disagreement between his writings and those of Campbell and Cook are more apparent than real, and arise largely because Campbell and Stanley (1963) and Cook and Campbell (1976, 1979) focus explicitly on research that has causal inference as its primary goal, and not on a more general theory of evaluation.

With Cronbach we agree that there are goals other than causal inference in evaluation. For instance, the National Institute of Education's (NIE) Compensatory Education Study largely involved descriptive research on such questions as how funds were being allocated and what types of services were being provided to what types of children (NIE, 1978). Descriptive research of this kind is often extremely useful to policy makers. Often, we admit, it is more useful than research on the program's effects.

We are also in agreement with Cronbach (1982; Cronbach et al., 1980) that different goals are appropriate at different stages of program development. We do not, however, believe there is any single, *best* sequence for research activities in program evaluation. Some programs will require extensive formative research prior to summative evaluation. In other programs, the evaluator's first order of business will be to prepare for and conduct a summative evaluation. More likely, this will be the case for programs involving relatively simple, well-defined treatments and for programs that have emerged from extensive work by program developers. (In the latter case, one might say that the formative research had already been done by someone other than the program evaluator.) Although it would be useful to have a theory of evaluation that specifies what research activities should be conducted at various stages of program development, such a theory would have to account for a wide variety of different sequences, and in any case might be premature in its prescriptions.

Nevertheless, we believe that any such theory would include summative evaluation—a rigorous evaluation of the program's effects—at one or more stages in the research sequence for nearly all noteworthy programs. Thus the conduct of randomized experiments and strong quasi-experiments is a critical component (though not the only aspect) of the evaluation enterprise.

Nevertheless, we strongly agree with Cronbach that there is a restricted role in evaluation for the summative use of randomized experiments and strong quasi-experiments. Even if one's current primary goal is causal inference, there is a great need for what we might call "front-end work" prior to summative evaluation. Before a summative evaluation, for example, outcomes must be selected, which will typically involve analysis of program goals, the theory behind a program, and the information needs of different stakeholder groups (Cook et al., 1984). A theory of the program should definitely be developed (Chen and Rossi, 1983; Cronbach et al., 1980) and used to determine whether the program is in a suitable state of development for a summative evaluation (Rutman, 1984). A system should be developed for monitoring treatment delivery (Mark, 1983). These and other front-end tasks are critical for successful summative evaluation, and the relative lack of attention to them in Campbell and Stanley (1963), Cook and Campbell (1976, 1979), and the present chapter should not be taken to mean they are trivial in the conduct of an evaluation. Indeed, we might say that evaluations' major sin of the past has been the premature use of experimentation. The summative use of experiments and strong quasi-experiments depends on extensive prior knowledge, including knowledge that the treatment is well developed and (will be) implemented as planned, measures are well developed, and the ecology of the program setting is well understood.

In short, we agree with much of Cronbach's criticism of a narrow-minded, exclusive allegiance to internal validity and randomized experimentation in evaluation. Nevertheless, there are areas of disagreement—or at least of differential emphasis—between Cronbach's position and our own. First, relative to Cronbach, we seem to see randomized experimentation, or strong quasi-experimentation, as appropriate more often in the series of studies that constitute an evaluation research program. More generally, while we agree with Cronbach that relevance is important, we do not wish to see external validity given general priority over internal validity in the design of evaluations when causal inference is one of the major research goals. To the extent that causal inference is of interest, we prefer to strive for external and construct validity within randomized experiments or the strongest available quasi-experiments. This can be done by conducting an experiment *and* also extensively examining the treatment's effects on heterogeneous, policy-relevant subgroups and by following the other recommendations we have given for enhancing external validity. Further, conducting a summative evaluation does not preclude addressing other evaluation issues. Though Campbell and Stanley (1963) and Cook and Campbell (1976, 1979) do not focus on multipurpose studies, it is possible to examine other research questions in a study designed to obtain valid causal inferences. For example, in a randomized experiment one could also conduct a process analysis (Judd and Kenny, 1981). It is also possible in a summative evaluation to examine whether naturally existing variations in the treatment are associated with differential impact (Cook, 1981). Finally, we believe that relevance in evaluation is best achieved by conducting research programs and by looking for convergence across multiple evaluations. We briefly discuss these strategies at the end of this chapter.

Cronbach (1982; Cronbach et al., 1980) also provides a third, less central criticism of Campbell and Stanley's (1963) and Cook and Campbell's (1976, 1979) emphasis on internal validity and randomized experiments. This criticism is based on the argument that a strong design often is not necessary for reasonable causal inference. For example, Cronbach et al. (1981) state that "when a study is being planned, whoever calls for a no-treatment control bears a burden of proof ,—the burden of making it plausible that practically significant change would occur in the absence of the treatment" (p. 290; also see Cronbach, 1982: 329). We readily acknowledge that all threats to validity are not plausible in all instances. To take an extreme example, the chemist studying the effect of some reagent on iron does not worry about spurious effects due to maturation. In contrast to metals, however, humans are often susceptible to maturation, history, and the other threats. Thus our position, unlike Cronbach et al.'s, is that when an evaluator elects not to use a control group or other design feature that would rule out internal validity threats, the burden of proof is on the evaluator to provide evidence or persuasive argument that the threats are not plausible in the evaluation.

We agree with Cronbach (1982; Cronbach et al., 1980) that simple quasi-experimental designs will sometimes allow for reasonable causal inferences (see the section on quasi-experiments below); however, we believe that in research on human subjects, this should be taken as the exception rather than the rule unless a strong background of knowledge in a particular research area renders particular threats implausible and it has been convincingly demonstrated that change does not occur because of motivation or external events that influence behaviors. Indeed, if costs are not prohibitive, it is wise to rule out deliberately all potential internal validity threats, even if they seem implausible at the onset of the evaluation. For example, even though history might initially seem to be implausible as an alternative interpretation in a given evaluation, evaluators have limited ability to foresee that historical events will not actually occur and affect the major dependent variables of interest.

The richness of Cronbach's (1982; Cronbach et al., 1980) recent writings warrants substantial attention. Regrettably, further discussion is beyond the scope of the present chapter, and we must return to our primary focus on the design of randomized and quasi-experiments.

RANDOMIZED EXPERIMENTS

Randomization can be used for two purposes in research. The first, *random sampling for representativeness*, was described as a method of increasing external validity. By drawing a random sample from a well-designated universe, we can generalize our results from the sample to the universe (within known limits of sampling error). Although the universe usually consists of individuals, it could also be composed of settings (e.g., public social agencies, schools, or hospitals). As noted in a previous section, random sampling for representativeness is a good method of increasing external validity, but it is often impractical.

The second use of randomization, *random assignment for comparability*, is achieved by randomly alloting experimental units to treatments. Random assignment for comparability is the defining characteristic of a randomized experiment. The value of random assignment is that it creates treatment groups that, at the beginning of the experiment, do not differ from each other *on the average* (see Reichardt, 1979). Such comparability rules out most of the internal validity threats listed above. Selection, selection-maturation, and the interactions with selection are ruled out because the groups are similarly constituted, on the average. Because the groups are comparable, maturation will not create spurious between-groups differences. Statistical regression is likewise made implausible by the comparability between groups. Each group should experience the same global pattern of history, so global history cannot create spurious difference between groups. If standard practices of research methods are followed, the groups will be assessed similarly, so that instrumentation is not a plausible threat. Therefore, few alternative explanations of posttest differences between groups are plausible—certainly fewer than with quasi-experiments where the researcher must consider explicitly all the relevant internal validity threats and then rule them out one by one.

Despite these advantages, planning a randomized experiment will not necessarily lead to a successful summative evaluation. Several problems can beset randomized experiments. In particular, (1) the program planners and staff may resist randomization as a means of allocating greatments; (2) the randomization process may not be carried out correctly, resulting in nonequivalent experimental groups; (3) random assignment may break down because different kinds of persons may refuse to participate in or may drop out of the different treatment groups; and (4) assignment to treatments may create a focused inequity because some treatments are more desirable than others, and this inequity may cause reactions that are falsely interpreted as treatment effects. We now discuss each of these four difficulties in turn, detailing ways in which they can sometimes be overcome.

RESISTANCE TO RANDOMIZATION

Sometimes resistance to random assignment among program sponsors or personnel threatens the successful implementation of a randomized experiment. Because resistance to randomization is a potential source of difficulty, it is useful to consider its causes and remedies. In addition, considering resistance to random assignment highlights some of the factors an evaluator should consider in deciding whether a summative evaluation with a randomized experiment is appropriate.

There are two common reasons why program sponsors and personnel may object to the use of randomization for treatment assignment. One is the belief that the treatment should not be withheld from *any* potential recipient. Resistance based on the belief that the treatment should not be withheld from the controls is fairly common, particularly if the treatment promises to be ameliorative in some way. In some cases, such resistance can be overcome by comparing one type of treatment, such as individual counseling, with another, such as group counseling. This obviously does away with the need for a no-treatment group and is useful when an evaluation of the relative merits of alternative treatments is appropriate. (But see our discussion below of evaluations without a no-treatment control group.) Alternatively, units might be assigned not to a no-treatment control, but to a "waiting list" control. The waiting list control group members serve as a control group for the treatment group and will later receive the treatment. This may satisfy the ethical concern that a potentially ameliorative treatment should not be withheld from eligible units, and it also allows a quasi-experimental replication by observing control group members after they receive the treatment. However, being on a waiting list may in itself be a sort of treatment and the treatment control contrast thus affected in complex ways. In other cases, resources are not sufficient to provide the treatment to all who want or need it. In such circumstances, a good case can be made that the lottery (i.e., randomization) is the most ethical principle of distribution, especially when the positive impact of the resource is not definitely known and the possibility of negative side effects cannot be ruled out. Moreover, in evaluations of pilot programs, a case can often be made that additional resources are more likely to be allocated in the future if valid, unambiguous evidence is provided regarding the effectiveness of the treatment—and such unambiguous evidence, we hold, is more likely to be obtained in a randomized experiment.

A second, related source of resistance to random assignment is the belief that a more appropriate criterion for allocation, such as need or merit, is available and should be used instead of random assignment. This point of view assumes that merit, need, or whatever the preferred criterion is can be explicated and can also be measured validly. To the extent that these conditions are met, random assignment may not be appropriate. Further, in the rare case where entry into the program is based strictly on some measured eligibility criterion, unbiased estimates of a treatment effect can often be obtained; see Cook and Campbell (1979), Reichardt (1979), Cronbach (1982), and Trochim (1982) for discussion of the so-called regression discontinuity design and its limitations. But to the extent that the merit or the need criterion is not used strictly for program assignment, it will be difficult to arrive at a causal inference that can be held as confidently as the inference that random assignment would have allowed. Recognition of the imperfection that follows from imperfect, poorly understood assignment processes may allow us to institute a randomized experiment, especially over that part of the range of program eligibility where uncertainty about assignment is greatest.

For example, a school district may wish to institute and evaluate a program designed to improve poor reading skills. A randomized experiment might be opposed on the grounds that admission to the program should be based on need as indexed by low scores on reading tests. All may agree that the very lowest scorers most deserve to enter the treatment. But there may be a range of children, all of whom need the program and whose scores are sufficiently similar that we are unsure who is neediest. Some such uncertainty is inevitable given that the measure of need is not perfectly reliable. Therefore, if the program has a limited number of openings, the neediest children could be admitted and a randomized experiment conducted using children in the range of need about which uncertainty exists. This randomized experiment would have limited external validity because participants come from a narrow range of need. However, conclusions about the program should be based on the pattern of results that emerges from the randomized experiment and from a quasi-experimental analysis using all children who receive the treatment.

Resistance to random assignment is generally based on the assumption that a treatment is beneficial. Thus resistance is sometimes reduced by pointing out that this is an assumption, and that similar assumptions about effectiveness have been incorrect in the past for other programs. However, in some instances the presumption of effectiveness might be unshakably powerful among all parties interested in the program. In such cases, one must ask whether a summative evaluation—including one that was carried out successfully and demonstrated no effect—would carry any weight in future decisions about the program. It might be more useful to forego a summative evaluation for extensive formative research. A similar course of action might also be considered when a program is universally endorsed by decision makers because of its symbolic value—that is, because it demonstrates concern for a particular social problem (Cronbach et al., 1980). Of course, one could alternatively argue that in such instances, if a well-conducted summative evaluation reveals that the program is ineffective, the result might be efforts to develop some alternative and perhaps more effective program.

When resistance to random assignment is expected or encountered, the evaluator may need to adopt the role of teacher. In this role, the evaluator will explain the nature and purpose of random assignment and illustrate its successful use and its value in ruling out threats to causal inference. Concrete, understandable examples will help, as will endorsement of random assignment by respected figures.

Sometimes, however, expressed resistance to random assignment may be a symptom of a more general resistance to rigorous evaluation. Such general resistance may be assuaged by developing good relations with program staff, involving interested parties in the planning stages of the evaluation, describing the potential value of evaluation for service delivery, and showing that the evaluation outcome does not threaten anyone's job security. Alternatively, the general resistance to summative evaluation might derive from the belief that a new program is not sufficiently established for rigorous testing of its effects. For this and other reasons, the evaluator who encounters widespread resistance to random assignment might profitably consider whether those voicing resistance have a valid case. If the answer is yes, random assignment of all perspective program participants may be inappropriate. Instead, random assignment might be replaced with a regression-discontinuity design, or random assignment might be restricted to a narrow range of eligibility, or summative evaluation might be delayed until formative research has been conducted.

Our comments should not be taken to imply that random assignment is generally inappropriate, or that resistance to random assignment inevitably imples that some alternative is preferable. Resistance to random assignment may sometimes be based on misconceptions that the evaluator should attempt to correct.

FAULTY RANDOM ASSIGNMENT

Procedural difficulties in randomizing. Random assignment is a procedure that ensures that each experimental unit has a known (and usually equal) chance of receiving a given treatment. In some cases randomization fails because of correctable flaws in the method of assignment. For example, in the 1969 military draft lottery, slips with the dates of the year were placed, in order from January 1 to December 31, into an urn from which they were then drawn. The urn was not adequately shaken, and the dates put in last tended to be drawn out first. As a result, men born later in the year had a higher chance of being drafted (Feinberg, 1971; Notz et al., 1971). Such problems are easily solved by consulting references that describe how to randomize correctly, such as Reicken and Boruch (1974).

Randomization sometimes breaks down because the personnel responsible for implementing the procedure do not fully complete their task. Often the job of processing applicants to a program falls to organizational staff or to temporary help, and these individuals may not be committed to systematic, random assignment. Processors may therefore deviate from random assignment to satisfy their personal conception of how selection should take place, or merely to satisfy "difficult" applicants who are particularly vocal in their desire to receive a certain treatment. Such well-meaning sabotage can usually be prevented by instituting randomization systems that are difficult to circumvent. For example, one can use a simple two-step randomization procedure, in which (1) the individual who processes applicants takes all of the needed information, and (2) applicants are subsequently assigned to conditions by someone who is unaware of the applicants' identity (see Conner, 1977, Reicken and Boruch, 1974). Regardless of whether this or some other system is used to reduce deviations from random assignment, the randomization process should be monitored carefully.

Sampling variability and the number and level of aggregation of units. Sometimes a treatment is delivered to aggregate units much larger than an individual. For example, a new computerized educational aid might be randomly assigned to some school districts, with other school districts serving as a no-treatment control group. Such decisions are sometimes made because of an interest in aggregate units, somethings for practical reasons, and also are often made to reduce respondents' awareness of other experimental conditions. (Such an awareness can lead to serious difficulties, which we shall discuss later.) However, the use of larger aggregate units typically results in fewer units for assignment to each treatment, and the random assignment of fewer but larger units is less likely to result in comparable groups.

One solution to this problem is to match or block units on variables that theory, prior research, or common sense indicate correlate with the primary dependent variable. Members of these matched sets are then assigned randomly to conditions. Pretest measures of the dependent variable are particularly desirable for such matching. (Matching or blocking prior to random assignment is useful even if a large number of cases are available.) An alternative (albeit rather mundane-sounding) approach is to use a larger number of smaller experiment units. For example, rather than assigning school districts, we might assign schools or classrooms to receive the new educational technology.

A third approach is to assign units to alternative treatments. For example, one group of schools might be assigned to use the new technology for mathematics instruction and the other schools to use it for reading instruction. If it is feasible that transfer is small (i.e., that improvement in math does not lead to improvement in reading and vice versa), the schools could serve as controls for each other. Another useful strategy is to implement a time-series design if possible. This strategy is particularly useful when one expects the treatment effect to build up over time.

TREATMENT-RELATED LOSS OF PARTICIPANTS

Treatment-related refusals. Sometimes experimental units will be assigned randomly to conditions and some units will choose not to receive the treatment selected for them. For example, Meyer and Borgatta (1959) studied the effectiveness of a particular method of rehabilitating individuals hospitalized with psychiatric disorders. The treatment was conducted at a live-in workshop in which the patients were expected to live for a year. Understandably, many people chose not to receive this assigned treatment, and only about a third of the assigned experimental subjects actually entered the program. Treatment-related refusals to receive the assigned treatment creates groups that, on the average, are composed of different kinds of individuals. The result is a selection problem that makes it difficult to interpret relations between the treatment and any of the dependent variables.

Self-selection is most likely to lead to treatment-related refusal if the treatments differ intrinsically in attractiveness, as in the case with guaranteed income experiments that offer guarantees of, say, $12,000 versus $3,600. Treatment-related bias in who enters treatment groups can also arise from processes other than self-selection. For example, there may be pressures to ensure that certain individuals (e.g., friends of the project director) receive a particular treatment.

Treatment-related attrition. Even though random assignment to treatments may be implemented successfully, program participants can still differentially drop out of a program before an evaluation is completed. This is especially a problem in longitudinal research where participants in different treatments perceive differential costs and gains associated with their participation. For instance, after a three-year period, attrition in the New Jersey Negative Income Tax Experiment ranged from 25.3% in the control condition to 6.5% in the highest payment condition. In a randomized experiment, differential attrition is itself interpretable as a treatment effect. Sometimes this can be of interest, as when evaluating a program designed to increase retention in college (Mark and Romano, 1982). More frequently, attrition will not be of great interest as an outcome variable. In any case, treatment-related attrition results in groups that differ in their composition, so posttest differences on any other outcome are difficult to interpret.

Possible solutions. Several methods exist for dealing with the problem of treatment-related refusals and attrition. Some of these involve actions that can be taken *prior to* an evaluation, to reduce the likelihood of treatment-related loss of participants. For example, pressures to provide some individuals with a certain treatment might be foreseen. If so, then the selective assignment should be monitored and the persons who benefit from it dropped from the study, although not from getting the treatment. This effectively redefines the experimental population, and random assignment is restricted to persons in the refined population.

Careful consideration prior to an evaluation can also help identify some sources of differential cost or reward to participants that can be dealt with quite simply. For instance, Hudson (1969) wanted to evaluate the effects of an autotelic teaching device that was located miles from where his respondents lived. To alleviate the potential attrition of the treatment group members, who had to travel to the machine (control group members did not), he simply provided them with transportation to the device. Another related way in which the problem of treatment-related loss of partcipants can be minimized is by adding inducements to participate in the less desirable treatment groups. In some cases, we may simply offer to pay those who are in less desirable groups for their cooperation.

Another strategy for avoiding treatment-related loss is to assign participants to alternative treatments, rather than having some people in a no-treatment control group. To the extent that the different treatments are perceived as equally attractive, differential refusal and attrition should be alleviated. Designs employing alternative treatments are often feasible. For instance, Atkinson (1968) studied the effects of computer-assisted instruction (CAI) by having children randomly assigned to CAI either in math or in English. Each group was tested on both math and English, so that the English scores of children receiving math instruction provided a no-treatment baseline for English instruction, and the math scores of children receiving English instruction served as a control for the math course. Alternatively, one can imagine situations where persons are assigned to one form of psychotherapy versus another, with everyone receiving some sort of treatment.

There are limitations to evaluations that compare alternative treatments aimed at the same problem (e.g., alternative forms of psychotherapy). One is that the alternative treatments may address somewhat different outcomes (e.g., Therapy A might focus primarily on self-esteem and Therapy B on a specific behavioral problem). Thus the issue arises whether measures should be tailored to each treatment's particular focus or should be aimed at their common focus. (It is probably best to do both if possible.)

Even if this problem is solved or does not arise because the alternative treatments address the same outcomes, there is a second problem with designs offering alternative treatments to all participants: We can assess the effectiveness of the treatments relative to one another, but we cannot readily assess how effective they are relative to no treatment. This is particularly problematic if the treatments are in fact equally effective (or equally harmful), for without a no-treatment control group the common effect of each treatment would go undetected. Thus it is important to try to establish what a no-treatment baseline would be when using a design in which all units receive a treatment. Methods other than a no-treatment control group are available for achieving this. The most desirable, but not necessarily the most available, is to use a pretreatment time series, as opposed to a single pretreatment measure, to estimate the no-treatment baseline. One can also resort to one of the cohort strategies that we outline later in the section on quasi-experimental designs.

Another strategy for reducing treatment-related loss of participants is to redefine the population from which random assignment is made. The question of how to define the population from which random assignment occurs is a difficult one involving issues of internal validity, external validity, and ethics. Reicken and Boruch (1974) discuss three alternative time points at which random assignment could occur: (1) as soon as the pool of available and eligible units has been identified, irrespective of whether participants agree to receive a treatment or be measured; (2) when units have agreed to participate with all the measurement activities of the study even though they have not agreed to receive a treatment; and (3) when the units have agreed beforehand to participate in the evaluation and to be in any treatment condition to which they might be assigned.

Randomization at the first time point presents the greatest threat to internal validity. This is because the participants have made no commitments and so the potential treatment-correlated dropouts have not been identified. However, assignment at this point may present the smallest limit to external validity, given that all of the available units are included in the study and the population is not redefined away from the population of initial research interest. However, generalizability is limited to the range of persons represented in the evaluation when it ends, so external validity may be limited by the loss of participants in studies that randomize at this time point.

Random assignment at the third, latest time point should most reduce the treatment-related loss of participants and is ethically satisfying, in that participants are fully informed about the evaluation's treatments and measurement demands. However, the participants' awareness of all conditions may lead to other problems. For example, the controls may react to inequities caused by the fact that they receive less than others, and these reactions could lead the researcher to make false interpretations of treatment effects. (Reactions to such focused inequities will be discussed later.) Further, generalization is limited to volunteers. On the other hand, the third alternative, in addition to being ethically satisfying, is desirable when a few aggregate units (e.g., schools or neighborhoods) are to be studied because the loss of even a few units would be serious. This alternative is also feasible when alternative treatments are being compared, as this will likely facilitate agreement to participate in any condition of the evaluation.

The second alternative strikes a middle ground between the other positions and is often preferable. In many instances, individuals will be continuing in the measurement framework naturally, as is often the case in educational or judicial settings, or they will agree to meet the study's measurement demands for small financial rewards.

As this discussion indicates, many practical and ethical concerns affect the decision about when to randomize. The evaluator must be sensitive to the particular issues in the evaluation at hand, weigh the trade-offs, and select the option that seems best in that case.

Despite the best precautions, some level of refusal and attrition is likely in an evaluation, especially if the program is of long duration. The question then arises whether the loss is treatment-related, for if it is not, the groups would still be comparable. There are three primary methods of inspecting for differential loss of participants. The first, and simplest, is to test whether the percentage of lost units differs across treatment groups. Equal loss rates suggest that refusal and attrition are not treatment-related, but this is not conclusive: Different *kinds* of people may have elected out of each treatment group. To illustrate this, imagine an effective ameliorative program for poor people. Members of a no-treatment control group might drop out because they could not afford to pay their rent and were forced to move, whereas experimental group members might drop out because they benefited from the treatment and moved on to better jobs or better apartments. Therefore, a second test of differential loss involves examining the *reasons* for loss, either by direct measures of the reason for refusal or attrition or, when these are not available, by informed speculation.

The third method of analyzing for treatment-related loss requires data collected prior to the treatment, and is generally more useful in testing for differential attrition than for differential refusals. The data to be examined will usually and most usefully be pretest data, but they may also be covariates or demographic information. Jurs and Glass (1971) discuss the analysis of pretest data for detecting differential attrition. Stated simply, they suggest that treatment-related loss is indicated by a condition (e.g., treatment versus control) × attrition status (still in the experiment at posttest versus dropped out) interaction, when analyzing *pretest* scores. Such an interaction in pretest scores would indicate that the units that dropped out of the experimental groups were initially different from those dropping out of the control. If sample size is insufficient for the analysis, Jurs and Glass (1971) suggest that an alternative analysis can be performed. This involves comparing the pretest data of experimentals and controls who provided posttest data. If such an analysis reveals a significant difference, differential attrition is indicated. An analysis of pretest data is particularly useful because it provides an estimate of the degree of bias created by attrition. Though not a perfect estimate, it provides a useful starting point in the analyses of an evaluation in which differential attrition has occurred. For this reason, a pretest should be considered essential in any evaluation employing random assignment.

Having determined that treatment-related loss occurred, the researcher must rely on post hoc data analysis strategies. One approach is to conduct the statistical analysis using all of the individuals who were assigned to a particular treatment group, even if some of them did not in fact receive the treatment. Thus to go back to the earlier example of the live-in workshop rehabilitation treatment, the strategy would involve including in the treatment group data from all who were assigned to that group, whether they attended the live-in workshop or not. Analyzing the data in this way is possible only when people self-select out of the treatment but do not leave the measurement framework and so provide posttest information. This situation occurs, for instance, in evaluations of judicial innovations, in which those on trial might select out of the treatment but still provide information about trial disposition.

Including in the analysis all the persons who dropped out is conservative and will tend to underestimate the program's effects because the analysis includes in the treatment group persons who received little or none of the treatment. However, omitting from the analysis persons who did not get the treatment will introduce a selection bias that might result in spurious differences. The issue is as follows: Which is preferable, a statistically conservative test with no bias or a statistically more powerful test with bias? Of course, one can and should do both analyses, one including the persons who did not actually receive their assigned treatment and another omitting them. If the analyses produce comparable results, causal inference is easy. If they do not, great caution is called for in drawing conclusions, particularly from the analysis that omits individuals, since selection biases have probably been introduced.

Another post hoc approach is to inspect the data to see if randomization has remained intact in some subgroups while not in others. For example, in evaluations that are conducted at several sites, the randomization may have broken down in some places but not in others, or it may have broken down with some age, gender, or race groups but not others. If subgroups are found for which random assignment did not break down, the data from them may be analyzed as coming from an internally valid randomized experiment. Cook et al. (1975) conducted a post hoc examination of the data for this purpose in their reanalysis of the Ball and Bogatz (1970) and Bogatz and Ball (1971) evaluations of *Sesame Street*. Cook et al. discovered that randomization had remained intact at some experimental sites but not at others, and the data analysis centered on sites where random assignment held up.

This strategy of searching for intact subgroups has two limitations. First, it requires focusing on a subset of the data and will therefore have reduced statistical power and limited external validity. Thus this strategy should generally be used in conjunction with quasi-experimental analyses that use all of the data but have lesser internal validity. By inspecting both the randomized experiment on a subset of respondents and a quasi-experimental analysis of all the data, one will emerge with clearer information about cause and about the level of confidence that is appropriate in one's conclusions. The use of a multiple analysis strategy is also important to avoid capitalizing on a second problem with the intact subgroup approach. The problem is that in examining multiple subgroups, the subgroup with apparent pretest comparability may simply appear comparable by chance, and thus posttest differences would appear in this subgroup by statistical regression. This problem is minimized by the judicious examination of meaningful subgroups and by reliance on a multiple analysis strategy.

The two data analysis strategies we have discussed for dealing with treatment-related loss of participants both involve quasi-experimental analyses as part of a multiple analysis approach. In addition, in some evaluations, a quasi-experimental approach will be the only available one, because dropouts will not remain in the measurement framework and there will not be intact subgroups. Some critics of randomized evaluations argue that because differential refusals or attrition may reduce a randomized experiment to a quasi-experimental analysis, beginning with a quasi-experiment would be equally as good as implementing a randomized experiment. We disagree for two reasons. First, the bias from treatment-related loss will generally be less than the bias in an alternative quasi-experimental design. Second, by analyzing pretest data, one can roughly estimate the bias due to treatment-related loss in a randomized experiment, whereas the bias in a quasi-experiment will be unknown to a far greater extent.

VARIATION IN TREATMENT IMPLEMENTATION

We have already discussed the problem of some participants not receiving the planned treatment to which they were assigned. A related problem occurs when program participants have the ability to determine how much of a treatment they wish to receive. For instance, in a test of an individualized counseling program for individuals newly on welfare, the number of face-to-face therapy contacts ranged from 1 to 129, with a median of 15; the number of telephone and mail contacts ranged from none to 81, with a median of 9.5 (Mullen et al., 1972). Thus exposure to the treatment ranged from no more than one initial face-to-face contact that was required of everyone to a rather high level of contact. Variability in exposure to the treatment is not necessarily due to self-selection by respondents. It can also occur because the people responsible for implementing the treatment (e.g., caseworkers, teachers, or counselors) differ in the degree to which they are available to individual respondents or to their caseload in general. Further, the persons implementing a treatment may differ in how well they conduct that treatment when contact occurs, or the quality and level of treatment implementation may vary from site to site.

Standardization of the treatment delivery, extensive training of those responsible for delivering the treatment, encouraging participants to have high levels of treatment exposure, and continued monitoring of all of these can greatly reduce the problem of heterogeneity in treatment implementation. Nonetheless, if such heterogeneity occurs despite these precautions, the best strategy is to perform an analysis analogous to the conservative analysis just discussed. That is, one should simply treat all those assigned to the treatment group as though they had received the (fixed) level of the treatment to which they were originally assigned. But to complement this analysis, a quasi-experimental analysis should also be conducted that relies on stratifying individuals according to the length or intensity of their exposure to the treatment.

However, the quasi-experimental analysis will include bias of unknown direction and magnitude. Thus it must be interpreted cautiously, unless the causes of treatment-related loss are well known and well measured, in which case these causes can be included in the quasi-experimental analysis (Mark, 1983).

REACTIONS TO THE FOCUSED INEQUITY CAUSED BY RANDOMIZATION

The implementation of a randomized experiment creates inequities between groups, particularly when a desirable treatment is compared to a no-treatment control group. If respondents and others involved in an evaluation become aware of this inequity, their reactions may cause spurious differences or obscure true differences between the treatment and control groups. Cook and Campbell (1976, 1979) describe four types of reactions to the inequity caused by the differential desirability of experimental conditions.

Diffusion or imitation of the treatment. Diffusion or imitation of the treatment occurs when members of the less desirable group (e.g., the no-treatment control group) become aware of the other treatment (or treatments) and gain exposure to the more desirable treatment. Such exposure reduces the planned contrast between experiments and controls and hence tends to obscure true treatment effects. For example, a caseworker whose colleague is administering some experimental counseling technique may learn of the technique and employ it with his or her control group clients. Or the intended no-*Sesame Street* controls might spontaneously tune into the show given its popularity (Ball and Bogatz, 1970).

In addition, control groups members will sometimes receive the treatment because of legal, ethical, or public relations considerations. For instance, in a randomized evaluation of the effectiveness of pretrial conferences between clients and their lawyers (Rosenberg, 1964), the treatment group had mandatory pretrial conferences, whereas controls were only asked to forego the conference. For ethical and legal reasons they could not be denied the right to the treatment, and over half of those assigned to the control group elected to have the experimental conference.

Compensatory equalization of treatments. Given the perception of unequal treatment of experimental groups, an administrator, perhaps under pressure from members of the less desirable group, may distribute other similar resources at his or her disposal in such a way as to equalize treatment groups. Consider, for example, an experiment in a social work agency to evaluate the effects of a reduced caseload. In this example an administrator might act so as to reduce the workload of control group members in other ways, to avoid a focused inequity between workers in the agency. Such an administrative response is most likely when the administrator is not deeply committed to the evaluation and anticipates or experiences vocal dissatisfaction about the differential treatment from members of the control group. Compensatory equalization, like diffusion or imitation of the treatment, tends to obscure any true treatment effects.

Compensatory rivalry. Those in a no-treatment control group sometimes learn that they are not receiving a treatment but that others are. Such awareness can sometimes motivate control group members to become competitive (i.e., to alter their behavior so that their group is not outperformed). Such a compensatory rivalry is most likely, first, if existing groups, such as intact work units, are assigned to a control condition while nearby work units receive the treatment and, second, if those in the control group stand to lose something if the treatment proves effective. As an example, Saretsky (1972) cites the

OEO Performance Contracting Experiment, which contrasted the performance of traditionally taught students with that of students taught by contractors who were paid according to the amount of improvement in students' test scores. Saretsky reasoned that the traditional teachers may have perceived that if the outside contractors were found to be more effective, their own job security would be threatened. As Saretsky (1972) notes, teachers of control group students could deal with this threat by doing an atypically good job of teaching in the year of the experiment, which would decrease the possibility of the experimentals performing the controls at the posttest.

Resentful demoralization of participants receiving less desirable treatments. The knowledge that others are in a more favorable treatment group will sometimes lead to resentment and demoralization, rather than to compensatory rivalry. Imagine an attempt to assess the effect of a special recreational program on the coping of depressed adolescents. The depressed youths in the no-treatment control group might observe the treatment that others receive, feel relatively deprived, and become even more depressed. If so, any posttest differences between groups would not really be due to the beneficial effects of the treatment, but rather to the resentment or demoralization of the control. Resentful demoralization, then, is likely to lead to pseudo-effects.

Solutions. Diffusion or imitation of the treatment, compensatory equalization, compensatory rivalry, and resentful demoralization are not ruled out by random assignment, unlike the threats to internal validity discussed earlier. As a result, in designing and conducting an evaluation one must attempt to minimize the likelihood of these four threats. One way to do so is to minimize the obtrusiveness of the experiment. A related strategy is to isolate experimental units from each other and to prevent them and other involved parties (e.g., administrators who could undertake compensatory equalization) from communicating about the experiment with each other. Individuals cannot react to a focused inequity if they are unaware of it. The isolation of experimental units will typically involve the use of fewer, larger units that do not regularly communicate with each other (e.g., using geographically separated schools rather than students from the same school). Sometimes, of course, it is not possible to prevent knowledge of the focused inequity. For example, in the Follow Through program it would have been impossible to prevent school district administrators from knowing that an experimental program had been implemented in one of their schools; thus no attempts to avoid knowledge of the inequity could have prevented administrators from compensating the no-treatment control schools with supplementary Title I funds.

Another important means of avoiding compensatory equalization, as well as diffusion or imitation, is by monitoring treatment implementation carefully. Data from the treatment monitoring system or from an implementation study are also useful for assessing, after the evaluation is completed, whether the four threats are plausible. Informal, qualitative observations may also be of assistance. Pretest data, particularly time-series data of the controls, is an additional aid in determining whether one of these four problems occurred. If imitation of the treatment, compensatory rivalry, or compensatory equalization occurred, then the control group should deviate markedly from its pretreatment no-cause baseline. If it does deviate, then these threats are rendered all the more plausible. If it does not deviate, then it is less likely that something atypical happened in the control group. Even a small number of pretest observations can be valuable in providing a reasonable estimate of what a no-cause baseline would be. Thus in the performance-contracting experiment, Saretsky (1972) sought to demonstrate that control students showed more annual improvement on standardized achievement tests during the experimental year than had their cohorts in two earlier years. Such evidence would strengthen the contention that compensatory rivalry may have occurred.

The researcher can also search for additional data from units that were not in the experiment but that are similar to the control units; again, time-series data are preferable. For instance, in the performance-contracting experiment we might retrieve data from classes that were similar to the control classes. If we were to find that these other classes registered the same achievement gain in the year of the experiment as in previous years, this would be quite consistent with the interpretation that compensatory rivalry arose among the control teachers and classes.

PUTTING THE DIFFICULTIES OF RANDOMIZED EXPERIMENTS INTO PERSPECTIVE

The preceding discussion of the difficulty of randomized experiments might make the reader wonder: If there are so many problems with implementing random assignment in evaluations, why not aim for a quasi-experimental design in the first place? A reply to this question might include several points. First, the problems that occur with random assignment are often manageable, provided they have been identified in advance and ways of overcoming them have been considered. Second, most of the problems that occur with randomized experiments can also occur with quasi-experiments. For example, members of control groups in quasi-experiments can also become aware of more desirable treatments, thereby experiencing resentment or demoralization. Attrition can occur in quasi-experiments as well as in randomized experiments. Third, our discussion has highlighted threats to validity in a self-conscious way that may inadvertently suggest that greater bias generally arises when a randomized experiment breaks down than arises with feasible, alternative quasi-experiments. Our firmly held opinion is quite the opposite. The bias that arises when an implemented randomized experiment breaks down will nearly always be less than the bias arising from the systematic self-selection and recruitment biases that characterize the treatment assignment processes in most planned or ex post facto quasi-experiments. Further, we can usually estimate much better the degree of bias in a randomized experiment that breaks down than in a quasi-experiment, and thus can arrive at more confident, better estimates of treatment effects.

QUASI-EXPERIMENTS

Sometimes randomized experiments are not feasible for summative evaluations. It may be unpractical or unethical to assign units at random. A program might be made universally available, precluding assignment to conditions. An evaluation might begin after units have already been assigned to conditions. For these or other reasons, an evaluation might not be able to implement a randomized experiment. In such circumstances, a quasi-experiment will have to be used for a summative evaluation. In a quasi-experiment, assignment to conditions is not random and usually occurs because units self-select into treatments or are assigned to treatments by officials or project personnel. The major problem with quasi-experiments is that, in general, the nonrandom assignment makes it more difficult to rule out internal validity threats and hence to draw strong causal inferences. However, the design of a quasi-experiment can rule out internal validity threats, and thus there are design features that can enhance one's ability to draw a less ambiguous causal inference.

Our primary focus in this section is on various quasi-experimental designs and their susceptibility to internal validity threats. Although not our primary focus, we will also comment on the role of theory, common sense, and supplementary data in ruling out threats to internal validity.

THE ONE-GROUP, POSTTEST-ONLY DESIGN

Imagine an evaluation in which a measure of the outcome is administered to individuals after they have received the treatment. Consider a new recreational program designed to decrease the number of fights in a home for delinquent youths. If the program were implemented and the only measure was a posttest assessment of fighting, one would have no real notion of the program's effect. The best that could be done would be to make subjective estimates of the level of fighting that would occur without the program. Typically this would involve trying to recall the level of pretreatment fighting. Of course, there is no guarantee that one's recollection of the pretest level of fighting would be very accurate. The underlying problem is that inference is comparative, and it is impossible to state whether a lone posttest observation represents a treatment effect when there is nothing with which to compare it.

Having said that, we can point out that there are very special circumstances in which the one-group, posttest-only design may allow reasonable causal inference. One is when background theory and knowledge give us confidence about what the outcome should be in the absence of a treatment effect. The chemist who studies the effect of a reagent on a chemical compound may need only a posttest observation, because theory and years of study of the compound allow the chemist to assume confidently what the level of the dependent variable will be in the absence of a treatment effect. Thus background knowledge suffices for the comparison standard against which the posttest can be judged. Unfortunately, most social variables are neither so well known nor so stable across time and respondent groups that background knowledge will suffice.

A related circumstance involves an extension of the design to multiple outcome variables. If the expected relative level of each outcome is reasonably well known, and the treatment is expected

events that operate in one institution but not in the other, such as a staff change in only the home receiving the program. Selection-attrition could also be a plausible threat. In fact, all of the problems we described in the context of randomized experiments can beset this design (with the obvious exception of difficulties in implementing random assignment).

Some of the threats to the pretest-posttest nonequivalent groups design can be addressed using techniques we describe elsewhere in this chapter. Further, sometimes threats can be rendered implausible based on substantive knowledge of a research area; for example, selection-maturation may be unlikely when studying a program designed to train computer skills to adult residents of isolated African villages. The particular pattern of outcomes achieved in a study also affects the plausibility of particular threats. For instance, instrumentation explanations are implausible if one obtains a disordinal interaction (i.e., a crossover interaction that graphs like an X); for further consideration of the plausibility of threats given different outcome patterns, see Cook and Campbell (1979). Of course, it is unwise to assume in advance that the results will fall into a particular pattern.

The final factor that affects whether one can obtain unbiased estimates of the treatment effect is the type of statistical analysis one applies. It is impossible to discuss the analysis of the pretest-posttest nonequivalent groups design in this chapter; the interested reader may wish to consult Reichardt (1979), Cronbach et al. (1977), Bryk (1980), Cronbach (1982), and Stromsdorfer and Farkas (1980: Section I). We wish merely to point out that, in general, one cannot specify a single analysis that will control perfectly for selection-related problems. Rather, the most reasonable strategy is to conduct multiple analyses. Cook and Campbell (1979), Cronbach et al. (1977, 1980), Reichardt (1979, 1983), and others have suggested that multiple analyses be conducted to bracket the unknown effect size. Reichardt (1983) uses the term "plausibility bracket" to refer to the resulting range of estimates. Like a traditional confidence interval, a plausibility bracket would, by taking into account the plausible magnitude of bias, indicate the range within which the true treatment effect most likely falls. Unfortunately, as Reichardt notes, there is no well-developed logic for creating plausibility brackets like that underlying the estimation of confidence intervals. Until such a logic or rationale is developed, multiple analyses should be performed, but we will be uncertain about how well and how tightly they bracket the true effect.

One of the advantages of implementing a randomized experiment is that even if random assignment breaks down, and one must consider the final design a pretest-posttest nonequivalent groups quasi-experiment, it will be possible to estimate the degree of bias introduced by random attrition and our plausibility bracket will generally be smaller and allow more confident inferences.

COHORTS AS CONTROLS

Many formal institutions regularly graduate one group of persons to another level of the institution, or out of the institution. Schools are an obvious example as children advance from one grade to another. In addition, less formal advancement also occurs—for instance, as in the family where children follow each other. By "cohorts," we mean groups of units that follow each other through formal institutions (e.g., schools) or informal institutions (e.g., families). Cohort groups can be useful controls in quasi-experiments because they tend to be similar in background characteristics. As an example, one might use cohorts in an educational evaluation to determine whether the third-grade class that received a special reading program showed more improvement in reading scores than did the previous third-year class, which did not receive the program.

In this as in many studies using cohorts, the major threat is history. In the example of an educational evaluation, one group could have been subject to different experiences during its third-grade year than the other group during its third-grade year. One of the best ways to control for history is to divide pairs of cohorts according to the length of exposure to the treatment. Dividing according to the length of treatment exposure is easy to do for the experimentals, but how does one do it for control cohorts that preceded the treatments? Sometimes the answer is obvious, as when the cohorts are siblings. For example, to study the effects of *Sesame Street* after its first seasons, one could pair siblings together and classify sibling pairs by the number of hours the younger sibling spent watching *Sesame Street*. This strategy controls for history because a treatment effect should be stronger for the experimentals most exposed to the treatment, whereas there is no reason why history should result in this difference. While controlling for history, partitioning cohorts according to exposure to the treatment will not necessarily rule out all the other threats, in particular selection: Respondents who self-select to highest level of treatment exposure may be those who differ more from their matched cohort. (For extended discussion of this strategy, see Cook et al., 1975; and see Cook and Campbell, 1979, for further discussion of the use of cohorts.)

NONEQUIVALENT DEPENDENT VARIABLES

It is sometimes possible to specify, along with the dependent variables in which we are principally interested, some other dependent variables that (a) should not be affected by the treatment but (b) would be affected if some plausible alternative (such as history or maturation) had affected the principal dependent variables. For example, a state might implement a program designed to reduce drunk driving and assess its effect with a one-group, pretest-posttest design. A nonequivalent dependent variable strategy might be implemented to rule out the explanation that any observed effect might be due not to the program but to history (e.g., a change in miles driven because of a gas shortage), maturation (e.g., a long-term decline in fatality rates), or some other threat. In this example, the nonequivalent dependent variable strategy could involve examining both alcohol-related fatalities and alcohol-unrelated fatalities. If history, maturation, or some other threat were operating, we would generally expect both alcohol-related and alcohol-unrelated fatalities to change. In contrast, if the program, and not some alternative threat, were causing changes, we would expect a decrease in alcohol-related fatalities but not in alcohol-unrelated fatalities.

The usefulness of nonequivalent dependent variables depends on selecting a dependent variable that *should not* be affected by the treatment but *should* be affected by most plausible alternative causal agents. It therefore requires a strong initial theory. Moreover, this strategy requires accepting the null hypothesis that the nonequivalent dependent variable has not changed. Thus one must be particularly concerned about ceiling or basement effects, unreliability, and other measurement problems that would prevent the nonequivalent dependent variable from demonstrating any true effect. The usefulness of nonequivalent dependent variables therefore increases if each outcome is assessed by multiple operations. Finally, the use of nonequivalent dependent variables presupposes that there will be no generalization from the primary outcome (in which one expects change) to the secondary, control outcome. If there is generalization—and remember that the design calls for similar dependent variables—then each outcome measure will be affected and no causal inference will be drawn even though a causal change could have occurred.

These problems suggest that nonequivalent dependent variables are best used not as the most basic feature of an evaluation, but rather as an adjunct to other features, such as a no-treatment control, or cohort groups, or a time series. For example, the anti-drunk-driving program described above could be evaluated better by adding a control state and by observing both dependent variables in time-series form. Further, the usefulness of nonequivalent dependent variables increases as more specific predictions are made about more dependent variables.

REGRESSION-DISCONTINUITY DESIGN

As noted in our discussion of randomized experiments, commitment to some allocative principle such as need or merit sometimes precludes the use of random assignment. In such cases, a regression-discontinuity design can sometimes be used to make relatively confident causal inferences. This design requires that units are classified on a quantitative dimension, and that a cutoff point on the dimension be specified such that all units on one side of the cutoff receive the treatment and all units on the other side do not receive the treatment. For example, Trochim (1982) describes the use of the design to evaluate Title I compensatory education programs. In principle, according to this design all students within a school district who scored below a cutoff on an eligibility test of achievement were to be assigned to the Title I program and students scoring above the cutoff were not to be admitted. A treatment effect would be inferred if students in the program have better scores on the outcome measure than would be predicted from their score on the eligibility test of achievement.

The primary internal validity threat to the regression-discontinuity design is a form of selection-maturation. The threat is that the relationship of the eligibility scores to the outcome is nonlinear, which could lead to a spurious treatment effect. Although theoretically very useful, the regression-discontinuity design is rarely used in practice. For further details, see Cook and Campbell (1979) and Reichardt (1979), as well as Trochim (1982, 1984), who illustrates additional obstacles to successful application of this design.

REMOVED TREATMENT

In some cases it is not feasible to obtain a nonequivalent control group, and the design has to be restricted to a single treatment group. Under these conditions, it may still be possible to obtain a conceptual approximation of a control group by using the treatment group as its own control in a removed treatment design. As an example, consider a token reward system designed to increase the amount of time that problem students sit at their desks. Imagine that we implement the program, and the amount of time students spend at their desks reliably increases from pretest to posttest. Then, after another posttest we remove the treatment and test whether there is a subsequent decline in the time spent at desks. Such a pattern of change renders history implausible; it is unlikely that a historical event with an effect in one direction would coincide with the introduction of the treatment *and* that a historical event with an opposite effect would coincide with the treatment's removal. Maturation is often ruled out by an initial increase and a subsequent decrease, although cyclical maturation patterns can remain a threat. Finally, testing is generally ruled out because it is implausible that the measurement increases scores at one time and causes them to decline at another.

Removed treatment designs are not without shortcomings. First, a construct validity (and ethical) problem arises if treatment removal is frustrating, for any change opposite in direction to the initial pretest-posttest change may be due to this frustration. Second, at least two measurements should separate the introduction and removal of the treatment, preferably with all measures being at equally spaced intervals. If there were only three measurement waves (i.e., pretest-treatment-posttest-removal of the treatment-second posttest), then a deviantly high first posttest mean would give the pattern of results that would be interpreted as a treatment effect, and interpretability would suffer. Third, the possibility of cyclical maturation patterns should be considered. The plausibility of such a pattern can be assessed best by observing whether a cyclical pattern occurs in a control group or in a longer series of pretest or posttest observations. Fourth, special caution must be taken in interpretation when the treatment removal is caused by respondents' self-selection out of the treatment, because the factors causing this self-selection out of the treatment may be responsible for changes in the outcome measures. Finally, it should be obvious that the removed treatment is applicable only when a treatment is expected to have a transient effect that will wear off as soon as the treatment is removed. Any effect that persisted over time would lead to false negative conclusions about the treatment's true impact.

REPEATED TREATMENT

It is sometimes possible not only to introduce the treatment and to remove it, but also to reintroduce it a second or even a third time. On some occasions, the reintroduction happens spontaneously, but at other times it might come about as policy because removing the treatment suggested that the treatment was initially effective. In any event, reintroducing the treatment is similar to removing it with respect to both advantages and problems. That is, most threats to internal validity are ruled out, but the possibility remains that apparent treatment effects may be due to cyclical maturation, or to the treatment removal causing resentment that disappears when the treatment is reintroduced. Further, the participants in the experiment may notice the change in their treatment status and become suspicious. The design is most suitable when the treatment is unobtrusive and is unsuitable unless the treatment effect is so transient that it disappears when the treatment is removed and can reappear when the treatment is reintroduced. Thus this design may not be widely applicable in evaluation research.

SIMPLE INTERRUPTED TIME SERIES

Our discussion of removed and repeated treatments suggests that under certain conditions, an experimental group can serve as its own control. The collection of multiple pretest and posttest measures over time is also useful in this regard. For example, Baldus (1973) examined the effect of state laws that require that the government be repaid when a recipient of old age assistance dies and leaves money or property. His concern was that elderly persons would not apply for aid for which they were eligible, if receiving aid would jeopardize their ability to bequeath their homes and other goods to their heirs. Baldus could simply have examined the number of Old Age Assistance (OAA) caseloads before and after new state laws were passed, but he did not do so because this would not control for many internal validity threats. Any observed decrease in the number of elderly persons applying for aid might, for instance, be due to statistical regression, as would be the case if state legislatures had enacted such laws because OAA caseloads were unusually high. The plausibility of this interpretation could be examined by plotting the level of OAA caseloads for an extended time before and after the law's enactment. If regression to the mean were occurring, the immediate pretreatment point would have a value abnormally high for the time series. Thus a single time series can rule out regression. Maturation also can be rendered implausible because the time-series data would reveal any linear or cyclical pattern of maturation (assuming the series is long enough to include the cyclical pattern).

Three internal validity threats remain plausible for the simple interrupted time-series design. Instrumentation is a possible threat because in some cases when a treatment is implemented, changes are also made in the way variables are defined or records are kept. For example, when the Michigan rape law was modified, the legal definition of rape was changed, raising questions about assessing the effect of the legal change on convictions (Marsh, forthcoming). The possibility of such changes is best assessed by careful study of record-keeping and by discussion with those responsible for data collection. A form of selection is also a possible threat if some members of the experimental group drop out when the treatment is introduced. Such attrition would mean that the composition of the group is not comparable for the pretest and the posttest periods. One solution to this attrition problem would be to conduct an analysis using only units that were measured at each time point. It is also helpful to assess whether the number or characteristics of the units providing data changed substantially at the time of the treatment. If so, the attrition explanation gains plausibility.

History is the single most serious threat to internal validity in the simple interrupted time-series design. In the Baldus case, history would be any event that could have caused caseloads to decrease and that occurred at the same time as new state laws on reimbursement were passed and enforced. It is sometimes possible to rule out specific historical threats by qualitative evidence or supplementary data. For example, if in the Baldus study the possibility arose that another kind of legal change (e.g., a new form of welfare began or social security payments increased) could have affected OAA caseloads, it would be possible simply to examine whether such a change co-occurred with institution of the OAA reimbursement law. More generally, to rule out history will require combining the simple interrupted time-series design with other design features we have previously considered. That is, one can use a complex interrupted time-series design.

COMPLEX INTERRUPTED TIME-SERIES DESIGNS

Interrupted time series with nonequivalent dependent measures. Suppose Baldus believed that a shift in the level of OAA caseloads from before to after enactment of the welfare repayment law was due to a general reduction in the funds being spent on welfare rather than to the specific law being studied. If the reduced level of aid to the elderly was due to reluctance to spend money on any welfare groups, we would expect to find decreases in the amount spent on other assistance categories at the same time as any decreases in OAA caseloads. This possibility could be tested easily by examining the time series for other assistance categories to see whether they also decreased at the time the law that enforced repayment was passed. In this and all other complex time-series designs, the possibility of selection $\times$ instrumentation and selection $\times$ attrition interactions should be examined, following the strategy described above for examining the simple instrumentation and history threats in the simple interrupted time-series design.

Interrupted time series with nonequivalent control group. History effects can also be checked by collecting data on control units as comparable to our experimental series as possible. The presumption is that the nonequivalent control units will experience the same historical forces as the experimental units, so that any history effects should affect both groups. Clearly, adding the nonequivalent control group series does not control for all history effects —merely for those that the groups share in common. Any unique events that affect one group but not another at the time of the treatment introduction will not be controlled for in the extended design. Likewise, the design will not control for any instrumentation change or attrition that affects only one group when the treatment is introduced.

Further, diffusion of the treatment may sometimes occur. For example, imagine a historical time-series analysis of the effect of the introduction of legalized abortion on the number of live births, examining state-level data and using adjoining states for controls. The problem is that large numbers of women in the control states may have crossed state lines to obtain abortions, reducing the planned contrast between the experimental and control groups. Nonetheless, the inter-

rupted time series with a nonequivalent control group series is generally a very powerful design.

Other complex interrupted time-series designs. A time-series design
can also involve a removed treatment or repeated treatment, two
design features discussed above. These design features bring to time-
series data the same advantages and problems noted earlier. Another
highly desirable design is the interrupted time series with "switching
replications." In this design, two nonequivalent groups each receive
the treatment, but at different times. Thus each group can serve as a
control group for the other. External and construct validity are
enhanced by the replication across groups, and most threats to internal validity are implausible (e.g., history is impluasible because it is
unlikely that both groups would experience a historical event that
coincided with the onset of the treatment and that could explain any
observed change).

Analysis of time-series data. An extensive discussion of the
analysis of interrupted time-series data is beyond the scope of this
chapter. McCain and McCleary (1979) and McCleary and Hay (1980)
provide relatively accessible accounts and can guide the reader to additional sources. We wish to note only two things about time-series
analysis. One is that whereas complex statistical analyses are often associated with the topic of time-series designs, time-series data can
greatly enhance internal validity even if the number of observations is
insufficient for the more sophisticated analysis methods. Second,
given a sufficient number of observations, it is possible to use analysis
techniques that can test for nonconstant, dynamic effects; that is, one
can test for treatment effects that build up over time, die down across
time, or do both in sequence. (See McCain & McCleary, 1979; Mc-
Cleary & Hay, 1980, for further details.) Testing for the temporal pattern of the effect in this way gives a better picture of how well a program operates over time, and may help us to understand better the
process by which the treatment operates.

RESEARCH PROGRAMS, REPLICATION,
AND META-ANALYSIS

As is suggested by our discussion of the many problems involved in
implementing a summative evaluation, no study is perfect. An evalua-

tion may be methodologically flawed in some way, limiting statistical conclusion or internal validity. An evaluation is based on a particular sample of units from particular settings, with a particular operationalization of the program and particular measures of a subset of possible outcomes of interest; thus external and construct validity may be limited.

In this chapter we have focused primarily on design issues that can enhance internal validity in an evaluation. We have also provided a brief description of procedures that can improve construct and external validity in a single study. Despite our focus on single summative evaluations, it is the case that cause-probing evaluations often do and generally should occur in the context of a larger program of evaluation research. As we noted earlier, one advantage of programmatic evaluation is that there are often multiple questions to be addressed about a program, and a series of studies may address these questions in a logical sequence with one study's results feeding into the following study's planning. For example, Cook (1981) suggests that for heterogeneous ongoing social programs randomized experimentation should be preceded by intensive study of the naturally occurring variation that exists across different types of local projects; this information then helps determine which "varieties" of the program to study experimentally. More generally, studies within a program of evaluation research can often be sequenced to address various questions about the program in an orderly, developmental fashion. For more information about this important issue, see Cronbach et al. (1980) and Cook et al. (1984).

REPLICATION AND META-ANALYSIS

In our discussion of validity within a single study, replication played an important role, particularly in the case of external and construct validity. Within a single evaluation study using a single design, one is concerned about replication across multiple analyses (internal validity); replication across respondent subgroups and across sites (external validity); and replication across multiple measures of each outcome and, if they exist, multiple implementations of the treatment (construct validity).

In addition, replication across designs can increase the confidence one can place in one's conclusions. When different designs, each with different shortcomings, converge on the same answer, it becomes implausible that design-related bias is responsible for one's findings. Thus it is often desirable to employ a variety of designs for answering the question of program effects rather than relying on a single design. For an example of this strategy, see Lipsey et al. (1981).

Replication within and across designs thus increases an evaluation's ability to address the question of program effects at a given stage of an evaluation research program. In addition, replication may be possible across phases of the research program when multiple studies are conducted in sequence. Although different studies may have different goals, it may be possible to estimate the program's effects even if this is not the primary goal of a particular research phase. Further, as a program develops from an initial proposal to a widely implemented program, the issue of program effects may be studied on more than one occasion (Cronbach et al., 1980). In short, an evaluator or evaluation team can enhance validity by seeking replication within a single design, across designs within a given phase of the evaluation research program, and across phases of the research program.

Some writers (e.g., Cronbach et al., 1980) have suggested further that validity can be enhanced by eliminating massive evaluations with a single evaluation team and replacing these with two or more smaller evaluation research programs conducted by independent evaluation teams. In this way it is possible to assess replication across different evaluation teams, who may formulate somewhat different research questions and employ different designs, different measurement devices, and so on.

The notion of multiple evaluation teams addressing similar questions can be expanded beyond one or two teams. For some sorts of programs, dozens or hundreds of relatively independent local evaluations may occur. In some cases, local evaluations may be mandated, as in the Title I compensatory education evaluation (Trochim, 1982). More frequently, numerous local evaluations may be planned and sponsored independently. Many independent evaluations have been conducted of school desegregation in local school districts, for example. (See Light, 1983, for additional examples.) Whether or not the local evaluations are centrally mandated, the procedures of data synthesis, meta-analysis (Glass et al., 1981), or meta-evaluation (Cook and Gruder, 1978) can be of great value when numerous evaluations examine the questions of effectiveness for different instances of a program at different sites. Essentially, the goal of these procedures is to summarize the results of a large body of studies. These procedures can also address such questions as whether effect size is larger for some subgroups than others.

Meta-evaluation should not be a mindless statistical aggregation of studies, as it sometimes appears to be in practice. Substantial thought and substantive knowledge may be required, for example, in deciding what differences across studies are important to examine as possible correlates of effect size. Nevertheless, careful synthesis of multiple studies conducted at multiple sites is an important strategy for assessing the limits of generalizability to a program's effects. With adequate information, one can assess generalizability across site characteristics, across respondent subgroups, across variations in program implementation, and across outcomes. Data synthesis is therefore a most important tool for informing policy decisions about the future. (For further details, see Cook and Gruder, 1978; Cook and Leviton, 1980; Glass et al., 1981; Light, 1983.)

Although research programs and synthesis across multiple evaluations is the ideal, it is an ideal for which individual evaluations are a necessary ingredient. Indeed, even in meta-analysis heavier reliance is placed on well-conceptualized and well-conducted individual studies: These are used as the criterion against which to assess whether any bias occurred in less rigorous studies (Cook and Leviton, 1980). Thus synthesis depends on individual studies in general and on superior individual studies in particular.

A CONCLUDING NOTE

In this chapter we have focused on important aspects in designing an evaluation; however, designing an evaluation involves far more than the issues on which we have focused. For example, measures must be selected and a sampling plan instituted. Most important, research questions must be selected, the appropriateness of summative evaluation considered, and trade-offs among various research goals weighed (Cook et al., 1984; Shotland and Mark, forthcoming). An understanding of validity issues and of the design of randomized experiments and strong quasi-experiments will not provide a simple answer to such complex questions; however, such understanding will allow one to consider the alternatives more wisely and to draw stronger casual inferences about a program's effects when that is one's goal.

NOTES

1. Actually, random assignment is not required. The essential feature that enhances internal validity is perfectly knowing the assignment rule that determines assignment to treatment (see, e.g., Reichardt, 1979). In a randomized experiment, the rule is known: random assignment. Another design in which the assignment rule is known is the regression discontinuity design, which is described in a later section. However, the regression discontinuity design requires additional assumptions which randomized experiments do not (see Cook and Campbell, 1979).

2. Sometimes, in an effort to control for a selection-maturation threat, an investigator might use matching—an analysis might be conducted using only treatment and control units with similar pretest scores. But pretest scores are measured with error and the treatment group members will regress back toward their group mean on the posttest. In other words, the unreliability leads to an underadjustment for existing group differences, and, consequently, a pseudo-effect may be obtained. The under-adjustment problem in matching and in regression techniques is documented amply elsewhere, as is the corresponding problem in related regression techniques (Campbell and Boruch, 1975; Campbell and Erlebacher, 1970; Cook and Campbell, 1979; Cronbach and Furby, 1970; Lord, 1960, 1967, 1969) and will not be considered further here.

REFERENCES

ATKINSON, R. C. (1968) "Computerized instruction and the learning process." American Psychologist, 23: 225-239.

BALDUS, D. C. (1973) "Welfare as a loan: the recovery of public assistance in the United States." Stanford University Law Review 25: 123-250.

BALL, S. and G. A. BOGATZ (1970) The First Year of *Sesame Street*: An Evaluation. Princeton: Educational Testing Service.

BOGATZ, G. A. and S. BALL (1971) The Second Year of "Sesame Street": A Continuing Evaluation (2 vols.) Princeton: Educational Testing Service.

BORUCH, R. F. and H. GOMEZ (1977) "Sensitivity, bias, and theory in impact evaluations." Professional Psychology 8: 411-434.

BRYK, A. S. (1980) "Analyzing data from premeasure/postmeasure designs," in S. Anderson et al. (eds.) Statistical Methods for Comparative Studies. New York: John Wiley.

CAMPBELL, D. T. " 'Degrees of freedom' and the case study." Comparative Political Studies September: 178-193.

———(1969) "Reforms as experiments." American Psychologist 14: 404-429.

——— and R. F. BORUCH (1975) "Making the case for randomized assignments to treatment by considering the alternatives: six ways in which quasi-experimental evaluations in compensatory education tend to underestimate effects," in A. Lumsdaine and C. A. Bennett (eds.), Evaluation of Experience: Some Critical Issues in Assessing Social Programs. New York: Academic Press.

CAMPBELL, D. T. and A. E. ERLEBACHER (1970) "How regression artifacts in quasi-experimental evaluations can mistakenly make compensatory education look harmful," in J. Hellmuth (ed.) Compensatory Education: A National Debate, Vol. 3: Disadvantaged Child. New York: Brunner/Mazel.

CAMPBELL, D. T. and D. W. FISKE (1959) "Convergent and discriminate validation by the multitract-multimethod matrix." Psychology Bulletin, 56: 81-105.

CAMPBELL, D. T. and J. C. STANLEY (1963) "Experimental and quasi-experimental designs for research on teaching," in N. L. Gage (ed.) Handbook of Research on Teaching. Chicago: Rand McNally.

CHEN, H. and P. H. ROSSI (1983) "Evaluating with sense: the theory driven approach." Evaluation Review 7: 238-302.

COHEN, J. (1970) Statistical Power Analysis for the Behavioral Sciences. New York: Academic Press.

COOK, T. D. (1983) "Quasi-experimentation: its ontology, epistemology and methodology," in G. Morgan (ed.) Beyond Method: Strategies for Social Research. Beverly Hills, CA: Sage.

———(1981) "Dilemmas in evaluation of social programs," pp. 257-286 in M. B. Brewer and B. E. Collins (eds.) Scientific Inquiry and the Social Sciences: A Volume in Honor of Donald T. Campbell. San Francisco: Jossey-Bass.

——— and D. T. CAMPBELL (1979) Quasi-Experimentation: Design and Analysis Issues for Field Settings. Chicago: Rand McNally.

———(1976) "The design and conduct of quasi-experiments and true experiments in field settings," in M. D. Dunnette (ed.) Handbook of Industrial and Organizational Psychology. Chicago: Rand McNally.

COOK, T. D. and C. L. GRUDER (1978) "Metaevaluation research." Evaluation Quarterly 2: 5-51.

COOK, T. D. and C. L. LEVITON (1980) "Reviewing the literature: a comparison of traditional methods with metaanalysis." Journal of Personality, 48: 449-472.

COOK, T. D. and C. S. REICHARDT [eds.] (1979) Qualitative Methods in Evaluation. Beverly Hills, CA: Sage.

COOK, T. D., A. APPLETON, R. CONNOR, A. SHAFFER, G. TAMKIN, and S. J. WEBER (1975) Sesame Street Revisited: A Case Study in Evaluation Research. New York: Russell Sage.

COOK, T. D., C. L. LEVITON, and W. SHADISH, Jr. (1984) "Program evaluation," in G. Lindzey and E. Aronson (eds.) Handbook of Social Psychology. Boston: Addison-Wesley.

CONNER, R. F. (1977) "Selecting a control group: an analysis of the randomization process in twelve social reform programs." Evaluation Quarterly 1: 195-244.

CRONBACH, L. J. (1982) Designing Evaluations of Educational and Social Programs. San Francisco: Jossey-Bass.

——— and L. FURBY (1970) "How we should measure 'change'—or should we?" Psychological Bulletin 74: 68-80.

CRONBACH, L. J. and P. E. MEEHL (1955) "Construct validity in psychological tests." Psychological Bulletin 52: 281-302.

CRONBACH, L. J., S. R. AMBRON, S. M. DORNBUSCH, R. D. HESS, R. C. HORNIK, D. C. PHILLIPS, D. F. WALKER, and S. S. WEINER (1980) Toward Reform of Program Evaluation. San Francisco: Jossey-Bass.

CRONBACH, L. J., D. R. ROGOSA, R. E. FLODEN, and G. G. PRICE (1977) Analysis of Covariance in Nonrandomized Experiments: Parameters Affecting Bias. Occasional paper, Stanford Evaluation Consortium, Stanford University.

FIENBERG, S. E. (1971) "Randomization and social affairs: the 1970 draft lottery." Science, 225-261.

FELDMAN, R. (1968) "Response to compatriot and foreigner who seek assistance." Journal of Personality and Social Psychology 10: 202-214.

GLASS, G. V, B. McGAW, and M. L. SMITH (1981) Meta-Analysis in Social Research. Beverly Hills, CA: Sage.

HENDRICKS, M. (1981) "Service delivery assessment: qualitative evaluation at the cabinet level," in N. L. Smith (ed.) Federal Efforts to Develop New Evaluation Methods. San Francisco: Jossey-Bass.

HUDSON, W. W. (1969) Project Breakthrough: A Responsive Environment Field Experiment with Preschool Children from Public Assistance Families. Chicago: Cook County Department of Public Aid.

JÖRESKOG, K. G. and D. SÖRBOM (1979) Advances in Factor Analysis and Structural Equation Models. Cambridge, MA: Abt.

JUDD, C. M. and D. A. KENNY (1981) "Process analysis: estimating meditation in treatment evaluations." Evaluation Review 5: 602-619.

JURS, S. G. and G. V GLASS (1971) "The effect of experimental mortality on the internal and external validity of the randomized comparative experiment." Journal of Experimental Education 40: 62-66.

KISH, L. (1965) Survey Sampling. New York: John Wiley.

KRUGLANSKI, A., W. and M. KROY (1975) "Outcome validity in experimental research: a reconceptualization." Journal of Representative Research in Social Psychology 7: 168-178.

LIGHT, R. J. [ed.] (1983) Evaluation Studies Review Annual, Vol. 8. Beverly Hills, CA: Sage.

LIPSEY, M. W., D. S. CORDRAY, and D. E. BERGER (1981) "Evaluation of a juvenile diversion: using multiple lines of evidence." Evaluation Review, 5: 283-306.

MARK, M. M. (1983) "Treatment implementation, statistical power, and internal validity." Evaluation Review 7: 543-549.

MARK, M. M. and J. J. ROMANO (1982) "The Freshman Seminar Program: experimental evaluation of an introduction to the liberal arts." Evaluation Review 6: 801-810.

MARSH, J. C. (forthcoming) "Obstacles and opportunities in the use of research on rape legislation," in R. L. Shotland and M. M. Mark (eds.) Social Science and Social Policy. Beverly Hills, CA: Sage.

McLAUGHLIN, M. (forthcoming) "Implementation realities and evaluation design," in R. L. Shotland and M. M. Mark (eds.) Social Science and Social Policy. Beverly Hills, CA: Sage.

MEYER, H. J. and E. F. BORGATTA (1959) An Experiment in Mental Patient Rehabilitation. New York: Russell Sage.

MORGAN, G. [ed.] (1983) Beyond Method: Strategies for Social Research. Beverly Hills, CA: Sage.

MULLEN, E. J., R. M. CHAZIN, and D. M. FELDSTEIN (1972) "Services for the newly dependent: an assessment." Social Service Review 46: 309-322.

NIE [National Institute of Education] (1978) Compensatory Education Study: Final Report to Congress. Washington, DC: National Institute of Education.

NOTZ, W. W., B. M. STAW, and T. D. COOK (1971) "Attitude toward troop withdrawal from Indochina as a function of draft number: dissonance or self-interest?" Journal of Personality and Social Psychology 20: 118-126.

PATTON, M. Q. (1982) Qualitative Evaluation Methods. Beverly Hills, CA: Sage.
REICHARDT, C. S. (1983) "On the logic and practice of assessing cause." Presented
    at annual meeting of the American Educational Research Association, Toronto.
———(1979) "The statistical analysis of data from nonequivalent group designs," in
    T. D. Cook and D. T. Campbel (eds.) Quasi-Experimentation: Design and Analysis
    Issues for Field Settings. Chicago: Rand McNally.
REICKEN, H. W. and R. F. BORUCH [eds.] (1974) Social Experimentation: A
    Method for Planning and Evaluating Social Intervention. New York: Academic
    Press.
ROSENBERG, M. (1964) The Pretrial Conference and Effective Justice. New York:
    Columbia University Press.
ROSS, H. L. (1973) "Law, science, and accidents: the British Road Safety Act of
    1967." Journal of Legal Studies 2: 1-75.
RYAN, T. A. (1959) "Multiple comparisons in psychological research," Psychological
    Bulletin 56: 26-41.
SARETSKY, G. (1972) "The OEO P.C. experiment and the John Henry effect." Phi
    Delta Kapan 53: 579-581.
SCHEIRER, M. A. and E. L. REZMOVIC (1983) "Measuring the degree of program
    implementation: a methodological review." Evaluation Review 7: 599-633.
SCRIVEN, M. (1976) "Maximizing the power of causal investigations: the modus
    operandi method," in G. V. Glass (ed.) Evaluation Studies Review Annual, Vol. 5.
    Beverly Hills, CA: Sage.
———(1967) "The methodology of evaluation," in R. E. Stake et al. (eds.) Perspec-
    tives on Curriculum Evaluation (AERA Monograph Series on Curriculum Evalua-
    tion, No. 1). Chicago: Rand McNally.
SHOTLAND, R. L. and M. M. Mark [eds.] (forthcoming) Social Science and Social
    Policy. Beverly Hills, CA: Sage.
STROMSDORFER, E. W. and G. FARKAS [eds.] (1980) Evaluation Studies Review
    Annual, Vol. 5. Beverly Hills, CA: Sage.
TROCHIM, W. M. K. (1984) Research Design for Program Evaluation: The Regres-
    sion-Discontinuity Approach. Beverly Hills, CA: Sage.
———(1982) "Methodologically based discrepancies in compensatory education evalu-
    ation." Evaluation Review 6: 443-480.
WINER, B. J. (1971) Statistical Principles in Experimental Design. New York: Mc-
    Graw-Hill.

5

DATA ANALYSIS

Robert F. Boruch and David Rindskopf

This chapter addresses the problem of estimating the effects of social program on its participants. We try to deliver two principal messages. First, there is a crucial tie between design of a program evaluation and data analysis. To the extent that the evaluation design is poor, simplistic, or absent, the data analysis will certainly be difficult and conclusions will be misleading, at worst. Randomized experiments are used here as a standard against which other designs for impact evaluation are judged.

The second message concerns strategy of data analysis. In particular, one ought to know or have good evidence about the way people behave in the absence of the new program to estimate the program's effect accurately. When theory or data are equivocal in this respect, and they usually are in applied social research, we invoke a third message: that multiple designs and competing analyses of the data are warranted.

These messages are not original. This chapter is designed as an introduction to the topic rather than an advanced treatise. Any merit it may have lies in its clarity, accuracy, and illustrations.

The discussion is nontechnical because the chapter was designed for individuals who are not especially interested in technical detail. Because its audience does include some methodologists, we reference some contemporary statistical work. The illustrations are taken from a variety of programmatic areas—welfare, health, rehabilitation, and others.

PEDESTRIAN BUT NECESSARY DEFINITIONS

The need to be explicit about what we mean by evaluation, by experiments, by quasi-experiments, and so on is not trivial. Lots of contemporary arguments about how to estimate program effects are based on confusion about what the terms mean. To avoid needless ambiguity, we begin with definitions.

The form of evaluation that interests us here focuses on the *relative effects* of the program on its target group. One asks whether the program, service, or delivery system works with respect to some alternative condition or program.

It should be obvious that this kind of evaluation is not the only legitimate way to assess a social program. Other kinds focus on different questions and are often more important in deciding whether a program should continue. Indeed, studies of relative impact are in the minority partly because they are so hard to do well (e.g., Leviton and Boruch, 1983). Process evaluation, monitoring program operations, and so on are crucial. We do not consider them here because they are treated ably in other articles (e.g., Scheirer and Rezmovic, 1983).

The stress here is on one kind of impact evaluation design: the randomized experiment. By this we mean the random allocation of experimental units to two or more program or treatment conditions, so as to permit a fair comparison (unbiased estimate) of program effects on some outcome variable, and to permit quantification of our confidence in that comparison. So, for example, we might randomly assign some members of a group of elderly persons to a novel day care program and some to conventional (control) services. The objective is to estimate the impact of day care and its costs relative to conventional services. The randomization guarantees long-run equivalence of the participants in the new program and nonparticipants, aside from program effect. And the process permits us to quantify our confidence in the resulting estimate of program effect.

A statistical *approximation to an experiment or quasi-experiment* refers to any technique that does not include randomized assignment but that does purport to yield fair comparisons and (possibly) quantification of confidence. There appears to be no easy way to classify the numerous approximations to experiments that have been created. For the sake of concreteness, the relevant methodologists may be split into three camps: adjusters, fitters, and designers. Adjusters dip into conventional statistics texts and use techniques like matching, grouping, and standardization to create comparison groups that are alleged to be equivalent to the program recipient group. Or they use regression and covariance methods to achieve the same end. Some adjusters actually recognize that the adjustments made to the data imply a statistical model and a theory of the way people behave in the absence of any special social intervention. If the model is made explicit, we cast them out of the adjuster's camp and into the fitter's camp. This is a promotion to a higher level of technical consciousness.

The fitter's group includes methodologists with an interest in structural equation models. Goldberger (1973) prescribes that the models be developed so that "each equation represents a causal link rather than a mere empirical association." A structural equation expert usually relies on previous research to identify the causal links. Where the structural equations are based on observational (nonrandomized) data, causal links are regarded as potentially testable assumptions in order to develop a better framework for understanding a complex process. To the extent that causal links or models are laid out adequately, the models ought to fit available data. Further, important parameters in the model should be estimable, and hypotheses about the size of a program effect will be testable.

The adjuster's group does not differ from the fitter's group in principle, of course. In practice, the adjusters usually assume that the statistical model that underlies their adjustment procedure actually generates the population data. The fitters regard this assumption with more suspicion; indeed, they make deliberate attempts to recognize explicit alternative models and to assess the tenability of alternative models if the data are sufficient (e.g., Goldberger, 1973).

The designer's group is exemplified by the quasi-experimentalists, notably Campbell (1969) and Cook and Campbell (1976). Its members confront situations in which randomization cannot be accomplished and deliberately plan data collection efforts that will reduce the level of inferential equivocality and bias to the lowest level possible. Unlike the adjusters or the fitters, this group does have some administrative power to structure the evaluation. The exemplary quasi-experimentalist regards estimates of program effect as tentative, a matter of examining competing explanations of an estimate of the program's effect.

Of course, these categories are not mutually exclusive. Good methodologists generally pitch their tents in each camp at one time or another. We offer the distinctions here only for convenience, and with the understanding that labels and duties will differ a bit from one substantive research project to another.

THE STANDARD FOR ESTIMATING
A PROGRAM'S EFFECT:
NULL CONDITIONS

Any good estimate of a new program's effect is based on an explicit standard or reference group. Most often, the standard is how people behave, or would behave, in the absence of the new program. Absence of a new program here does *not* imply that individuals would normally receive no services at all. It does imply normal or control services or some program other than the one under special investigation.

For the analyst, the problem of making a fair estimate of a program effect turns around the problem of assuring the accuracy of that standard. That is, we would like to assure that our conception of the way people behave without the program in which we have a special interest is reasonable. Roughly speaking, three kinds of strategies are used in sustaining the argument for "reasonableness"—procedural, evidentiary, and rhetorical—and each is considered below.

PROCEDURAL STRATEGIES: CONTROLLING DESIGN
FOR CLARITY IN ANALYSIS

Consider a setting in which eligible members of a group of elderly persons are assigned *randomly* to a novel day care program or to conventional services. The random assignment procedure carries a guarantee that in the long run, if the experiment is conducted properly, participants and non-participants do not differ. This procedural guarantee is limited, of course: chance alone will produce differences in the group at hand. But the chance variations can be accommodated with conventional statistical methods. The main point is that because the long-run equivalence of groups is assured, long-run effect will be fair and unbiased. A difference in health status or in medical expenditures between groups will be attributable to the new program rather than to preexisting, systematic, and unrecognized differences between groups.

Of course, if randomization is not carried out properly, if attrition from the program degrades the comparability of groups, and so on, the guarantee no longer holds. The management of randomized field tests of social programs is no less important in this regard than is technology. To the degree that the management is poor, randomization will be imperfect and data will be suspect. The analyst will not be able to rely on the design guarantee.

EMPIRICAL STRATEGIES

One obvious alternative to procedural guarantees is an empirical approach. Health status of the elderly might, for example, be observed over an extended period prior to the program's introduction. Following or during their participation in the program, their health status is again observed periodically. In this instance, preprogram measures provide a basis for predicting the way they would behave without the program. The difference between that estimate and their actual status after the program's introduction would, in the simplest case, reflect the program's impact.

Regression-discontinuity approaches are similar in spirit to time-series analyses, but they are safer in the sense that control is exercised over selection of individuals into programs in the latter. That is, the design involves building an explicit multivariate analytic model that can include such important client characteristics as control variables. Thus statistical controls can be exercised over the way individuals are selected into or rejected from programs.

A statistical method that tries to help determine the effect of treatment by estimating what would have happened without the treatment is called the *value-added model* (Bryk and Weisberg, 1976, 1977; Bryk et al., 1980). No control group is needed for the application of this model, although the use of a control group can help reduce the possibility of bias in the estimation of the treatment effect. In order to use the method, one must have scores on a pretest and (parallel or identical) posttest and the age of each subject at pretest and posttest. The procedure is to develop a model for predicting pretest score from age—that is, a model for growth. This information is then used in predicting what the posttest score would have been if the same growth pattern continued over the treatment period. The difference between this predicted value and the observed score is the value added by the treatment. The average treatment effect can be calculated, and the variance in treatment effect, which is considered a random (not fixed) variable, can also be estimated. Although the standard error of the average treatment effect is not simple to calculate, empirical techniques such as the jacknife can be used in order to perform a statistical significance test of the average treatment effect.

As has been noted by the originators of this method, validity of the method rests on a large number of assumptions, many of which might not be tenable. Also, one must have a fairly large sample in order to estimate well the form and parameters for the growth model. The large number of assumptions necessary leads us to be cautious about recommending this method of analysis, unless there are empirical reasons in a given case for believing the assumptions to be (at least approximately) true.

The strategies carry no guarantee analogous to that provided in randomized experiments. Indeed, the frame of reference is different. To the extent that the prediction based on the prior data is accurate, the estimate of program effect will be accurate. To the extent that it is a poor prediction, the estimate will be poor.

The problems in relying on this frame of reference are not difficult to identify. In the crudest cases, the data available may be too puny to make a good estimate. At their nastiest, the problems involve fitting rather complicated models to the data so as to accommodate various cycles, auto-correlated error, the effect of repeated measures per se on the target population, and so on (see Glass et al., 1975; Trochim, 1982).

For *novel* social programs, it is often the case that data are insufficient to sustain a time-series or regression-discontinuity approach. It is partly for this reason that randomized experiments are an attractive option.

RHETORICAL APPROACHES: SPECIFYING THE NULL CONDITION BY ASSUMPTION

We might simply assume that some null condition is an accurate standard and then test the observed estimator of treatment effect against the assumed value.

The simplest example is the usual posttest in design: Measurement occurs only after a program is emplaced. Here one makes the often implicit assumption that in the absence of any program effect, the characteristics of the participants that reflect their response to the program will be at a specific level. It might be assumed, for example, that a group of high school students will know virtually nothing about health following the program if the program is ineffective.

In this simple case, it is easy to see that if the assumption of zero knowledge, aside from information obtained in class, is incorrect, then any estimate of program effect is also incorrect. Any test of the null hypothesis is incorrect because that null condition—the assumption of stable ignorance—is incorrect. In the absence of any extraordinary intervention, there may be deterioration or advancement in knowledge.

This classification scheme is imperfect. All procedural and empirical strategies require some assumptions. Rhetorical specification may be based on individual experience, and so on. But it does help anticipate crude problems in analysis. In particular, where there are no procedural guarantees of fairness in estimating the program's effect, one must rely on projection from data. Where data useful for projection are scanty, one must rely on assumption, theory, or rhetoric to argue that the standard one chooses is reasonable.

EXPERIMENTS AS PROPERLY PACKAGED IGNORANCE, AS ASPIRIN, AND AS PROPHYLACTIC

The alternatives to a procedural guarantee of the fairness of comparisons are demanding. They require more substantive knowledge about the social phenomena than randomized tests, more technical sophistication, and more wariness about the invidious effects of unrecognized weaknesses in the analysis.

As properly packaged ignorance. McLuhan and Nevitt (1973) observe that all elementary particles in modern physics are packets of ignorance. So too is error in statistics an elementary particle, a packet of ignorance that consolidates unknown and possibly unknowable causes of human behavior. What is unique about randomized experiments is that they put our ignorance in an explicit form—random error—and, more important, structure our ignorance so that it does not systematically distort our estimate of a program effect. It is a form that requires the evaluator to know little but distributes his or her ignorance equitably across treatment and control groups.

This is not to say that the evaluator cannot or should not capitalize on prior knowledge; one can use randomized block designs or randomized covariance designs to increase the power of one's experiment considerably. But with strictly observational data, one can never be sure if ignorance is working systematically against one, for one, or in a neutral fashion. Randomization guarantees in the long run that the work is neutral in the sense that it exerts no systematic impact on the accuracy of an estimate.

As aspirin. A fundamental sense in which planned randomized experiments are ideal is that "randomization relieves the experimenter of the anxiety of considering and estimating the magnitude of the innumerable causes by which his data will be disturbed" (Fisher, 1935: 44). This quote from the scripture does not mean that Sir Ronald was terribly interested in mental health, of course. It does mean that his interest lay in a fair and equitable comparison of, say, two treatments, a comparison of groups that are not free from innumerable causes but that are affected equally by those causes.

Explicit in Fisher's statement are two sensible but anxiety-provoking activities: identifying and estimating the causes of disturbances in the data. Merely identifying plausible causes of variation in nonexperimental data is difficult, of course. But we have had little guidance from the formal statistical community on how to go about doing so. If we look to the econometric curve-fitting tradition for advice, we find numerous pointers on the consequence of misspecification but virtually nothing about the character (statistical or otherwise) of the missing variables.

We might then call on substantive experts to make some judgments about what variables have been ignored. But then we find ourselves relying on idiosyncratic faith in an individual (or an advisory board). Their opinions may or may not be verifiable, and to the extent that they are not, the opinions are of less value.

The only general taxonomy for classifying these causes in evaluative research was produced by Campbell (1957) over twenty years after Fisher made his remarks. Campbell's so-called threats to validity are an important first step in the direction of systematizing the innumerable causes of disturbances in the data and in speculating about their existence and their effect (see the section on data analysis). These threats are, in fact, chronically unrecognized influences on the estimates of program effect obtained on observational studies.

As prophylactic. Experiments can be prophylactic in the sense that they can prevent subtle analytic biases from appearing. There will be no specious pessimism to the extent that randomization prevents population differences from occurring and prevents the chronic underadjustment problem. In particular, a point reiterated consistently by Campbell (1974) is that conventional methods of analyzing observational data in evaluative research can actually make a social program appear harmful when it has no effect at all, and can make a program appear ineffective when the program impact is large and positive.

Any commonly used technique can result in misleading conclusions. But one such technique appears to be chronically misused in evaluative research: covariance adjustment of differences between preexisting groups. It is easy to show (Campbell and Boruch, 1975) that covariance adjustments are inadequate when (a) populations from which experimental and control groups are drawn differ and the differences persist in the absence of extraordinary intervention, and (b) the covariates used to account for those differences are measured imperfectly and/or incomplete.

In most nonexperimental studies, condition a will to be true for reasons of self-selection and/or voluntarism of program participants, differences in history and development of comparison groups and program participants, and so forth. Condition b is typically true in social and educational research, but exceptions do occur. Imperfectly measured covariates—be they cognitive test scores, demographic characteristics, or other variables—are the rule rather than the exception. We usually know very little about the degree of incompleteness of the covariate set, but this does not seem to prevent many evaluators from making a veritable act of faith that we can define population differences (between participant and nonparticipant groups) in any given evaluation setup with the covariates at hand. When the covariance adjustment is imperfect, as it must be under these conditions, and one computes "adjusted means" for experimental and comparison groups, the magnitude of those statistics can make it appear that the program's effect has been considerably smaller (and even negative) relative to the true effect (see, for example, Director, 1974).

FEASIBILITY OF RANDOMIZED EXPERIMENTS[1]

We often presume that approximations to randomized experiments are desirable. If experiments themselves are approximations to reality, why do we need further approximations? Are experiments not feasible? Are they unethical and therefore inappropriate? Do they fail to be sufficiently broad in scope to be useful? Answers to these questions are given elsewhere, so we focus very briefly on them here.

Feasibility. Just a little homework reveals that a considerable number of experiments for planning and evaluation have been mounted successfully. Our list of over 300 field experiments (in Boruch et al., 1978) illustrates the remarkable variety of novel programs subjected to experimental test. Randomized experiments have been mounted to evaluate new income subsidy and housing subsidy programs; law enforcement strategies and court procedures; training programs for police, military, and industrial workers; health care delivery systems and preventive medical programs; new social service strategies, and a range of others. Not all have been successful in carrying out the evaluation design, but the number and variety of experiments that have been mounted suggests that randomized tests are more feasible in the social sector than one might suspect.

Scope and limitations. Nothing in experimental design demands that anthropological and similar narrative information be ignored. The various kinds of information have been combined quite nicely in some studies (e.g., Weikert's, 1972, educational experiments). Similarly, nothing in classical experimental design precludes the use of crude qualitative or ordinal variables, and in fact most experiments capitalize on expert observation of "improvement" versus "no improvement," "change" versus "no change," and the like. In fact, the state of the art in using qualitative variables has expanded considerably over the past few years (see Bishop et al., 1975). That differences in individuals' reaction to treatment can be accommodated in experiments is also clear, given our experience with randomized block designs and block-by-treatment interaction (see Molof, 1967; Warren, 1967; and other juvenile corrections experiments). Experiments can also capitalize on important auxiliary data, notably social and archival indicators. We know that such data can be and have been used to optimize designs (in the negative income tax experiments), to improve precision of the experiment (where social indicators serve as covariates), and to accomplish other tasks in randomized field tests (see Boruch, 1973, for more detail).

Ethicality and legality. Some ethical issues here appear to be no different in experiments and approximations to experiments *except* insofar as experiments permit one to identify and estimate the magnitude of the negative effect less equivocally. In this sense, randomization can be a more ethical approach than others. To accommodate ethical or legal implications of random deprivation of a potentially necessary program, a variety of strategies can be considered: short delays in receipt of the program where these are acceptable, random assignment for the marginally needy to treatment, comparison among levels of program intensity rather than simple comparisons of presence and absence of programs, and so forth. Ethical issues are well treated in Beauchamp et al. (1982). Legal issues and solutions have been discussed with formidable expertise by Breger (1983).

Reprise. The main point we make here is that *if we accept bold criticism of experiments without question, we will compromise our goals without ever having tried to reach them*. Randomized field experiments are mounted more frequently than we might suspect, and the feasibility is demonstrable in a variety of settings. Insofar as the usual criticisms of experiments are weak or specious, we cannot and must not justify approximations to experiments on these grounds.

This is not to say that developing alternatives to randomized experiments is unjustified, of course. There will always be situations in which randomization is physically impossible, politically impractical, ethically unacceptable, or entirely unnecessary. The crucial issue is determining whether these conditions actually prevail and uncovering their nature so that high-quality evaluations can be designed around these constraints.

METHODS OF ANALYSIS: SIMPLE COMPARATIVE STRATEGIES FOR THEIR APPRAISAL

Some simple techniques are often advertised as useful in obtaining estimates of a program's effect—before-after approaches, matching or covariance analysis to produce statistically equivalent control and comparison groups, and so forth. Given the variety of competing methods, it is not unreasonable to ask how the estimates of program effect obtained from using each method stand against one another in live evaluations. To answer the question simply, we might choose one of three approaches.

First, we might identify instances in which a randomized test *and* a nonrandomized test have been run on the same program and target population. If the quality of each test is similar, and if we use the estimate of effect stemming from the randomized test as a standard, then we might judge the quality of competing estimates by their similarity to the standard. The results of our search for instances and comparisons of estimates stemming from *conventional* quasi-experimental designs are given in the next section.

A second approach, developed by Steven Director and Donald T. Campbell as dry-run experimentation and by Boruch as multiple pretesting, involves a dummy evaluation with live data and a prescribed analytic technique but no real program. The approach is used to check the biases in estimates likely to occur in identical analysis of live data based on a real program. This technique can be used in both design of new program evaluations and salvaging a poorly designed evaluation: The first approach can be used similarly.

The final approach is less formal. Articulated by John Gilbert et al. (1975), its main purpose is to consolidate previous evaluations with some similarity, compare them with respect to their equivocality, and reach some judgments about the character of the statistical methods that are most useful under various conditions.

All the approaches point to the linkage between evaluation design and the results of data analysis. More important, they illustrate in concrete fashion the way in which estimates of effect based on alternative methods can differ or be biased, sometimes dramatically, relative to a standard.

COMPARING ESTIMATES FROM RANDOMIZED EXPERIMENTS AND APPROXIMATIONS TO EXPERIMENTS[2]

This approach is geared chiefly toward understanding the limits of statistical manipulation. One locates (or conducts) a randomized experimental test of a program and, in addition, collects sufficient nonrandomized data to support ostensibly appropriate quasi-experimental assessment of the same program.

Suppose, for example, that data are obtained on individuals who have been assigned *randomly* either to a treatment program (T) or to a control condition (C). Similar data are also collected on an additional group (C') whose members, though not assigned randomly, are regarded as similar to members of the C group and T group prior to treatment. The question is then posed: How does the estimate of program effect based on ordinary analysis of variance of the T-C groups compare with an estimate of effect based on the T-C' groups and conventional statistical techniques such as matching, covariance analysis, or change scores analysis? The answer is important insofar as it helps us to understand the empirical nature of bias that may be obtained when using techniques such as covariance analysis that purportedly yield unbiased estimates of effect without randomization.

That estimates of effect will often be biased if we rely solely on nonexperimental evidence because obvious with some examples. Consider the simplest form of nonexperimental analysis—comparing the condition afterward. This before-after (or pretest-posttest) approach is common despite the fact that any increase or decrease in average condition may be attributable entirely to unrecognized growth or development processes.

In the Michigan arthritis studies, for example, severity of condition *increased* after the introduction of an arthritis treatment program. Based on this information alone, we might erroneously conclude that the program's effect was negative—that is, it actually harmed program participants. In fact, we know from randomized experimental tests that the equivalent control group's condition deteriorated even further, and consequently, the proper inference is that the program did indeed have a beneficial effect (see Deniston and Rosenstock, 1972).

Usually, one attempts to find a comparison group against which to gauge the condition of program participants and also to reduce the equivocality underlying most before-after designs. But this is also hazardous when the comparison group differs systematically and (often) in unknowable ways from the participant group.

For example, one facet of the Salk vaccine trials involved comparing volunteer vaccine recipients to an allegedly equivalent, "natural" comparison group of nonrecipients. The vaccine's effect in this nonrandomized quasi-experiment was positive. But estimates based on a second facet of the trials—randomized tests—gave estimates of effect that were 14% higher than the value based on the nonrandom tests. Given only the evidence from the nonrandom groups, then, we would have concluded that the vaccine was notably *less* effective than it actually was in reducing polio incidence (Meier, 1972).

At this point, the critical reader might observe that techniques exist that purportedly "adjust out" differences between groups and that equate groups that differ initially, in order to avoid biases such as these. The techniques—matching program participants and nonparticipants with respect to their demographic or other characteristics, covariance or regression analysis—are sophisticated but do require strong assumptions about the underlying nature of the data (e.g., Rubin 1976a, 1976b, 1976c). More important, those assumptions may not be an adequate picture of reality—of how individuals will behave in the absence of any program intervention. To be specific, when groups differ intially and the difference persists, then these methods will *not* perform adequately if the matching variables or covariates are measured imperfectly or incompletely. Some of the more advanced techniques accommodate the problem of fallible measures reasonably well, provided that reliability of the data is not too low (e.g., Porter, 1967). But none accommodates the specification problem satisfactorily: In many cases, we are likely to leave out variables that are important but that are unmeasured or unmeasurable. In either case, the adjustment process is imperfect, and estimates of program effect will often be biased. How often will they be biased? It is impossible to say, but a few examples may help to illustrate the problem.

In the Michigan Arthritis Study, a comparison group was identified, differences between this group and program participants were reduced by matching individuals, and estimates of program effect were obtained. The estimate of effect based on this comparison is near zero; that is, despite selection of a matched group, the estimate obtained by comparing these individuals to the program participants is biased, relative to the estimate obtained from the completely randomized data (Deniston and Rosenstock, 1972).

The Middlestart program was designed by Yinger, Ikeda, and Laycock (1977) as a special precollege program for promising high school students. In the original evaluation, some students were assigned on the basis of post facto matching. In the latter, five sets of treatment and comparison groups were constructed; they were not randomized and were equivalent only in the sense that they were matched on the basis of their demographic characteristics. If one examines the pooled data, one finds a significant difference of about six months in grade equivalent achievement test scores between participants and nonparticipants. However, if one examines only the randomized set of students, the estimate is far lower and quite negligible. In this case, the nonrandomized comparisons yield estimates of effect ranging from zero to a two-year difference in achievement test scores (Boruch et al., 1975).

Time-series designs are also a promising approach to estimating program impact. Here one observes some outcome variable over time (e.g., rape rate over the last three years), introduces the program, and then tries to detect subsequent change in the variable (e.g., a drop in incidence of rape). The time-series approach is promising to the extent that there is no good competing explanation for the change in the outcome variable, such as changes in the accuracy of measuring the incidence of rape, and to the extent that the time series is stable, so that discontinuity will be obvious if it occurs. However, time-series analysis is not always possible, and it can yield estimates that differ from those based on experimental evidence.

In the Cali (Colombia) evaluation of nutrition and education programs, we find that an estimate of program effect based on short time-series projection from the control group is biased downward drastically. The time-series estimate of effect on children's cognitive skills is half the size of the effect based on test scores of randomized recipient and nonrecipient groups. The bias would be smaller if a much longer time series had been available (see McKay et al., 1973).

In the Michigan Arthritis Study, time-series estimates of effect were 10% higher than estimates based on randomized experimental tests in the same populations.

Of course, there have been studies employing much less competent methodology than even the ones we have described and that have also led to erroneous conclusions. The more dramatic examples have occurred in medicine, where medical or surgical remedies, adopted on the basis of weak evidence, have been found to be useless at best or damaging to the patient at worst. The so-called frozen stomach approach to surgical treatment of duodenal ulcers, for example, was used by a variety of physicians who simply imitated the technique of an expert surgeon. Later experimental tests showed prognoses were good simply because the originating surgeon was good at surgery and not because his innovation was effective. It provided no benefit over conventional surgery (Ruffin et al., 1969).

Anticoagulant drug treatment of stroke victims prior to 1970 had received considerable endorsement by physicians who relied solely on informal observational data for their opinions. Subsequent randomized experimental tests showed not only that a class of such drugs had no detectable positive effects but that they could be damaging to the patients' health (see Hill et al., 1960, and other examples described in Rutstein's, 1969, excellent article).

None of this should be taken to mean that estimates of program impact based on experiments will always differ in magnitude from those based on non-randomized assessments. The estimators will be close, for example, if there is no systematic difference between characteristics of the individuals assigned to one program variation and those assigned to another. If in a particular research project there is no sytematic association—that is, there is a kind of natural randomization process—or if such differences can be removed statistically, then we may expect various types of designs to produce similar results.

We have been able to document few instances of this, however. The first stage of Daniels et al.'s (1968) evaluation of the DANN Mental Health program, for instance, involved allocation of incoming patients to the experimental treatment ward on the basis of number of beds available in each. Controlled (deliberate) randomization was introduced after ward turnover rate had stabilized. Comparisons of the characteristics of ward entrants prior to their treatment in the first nonrandomized stage to the characteristics of entrants admitted in the second (deliberately randomized) stage showed no important measurable differences between the groups. More important, separate analyses of the nonrandomized and randomized groups yielded very similar estimates of program effect.

An essential condition for similarity of estimates is that prior to program introduction, there be no systematic association between characteristics of eligible program candidates and their participation in the program. The association may be slight enough at times to give us some confidence that the program effect is in the proper direction even if we recognize that the magnitude of the estimator is likely to be in error. Holt's (1974) evaluative studies of sentence reduction in prisons is informative in this respect. A number of nonrandomized studies on early versus late releases of individuals from prison suggested that length of sentence (within certain limits) had no impact on postprison behavior. Later randomized experimental tests demonstrated that the magnitude of early estimates of the effect of early release was reasonable.

In each of these cases, as in others (see Boruch, 1975), randomized tests were needed to verify that unobserved influences were not entirely responsible for the results obtained in nonexperimental studies. More specifically, the Daniels experiment helped to rule out the possibility that program effects estimated from the nonexperimental data of the first stage was attributable to subtle differences in patients assigned to each ward rather than to the ward program itself. In the Holt work, the experiment helped to demonstrate that the success of early releases was not entirely attributable simply to expert judgments by parole boards about the likelihood of a parolee's returning to prison, but that the length of sentence actually has no discernible effect, within certain limits, on recidivism.

DRY-RUN EXPERIMENTS AND MULTIPLE PRETESTING

Recall that one of the main problems in nonrandomized studies is that null conditions—the way people behave in the absence of the program—often cannot be characterized well. One simple vehicle for helping to specify null conditions *and* to establish flaws in analysis based on erroneous assumptions in the nonrandomized studies has been described under the rubrics of "dry-run experimentation" and multiple or dummy pretesting.

To illustrate the dry-run approach, consider an evaluation in which observations are made before (at time T_1) and after (T_2) the program's introduction, and on both program participants and on a control group. Assume, as will usually be the case in nonrandomized designs, that the procedure by which individuals enter the program is ambiguous. The comparability of the groups will then be suspect, and so it is not unreasonable to check for biases in the analysis. Finally, suppose that some conventional method, such as covariance analysis or matching, is used to estimate effects.

Under these conditions, it is sometimes possible to retrieve additional data on the same groups, for points earlier in time (say, T_0). If so, analysis of the data based on the measures over the interval T_0-T_1

should show no program effect, for after all, no program exists during T_0-T_1. Because of errors in the assumptions underlying the analytic method, however, such as a poor projection of null conditions or incomparability of groups, the estimate of effect based on the T_0-T_1 data will not be zero. The dry-run analysis can help to reveal flaws in the analytic strategy proposed for the live T_1-T_2 data, notably by demonstrating sizable program effects when no program exists.

The tactic can sometimes be incorporated formally into evaluation design. One obtains data on individuals who are *likely* to be members of treatment and control groups over at least two time points prior to the program's introduction. After program imposition, actual treatment and control group members are sorted out, and data from the double pretests are analyzed using exactly the same technique that is planned for the main evaluation. This analysis should show no effect—the data are, after all, collected before the program's introduction. If an effect does show up, then the analytic approach and the model of null conditions underlying that approach must be re-examined. Some concrete examples may help to illustrate the approach.

In many evaluations of manpower training programs, the increase in salary levels of trainees based on before-after observations is used to argue that the programs were successful. In fact, we know from other evidence that salary level is quite likely to have increased even in the absence of a special training program. That evidence may include two spaced observations of program participants' salary levels *before* introduction of the program. Or it may include multiple observations on salary level increases prior to the program's introduction on groups very similar to those actually participant in the program (Director, 1974).

In the evaluation of programs by the Manpower Training and Development Act, Borus and Hardin estimated that the program's effect was to *decrease* the income of trainees. They used covariance analysis to "adjust preexisting differences" between program participants and nonparticipants in a nonrandomized study. Director (1974), however, conducted exactly the same analysis on data from similar groups in prior years, before the program's introduction. He found that in the absence of any program at all, the analytic technique yielded nearly the same negative estimate of program "effect." That is, the technique failed, in both the original live evaluation and in the dry run, to yield unbiased estimate of program effect. Indeed, the estimate was biased in a direction that made the program look harmful; the bias is attributable to a seldom-recognized statistical artifact.

More recent examples stem from the evaluation of special compensatory education programs and illustrate that even without elaborate statistics, it is possible to appraise the credibility of an analytic approach using the dry-run method. Wortman and St. Pierre (1975), for example, were concerned with estimating the effect of so-called voucher programs, an educational innvoation designed, in part, to increase the achievement level of third-grade students. They used data from the same students, collected during the first and second grades, as a basis for determining which of several different analytic approaches would produce the least biased estimate of program effect. That is, an analysis was run, an estimate obtained and judged as to its size for the dry-run data. The analytic approach finally identified yielded the least biased estimate and so was applied to the live data.

The results of such an analysis may still be very equivocal. Indeed, Wortman and St. Pierre report that their own analysis is subject to some major threats to validity that are not accommodated by the dry-run approach. Still, the matter of data analysis, especially in the absence of randomized experiments, must be a matter of successive approximation to an unbiased estimate of program effect, and the Wortman-St. Pierre example is admirable in that respect.

Rindskopf (1976) presented a similar type of analysis. His secondary assessment of data from evaluation of Title I-supported compensatory education programs suggested that a covariance analysis, adjusting out individual differences between nonrandom treatment and control groups, might be useful. However, in order to avoid well-known biases, the analysis would have to be corrected for unreliability in the covariates. Deciding which reliability estimate to use—a measure of internal consistency of the variables, or test-retest correlations, or others—was difficult. To better understand the biases engendered by each correction factor, Rindskopf used background variables to predict the pretest variables like parental income and social status as a surrogate for the measure. A conventional covariance analysis showed that these predictors would yield biased results: Pretest differences using background characteristics as covariates persisted in the form of significant F ratios. When that analysis of pretest and (surrogate) pre-pretest data was corrected for internal inconsistency in the achievement measures, biases still persisted. When, on the other hand, the correlation between background variables and the pretest was used as an estimator of reliability, the bias (at least as reflected in the test statistics) disappeared.

This multiple pretesting approach is simple, and it can protect the analyst from making faulty assumptions about the way people behave in the absence of a program, about the comparability of comparison and treatment groups, and so on. It is better than a simple before-after approach in this respect. But it is still weaker than a strategy that employs randomized assignment or a long time series for analysis. In fact, it is a kind of weak time series, although it may not deserve the dignity of the label.

RATING INNOVATIONS AND MAJOR THREATS TO VALIDITY

Gilbert et al. (1975) set out to understand evaluative data and methods of analysis by examining rigorous evaluations that have been implemented successfully. The examination gives the analyst some feel for the likelihood of success in well-controlled settings, a frame of reference for judging the realism or credibility of claims of success based on other, less rigorous evaluations. Conducting such an examination of education programs, welfare programs, sociomedical and surgical treatments, all evaluated using randomized experiments, the authors find that success rate is low. They observe that this is not unexpected, for successes are probably as rare in physical sciences and medical research as well.

Having obtained some feel, based on well-designed evaluations, for the incidence of success, they then examine the evaluations based on poorer designs but that are often advertised as a success. Gilbert and his colleagues reiterate evidence from the medical sector showing that the poorer the evaluation design, the more likely it is that the program director-evaluator is enthusiastic about the program. They argue further that if, in these instances, a major competing explanation is found that might explain away the success, judgments about the impact of the program ought to be suspended. This suspension of judgment may not be pleasing to the policy maker, but in the absence of any real evidence against a plausible competing explanation, it must be regarded as fair. In examining a small array of ostensibly successful programs in medicine, education, and welfare, evaluated under less rigorous design, they do indeed find it easy to explain how "impact" of the programs may be attributable entirely to factors operating outside the direct intervention. Successful housing programs, for example, can be made to appear successful simply by choosing residents carefully and by keeping no records on the criteria for selection. Medical or surgical treatments can be guaranteed to show positive impact, as they have in the past, by selecting patients who are improving in any event. The only major exceptions to the perspective are so-called big bang effects; the program effect is so large, relative to normal variation in the social system and to naturally operating social factors, that it obviously overrides competing explanations. But this event is rare.

The point is that in examining data from a contemporary program evaluation, precedent can be important. One should know something about the incidence and size of effects under rigorous evaluation to gauge reasonably the credibility of claims based on designs that are likely to yield equivocal results. One ought to recognize, as well, the obvious criticisms leveled against previous nonrandom evaluations of programs similar to those of current interest. It is not unreasonable to expect that competing explanations of the past will be the competing explanations for current and future impact studies. By failing to recognize them, we do the public a disservice; the growth of applied social science is served no better.

DATA ANALYSIS:
MORE GENERAL STRATEGIES

Much of what has already been said, of course, concerns data analysis in one way or another. The following discussion is tied less to evaluation design than to the problem of making sense of the data stemming from non-randomized studies, including surveys. The review is brief but, we hope, not provincial. It ranges from the simpler devices, such as checklist approaches to making inferences about a program's impact, to those statistical methods that yield a better-qualified inference but are technically demanding. None guarantees unbiased estimates of program effect, but all help to establish the plausibility of any given interpretation of the data.

CHECKLIST APPROACHES

Given some data bearing on a program's impact, the idea behind many checklist approaches is to make some judgment about the existence of an effect, then to enumerate all the competing causes or explanations for the effect *other* than the program itself. The final step is to attach some level of plausibility or import to those competing explanations.

Consider, for example, data on a novel treatment for schizophrenics undertaken in one ward of a hospital and data on schizophrenics treated in another, nonequivalent ward. One might look first at levels of severity following treatment for each group and infer that because severity is higher for the novel treatment group, that treatment harmed rather than helped people. There are a number of competing explanations for a between-groups difference, of course. The type of patient normally assigned to the novel ward may, for example, differ from those assigned to the regular ward. And enumerating these explanations is easier if we have at our disposal a checklist of threats to internal validity such as the ones enumerated by Campbell (1957), Campbell and Stanley (1966), and Cook and Campbell (1976). Their lists are elaborate, so we provide only a brief description of major themes.

The *maturation* of each group may differ notably. Participants in the novel program, for example, may have been deteriorating over the past few years, whereas the comparison group condition may have been relatively stable. The *selection* process for each ward may be designed deliberately or accidentally to assign those with differing severity to each ward. Even when their history is similar, if initial severity is different in each ward, their rate of deterioration may differ irrespective of the program's impact. *Testing* patients in the new program may also produce artificial effects—for example, by heightening patient and staff awareness of their condition. And if the instrumentation changes during the process, if different raters are used at different stages of the evaluation, the resulting differences in ratings may be mistaken for program effects. *Regression artifacts* may also be critical: If individuals are assigned to the new ward on the basis of their high initial severity, in the absence of any program effect and any major trend in the overall population, that subgroup will have a lower severity score at the second testing. The drop is attributable to a regression to the mean that affects any measure with imperfect reliability, rather than to the program. *Dropout rate* or *attrition* may produce artificial differences between groups if, for example, the least severely ill members of the new treatment group reject the new treatment and leave the ward and perhaps even check themselves into the regular ward.

The recent list of threats to validity issued by Cook and Campbell (1976) is complex, and its completion can be tedious. Nonetheless, in the informal impact evaluation, an approach like this can be enormously helpful in avoiding egregious errors in *qualitative* analyses of the data.

APPROACHES BASED ON STEREOTYPICAL ERRORS

Any checklist is inefficient to the extent that the list is long and contains items that are irrelevant for the evaluation at hand. To accommodate the problem, it is sometimes possible to identify stereotypical ways in which inferences about program impact may be wrong and so narrow the list down. The literal stereotypes may apply to only one class of evaluative settings—in compensatory education, for example —but they can be more useful in developing prescriptions that are quantitative *and* qualitative rather than solely qualitative to deal with the problem of estimating impact.

The basic objective is to recognize chronic problems of data analysis in a given substantive area and to determine their severity for the evaluation at hand. For example, Campbell identified six such problems, and Campbell and Boruch (1975) furnish some procedures for detecting and accommodating them. Those problems, identified as chronic in the evaluation of compensatory education programs using covariance or matching design and observational data, are generalizable to other settings. They include regression effects, differential growth rates, differences in reliability of measurement over time and with subgroup, and ceiling and floor effects on measurement.

To make matters concrete, consider an actual cultural enrichment program to which economically deprived preschool children have been exposed. The comparison group, selected after the fact, consists of children from families whose economic condition is better and who are thus ineligible for the program. Understanding the specific mathematical character of the setting is essential to estimating program effects but not essential for understanding the problems and prescriptions given next.

The *regression effects* problem turns on the fact that unreliable measurement in surveys sets the stage for biases in estimation of program effects when covariance, regression, matching, or similar conventional techniques are used. So, for example, a covariance technique might be used by the conventional analyst to adjust out preexisting differences between a treated group and the control group, without recognizing that imperfections in measurement of the covariates or matching variables often lead to estimates of program effect that are seriously biased. Some conditions, which are common but do not always prevail, can lead to estimates of program effect that are biased downward—that is, estimated effects are small even where actual effects are large, and estimates are negative, making the program look harmful when actual program effects are negligible. The conditions under which the problem occurs are described mathematically and literally in Campbell and Boruch (1975).

To help assure that the problem is detectable, it is essential that the program evaluator have information on (a) the process underlying assignment of treatment and comparison group members, (b) statistical data bearing on the character of both groups before the program begins, and (c) reliability of matching variables, covariates. Estimates of reliability can sometimes be used to adjust conventional analyses for the presence of measurement error. The other information is helpful in understanding whether particular approaches can or should be used by the analyst (see remarks below).

Differential growth of the treated and comparison groups appears to be a chronic problem that cannot be remedied without strong theory and good data on growth processes. When tested repeatedly over time, for example, middle-class children's achievement test scores ofen increase more rapidly than do scores of children from economically deprived settings. The stereotype occasionally identified here is a "fan spread" pattern of mean achievement for economic groups when plotted over time (Kenny, 1975). If the phenomenon goes unrecognized by the conventional analyst, then estimates of program effect will be biased. An analysis that looks only at change scores in the program group relative to the middle-class children will lead to a declaration that because the middle-class group is increasing at a faster rate, the program must have had a negative impact on participants. The declaration will be wrong unless the differential growth rate has been recognized and accommodated.

There is evidence to suggest that the less privileged child is measured with somewhat less reliability, using standard achievement tests, than the middle-class child and, further, that the reliability of measurement of each group will increase (depending on age, grade, and other factors) as children and testers become more familiar with the test. One of the stereotypical problems that may emerge in the field setting, then, is that the differential rate of errors in measurement produces a small difference between groups when in fact the difference is large. That is, the unreliability obscures real differences, especially on initial testing. If children are tested a second time and reliability of measurement of both groups is higher on that testing, the difference between groups will, under certain common conditions, increase. The increase will be attributable to the properties of the test and to practice effects rather than to any real program effect. But if the differentials in reliability of measurement go unrecognized by the conventional analyst, then the postprogram had a negative effect. Again, the exact conditions under which the problem occurs and evidence are given in Campbell and Boruch (1975). The simplest prescription that we can offer to establish the existence and magnitude of the problem is to obtain hard data as a check on its character: pilot tests or side studies in which intergroup differences in reliability or intertime differences are estimated, on-site studies of the test process, post facto estimates of the internal consistency of test responses estimated by group and by time period. Without the estimates, it is unlikely that adequate corrections can be made to conventional analyses.

Floor effects refer here to the problem of inadequate measurement of children whose ability level is considerably lower than that measured accurately by the achievement test used in the evaluation. That is, children in this range score near the zero or chance level on a test not because they know nothing but because the test is insensitive to ability in the lower range. The consequences can be obvious: Even if the compensatory program has a notable effect, that effect may still be too small to be reflected by an insensitive test—that is, the effect may not be sufficient to boost children into a measurable range. The problem is not a new one, nor is it confined to education. It is a dangerous one to the extent that conventional analysts who do not recognize it will be tempted to declare that a program estimate that is near zero means the program had no effect, rather than that the measurement was faulty. Worse, the problem can lead, under certain conditions, to estimates of effect that are negative. Again, the only reasonable prescription to follow, especially when the tests' properties are not well documented or are suspect, is to run pilot tests prior to the program evaluation to establish their sensitivity and validity.

To summarize, it is clear from case studies of evaluations that some conventional data analyses are susceptible to stereotypical problems that often go unrecognized. These problems can be anticipated and documented with side studies and pilot tests. The idea, to identify stereotypes, can be helpful in avoiding serious problems in estimating program effects, especially when unrecognized problems engender estimates that are negatively biased. The hazard, as in any such effort, is that the stereotypes themselves may be irrelevant or misleading in the particular case (see Cronbach, 1976). The approach generally requires expertise of two kinds: substantive, as in social program development and applications; and mathematical-statistical, as in establishing presence and character of the stereotype and in accommodating the problem it generates. Similar approaches have been developed around particular evaluation designs—for example, by Linn and Slinde (1977) in analyzing time-series data, by Linn (1976) in analysis of the use of standardized test norms, and by Glaser (1973) in evaluating criminal offender programs.

ANALYTIC MODELS AND METHODS OF ANALYSIS

Regardless of which broad approach one uses—checklists, stereotypes, or comparative assessment—the problem of numerically estimating the impact of a program remains. That is, the literally stated threats to validity, our understanding of how people behave in the absence of a program, and so on must be translated into mathematical form to uncover the size of the program effect and to attach some level of confidence to the estimate. Having capitalized on substantive experts to learn about qualitative reality, the analyst must then match the mathematical models, which underpin any data analysis, to that reality.

The analyst faced with the prospect of estimating program effects based on nonrandomized data is, with some exceptions, not in an enviable position. There is a wide choice of methods that are alleged to be pertinent. For each, however, there is a set of assumptions that must be met in order for the analysis to be valid—to produce an unbiased estimate of effect. In many cases it is difficult to check assumptions, and for naively designed field surveys, checking their tenability may be impossible.

Most often a piecewise approach to verifying their tenability is warranted. Scales of measurement in many analyses are supposed to have interval properties, for example. Roughly speaking, this means that the validity of measurement at any given point in the scale is as good as validity at any other point. Attrition from treatment and comparison groups, if it occurs at all, is usually supposed to be random or at least predictable on the basis of simple statistical models. The fact that a program is in place and has additive effects rather than, say, multiplicative effects also must be verifiable both at the structural level and at the level of the individual participant. The structure of variances and covariances for any given analysis must have a well-specified form, and evidence on the matter can determine which analysis is appropriate.

In some cases, there may not be a method that can be used without violating some assumption. Two strategies can then be used. One is to use the results of a sensitivity analysis, which is a test of how much a violation of a particular assumption will affect the outcome of the analysis. Occasionally this can be done through algebraic derivations, but usually it is done using simulation of data in which the assumption is violated. For example, analysts are aware that violating the assumption of normal distribution of residuals often has little effect on the F statistic in analysis of variance. This was established through simulations of data in which various different distributions of data were used.

The other strategy that can be used when assumptions are violated is to try various methods of analysis, each of which involves a different set of assumptions. Under some circumstances, the pattern of results will enable the researcher to educe not only the probable treatment effect but also which assumptions were actually violated. Utilization of this method requires that the researcher be able to list every assumption of each analytic method.

Certain methods are suspect because it is unlikely that their assumptions will be met in many evaluation studies, and violation of the assumptions can result in large biases. As indicated earlier, many of these methods are similar in principle, although they look different on the surface; blocking (matching), analysis of covariance, standardization, and multiple regression are all used to adjust for differences in background of the groups being compared. But using these procedures to analyze nonexperimental data is fundamentally different from using the same techniques to analyze data from randomized experiments. When data are gathered from a randomized experiment, the purpose of using various adjustment techniques is to provide a more powerful statistical test. With random assignment there are fewer problems of bias in the sense of correcting for initial group differences, either in terms of problems caused by errors of measurement or misspecification of the model. With nonexperimental data, on the other hand, the purpose of many adjustments is to correct for these factors, for errors of measurement and misspecification can cause large biases. Statistical power is typically of secondary importance here.

Some application of *covariance analysis* to nonrandomized data will give unbiased results, but it is not always possible to check the assumptions underlying the application. Cronbach et al. (1976) indicate that if the analyst knows either the complete covariate (one which predicts within-groups outcome as fully as possible) or the complete discriminant (which fully represents initial group differences), then unbiased estimation is possible. The problem is that, in practice, the analyst seldom knows whether imperfect prediction is due to errors of measurement or misspecification. A subset of cases in which the complete discriminant is known occurs when the covariates have been used to assign subjects to treatment groups. In this case, covariance and regression estimates will be unbiased (see Rubin, 1975, 1976a; Kenny, 1975; Overall and Woodward, 1977). A discriminant analysis may be useful in detecting the implicit rules for assignment, which can then be used in analysis of covariance or a matching design.

Because assignment on the basis of a covariate (even if measured imperfectly) can provide unbiased estimates of treatment effect without randomization, the regression-discontinuity design advocated by Campbell (1969) is an important tool for evaluators. In the regression-discontinuity design, a continuum of need or merit is established, and subjects scoring above the dividing line are assigned to one group and those below the dividing line are assigned to the other group. For example, students might be rated on need for compensatory education, and those above a certain point would receive it, whereas those below would not. In this case, an analysis of covariance would not be biased *if* certain additional assumptions hold. Such clear-cut assignment rules seldom exist, so biases are probably the rule rather than the exception in present-day research.

If the data satisfy all of the other criteria for ANCOVA (in particular, the slopes of the regression line for each group should be the same), and the covariate set is complete except for random errors of measurement, then it is possible to do an ANCOVA with corrections for unreliability. To ameliorate problems of fallibility in the covariate, for example, Lord (1960) has developed a large sample test statistic (for assessment of treatment effects) that relies on auxiliary data as a vehicle for accommodating the fallibility. The technique, which is restricted to the single covariate situations, yields results similar to Porter's (1967) methods for estimating true covariates for any number of groups, given test-retest reliabilities. Stroud (1972) derived a large sample test statistic for assessing differences between regression lines when the reliability of the covariate is known for the population; reliability in this case appears to correspond to internal consistency. Implicit in the Cronbach et al. (1976) work is the idea that generalizability coefficients can be used for the adjustment. Still other approaches involve a combination of both blocking and covariance in which matching is conducted on regressed pretest scores (i.e., pretest regressed on posttest and estimates made of pretest scores); the regression might ignore unreliability altogether. There has been no attempt to compare results using these alternative methods or to lay out relations among them. Moreover, the usefulness of these approaches has not been assessed relative to matching and standardization strategies based on fallible qualitative or quantitative variables. At this point, expert statistical help may be necessary (but seldom sufficient), as there is disagreement about what kind of adjustment is appropriate in different situations (see e.g., Campbell and Erlebacher, 1970; Kenny, 1975; Linn and Werts, 1977; Cronbach et al., 1976).

In doing an analysis of covariance, it is particularly helpful if the covariate is the same as the dependent variable. This is because one of the assumptions that must be made is that the dependent variable and the covariate measure the same traits and in the same proportions. If not, there is no way to correct for initial differences. For example, suppose the covariate measures both mathematical ability and verbal ability in the ratio of 2 to 1; that is, the covariate measures mathematical ability more than verbal ability. Suppose that the dependent variable is just the opposite; it measures the same abilities but in a ratio of 1 to 2. What we want to do is to correct scores for initial differences between the groups on the dependent variable. But if we correct for differences in mathematical ability, we will overcorrect for differences in verbal ability, whereas if we correct for differences in verbal ability, we will undercorrect for differences in mathematical ability. We can minimize the change of this occurring, as well as the probability of the covariate being incomplete, by using the same test (or a parallel test) as the dependent variable for a covariate.

Blocking or *matching* in evaluation studies involves matching each member of the program participant group with a partner in a comparison group. Partners are generally matched on qualitative or quantitative variables, such that the absolute difference between their respective scores on matching variables is minimum or zero. A variety of sophisticated strategies for matching samples has been suggested, including individual matching, precision matching, pair matching, and mean matching. Those who want a more complete discussion of matching should consult the work of Rubin (Cochran and Rubin, 1973; Rubin, 1974, 1976a, 1976b, 1976c), which discusses the problems of reducing bias due to initial differences, the effects of unreliability in the matching variables, and techniques for matching. Note, however, that when Rubin discusses reducing bias, he usually means bias due to initial group differences, not bias due to unreliability of matching variables. One instance in which matching can cause problems that may not be correctable is when matching is incorporated into the design of a non-randomized study. If matched pairs are selected to be studied and no data are collected on other subjects, the extent of bias in test statistics may be impossible to estimate or correct for due to these selection biases. Thus our recommendation is that if matching is used, it should be used after the fact, so that the results can be compared with other analytic methods.

Tactics related to matching, such as *standardization* adjustments, often involve weighting the mean difference between comparison and treatment group means within a given range of scores; the sum of the weighted product is an estimate of the program effect. The weights are chosen to minimize variance of the treatment estimate. Wiley's (1976) direct and indirect standardization methods constitute one related approach; means of subgroups in control and comparison groups are weighted according to the proportion of children, say, in those subgroups in the population. Other related standardization procedures, more commonly applied, include age-grade equivalents and the like, although these do not use a variance criterion for their development. Both matching and these standardization strategies may remove between-cell bias but may do little to remove within-cell biases. In some cases, they will yield results similar to covariance adjustment, but predicting the conditions under which they do so is not easy.

There are more complicated methods that allow for errors in measurement, but for the most part they still require many of the assumptions of other methods. For example, *structural equation models* approaches (Joreskog, 1974; Duncan, 1975; Goldberger and Duncan, 1973) involve translating verbal descriptions of causal relationships between variables into a mathematical description. This mathematical model can then be tested to see if it fits the data.

Work on these methods has been summarized in Goldberger and Duncan (1973), Joreskog and Sorbom (1979), and Joreskog and Wold (1982), and one can rely on the papers appearing in those volumes to guide analyses. The Joreskog and Wold two-volume series contains research by Joreskog, Sorbom, and others on the LISREL model; Bentler on his structural equation model systems; Muthen on LISREL-like models that mix categorical and continuous variables; Wold and others on the partial least-squares method (which requires fewer assumptions than LISREL); and by Mooijaart, Duncan, and others on latent class models.

Structural equation model methodology has been applied in evaluation research by Magidson (1977-1978) and Magidson and Sorbom (1982), among others. In a reanalysis of the Westinghouse-Ohio Head Start data, Magidson developed a model in which background factors of educational status and occupation-income were used, along with a dummy variable for treatment condition, as independent (latent) variables, with scores on tests of cognitive ability as dependent variables. Bentler and Woodward (1978) proposed alternative structural equation models for the same data set. Several problems are especially salient in this type of analysis: the possibility of an interaction between background factors and between background and treatment condition, and the dichotomous nature of the treatment condition variable (i.e., the program). Magidson and Sorbom (1982) demonstrated a method for dealing with some of these problems: The program recipient group and control group are modeled separately. The addition of terms for the means of each variable allows an analysis that is very much like the analysis of covariance but with latent instead of observed variables. This helps to solve the problem of unreliability in the observed variables.

Another solution to the problem of categorical variables (such as program condition) is to develop models that are appropriate for such data. One approach was developed by Heckman (1978, 1979) in which a dichotomous variable is assumed to be related to an underlying continuous variable. When the underlying continuous variable takes on a value greater than some threshold, the value of the dichotomous variable is one but is zero otherwise. Heckman's (1979) paper is reprinted in Stromsdorfer and Farkas (1980), along with several other papers that discuss or apply similar methods. The methods can be used not only to help model cases in which they are needed solely because there is a dichotomous variable but also in cases where there is a truncated dependent or independent variable (because of selection criteria), differential attrition, and differential recruitment (selection) into groups.

More general methods for dealing with ordered categorical variables, as well as a mixture of categorical and continuous variables, have been developed by Muthen (1978, 1979, 1982, 1983; Muthen & Christoffersson, 1981.) In general, these methods parallel the development of methods by Joreskog and Sorbom (1979) for continuous variables. Muthen first developed methods for confirmatory factory analysis of dichotomous variables in one group (Muthen, 1978) and several groups (Muthen & Christoffersson, 1981). He has now expanded his system to include a mixture of variables, with a complete structural equation model system (Muthen, 1982, 1983). He has also developed a computer program, the latest version of which is called LACCI, to perform these analyses.

These models are general enough to allow for measurement error and for omitted variables, although the omitted variables must be uncorrelated with the underlying independent variables. There is still a possibility of bias entering, although less so than with the models described previously. There is a price to pay for using these models: More data must be collected. To get a good measure of errors in variables, underlying independent variables must usually be measured by at least two observed variables (exact rules for prescribing how many observed variables are necessary are usually complicated). Thus if the researcher feels that socioeconomic status influences test scores, he must usually have at least two, and preferably three or more, measures of socioeconomic status, such as mother's or father's education and family income. Other complications in the particular model will determine exactly how many measures of each underlying variable are necessary, but good planning (or good luck) is necessary in order that all of the plausible causal models can be tested. For this reason, although the structural equation models approach is the most powerful one yet devised to analyze nonexperimental designs, it cannot be used on all data sets because not enough data are always available, nor are the assumptions always plausible.

NOTES

1. Material in this section has been excerpted from Boruch (1975) and updates material in Rutman (1977).

2. Background research has been supported in part by National Institute of Mental Health Training Grant.

REFERENCES

BENTLER, P. and J. A. WOODWARD (1978) "A Head Start reevaluation: positive effects are not yet demonstrable." Evaluation Quarterly 2: 493-510

BISHOP, Y. M. M., S. E. FIENBERG, and P. W. HOLLAND (1975) Discrete Multivariate Analysis: Theory and Practice. Cambridge: MIT Press.

BORUCH, R. F. (1975) "On common contentions about randomized field experiments," in R. F. Boruch and H. W. Riecken (eds.) Experimental Testing of Public Policy. Boulder, CO: Westview.

——— (1974) "Bibliography: illustrative randomized field experiments for program planning and evaluation." Evaluation 2: 83-87.

——— (1973) "Problems in research utilization: use of social experiments, experiments, and auxiliary data in experiments." Annals of the New York Academy of Sciences 218: 56-57.

——— and H. RIECKEN (1975) Experimental Testing of Public Policy. Boulder, CO: Westview.

BORUCH, R. F., J. MAGIDSON, and S. DAVIS (1975) "Interim report: secondary analysis of Project Middlestart." Presented at the annual meetings of the American Psychological Association, September.

BORUCH, R. F., A. J. McSWEENY, and E. J. SODERSTROM (1978) "Randomized field experiments for program development and evaluation: an illustrative bibliography." Evaluation Quarterly 4: 455-695.

BREGER, M. (1983) "Randomized social experiments and the law," in R. F. Boruch and J. S. Cecil (eds.) Solutions to Ethical and Legal Problems in Social Research. New York: Academic.

BRYK, A. S. and H. I. WEISBERG (1976) "Value-added analysis: A dynamic approach to the estimation of treatment effects." Journal of Educational Statistics 1: 127-155.

BRYK, A. S. and H. I. WEISBERG (1977) "Use of the nonequivalent control group design when subjects are growing." Psychological Bulletin 84: 950-962.

BRYK, A. S., J. F. STRENIO, and H. I. WEISBERG (1980) "Value-added analysis: a dynamic approach to the estimation of treatment effects." Journal of Educational Statistics 5: 5-34.

BRYK, A. S. and E. WOODS (1980) An Introduction to the Value-Added Model and Its Use in Short Term Impact Assessment. Cambridge, MA: The Huron Institute.

CAMPBELL, D. T. (1974) "Making the case for randomized assignment to treatments by considering the alternatives." Research memo #Pre 627. Evanston, IL: Northwestern University, Psychology Department.

——— (1969) "Reforms as experiments." American Psychologist 24: 409-429.

————(1957) "Factors relevant to the validity of experiments in social settings." Psychology Bulletin 54: 297-312.

———— and R. F. BORUCH (1975) "Making the case for randomized assignment to treatments by considering the alternatives: six ways in which quasi-experimental evaluations in compensatory education tend to underestimate effects," in C. A. Bennett and A. Lunsdaine (eds.) Central Issues in Social Program Evaluation. New York: Academic.

CAMPBELL, D. T. and A. E. ERLEBACHER (1970) "How regression artifacts in quasi-experimental evaluations can mistakenly make compensatory education look harmful," in J. Hellmuth (ed.) Compensatory Education: A National Debate, Vol. 3: Disadvantaged Child. New York: Brunner/Mazel.

CAMPBELL, D. T. and J. C. STANLEY (1966) Experimental and Quasi-Experimental Designs for Research. Chicago: Rand McNally.

COCHRAN, W. G. and D. B. RUBIN (1973) "Controlling bias in observational studies: a review." Sankhya (Ser. A) 35: 417-446.

COOK, T. D. and D. T. CAMPBELL (1976) "The design and conduct of quasi-experiments and true experiments in field settings," in M. D. Dunnette (ed.) Handbook of Industrial and Organizational Psychology. Chicago: Rand McNally.

CREAGER, J. A. and R. F. BORUCH (1969) "Orthogonal analysis of linear composite variance." Proceedings, Annual Meeting of the American Psychological Association (Washington, D.C.).

CRONBACH, L. J. (1976) "Notes on temptress and Campbell-Boruch." Unpublished memo, Stanford University, Department of Education, January 18.

————D. R. ROGOSA, R. D. FLODEN, and G. G. PRICE (1976) "Analysis of covariance: angel of salvation, or temptress and deluder?" Occasional paper, Stanford Evaluation Consortium, Stanford University.

DANIELS, D. N. et al. (1968) DANN Services Program. Research report, National Institute of Mental Health, Grant No. 02332.

DENISTON, O. L. and I. M. ROSENSTOCK (1972) The Validity of Designs for Evaluating Health Services. Rsearch report, University of Michigan, School of Public Health.

DIRECTOR, S. (1974) "Evaluating the impact of manpower training programs." Ph.D. dissertation, Northwestern University.

DUNCAN, O. D. (1975) Introduction to Structural Equation Models. New York: Academic.

FISHER, R. A. (1935) Design of Experiments. New York: Hafner.

GILBERT, J. P., R. J. LIGHT, and F. MOSTELLER (1975) "Assessing social innovations: an empirical base for policy," in A. Lumsdaine and C. A. Bennett (eds.) Central Issues in Social Program Evaluation. New York: Academic.

GLASER, D. (1973) Routinizing Evaluation: Getting Feedback on Effectiveness of Crime and Delinquency, NIMH.

GLASS, G. V., V. L. WILLSON, and J. M. GOTTMAN (1975) Design and Analysis of Time-Series Experiments. Boulder: Colorado Associated Universities Press.

GOLDBERGER, A. S. (1973) "Structural equation models: an overview," in A. S. Goldberger and O. D. Duncan (eds.) Structural Equation Models in the Social Sciences. New York: Seminar.

GOLDBERGER, A. S. and O. D. Duncan [eds.] (1973) Structural Equation Models in the Social Sciences. New York: Seminar.

GRANGER, C. W. J. and P. NEWBOLD (1974) "Spurious regressions in econometrics." Journal of Econometrics 2: 111-120.

HEBER, R., H. GARBER, S. HARRINGTON, C. HOFFMAN, and C. FALENDER (1972) Rehabilitation of Families at Risk for Mental Retardation. Madison: University of Wisconsin Rehabilitation Research and Training Center.

HECKMAN, J. J. (1974) "Sample selection bias as a specification error." Econometrika 47: 153-161.

———(1978) "Dummy endogenous variables in a simultaneous equation system." Econometrika 46: 931-960.

HILL, A. B., J. MARSHAL, and D. A. SHAW (1960) "A controlled clinical trial of long-term anticoagulant therapy in cerebrovascular disease." Quarterly Journal of Medicine 29: 597-609.

HOLT, N. (1974) "Rational risk taking: some alternatives to traditional correctional programs." Proceedings: Second National Workshop on Corrections and Parole Administration. (College Park, MD: American Correctional Association.)

JORESKOG, K. G. (1974) "Analyzing psychological data by structural analysis of covariance matrices," in R. C. ATKINSON, D. H. KRANTZ, R. D. LUCE, and P. SUPPES (eds.) Contemporary Developments in Mathematical Psychology, Vol. 2. San Francisco: W. H. Freeman.

KENNY, D. A. (1975) "A quasi-experimental approach to assessing treatment effects in the nonequivalent control group design." Psychological Bulletin 83: 345-362.

———(1973) "Cross-lagged and synchronous common factors in panel data," in A. S. Goldberger and O. D. Duncan (eds.) Structural Equation Models in the Social Sciences. New York: Seminar.

LEVITON, L. C. andR. F. BORUCH (1983) "Contributions of evaluation to educational programs and policy." Evaluation Review 7: 563-598.

LINN, R. L. (1976) The Use of Standardized Test Scales to Measure Growth. Reproduced report, University of Illinois, Psychology Department.

———and J. A. SLINDE (1977) "The determination of the significance of change between pre- and posttesting periods." Review of Educational Research 47: 121-150.

LINN, R. L. and C. E. WERTS (1977) "Analysis implications of the choice of a structural model in the nonequivalent control group design." Psychological Bulletin 84: 229-234.

LIPSEY, M. W., D. S. CORDRAY, and D. E. BERGER (1981) "Evaluation of a juvenile diversion program: using multiple lines of evidence." Evaluation Review 5: 283-306.

LORD, F. M. (1960) "Covariance with fallible covariates." Journal of the American Statistical Association.

MAGIDSON, J. (1978) "Reply to Bentler & Woodward: the .05 level is not all-powerful." Evaluation Quarterly 2: 511-520.

———(1977) "Toward a causal model approach for adjusting for preexisting differences in the nonequivalent control group situation: a general alternative to ANCOVA." Evaluation Quarterly 1: 399-420.

———and D. SORBOM (1982) "Adjusting for confounding factors in quasi-experiments: another reanalysis of the Westinghouse Head Start Evaluation." Educational Evaluation and Policy Analysis 4: 321-329.

McKAY, H., A. McKAY, and L. SINESTERRA (1973) "Stimulation of intellectual and social competence in Colombian preschool-age children affected by the multiple deprivations of depressed urban environments." Second progress report, Universidad del Valle, Human Ecology Research Station, September.

McLUHAN, M. and B. NEVITT (1973) "The argument: causality in the electric world." Technology and Culture 14: 1-18.

MEIER, P. (1972) "The biggest public health experiment ever: the 1954 field trial of the Salk poliomyelitis vaccine," in J. M. Tanur, F. Mosteller, W. B. Kruskal, R. F. Link, R. S. Pieters, and G. Rising (eds.) Statistics: A Guide to the Unknown. San Francisco: Holden-Day.

MOLOF, M. J. (1967) Forestry Camp Study: Comparison of Recidivism Rates of Camp-Eligible Boys Randomly Assigned to Camp and to Institutional Programs. Research Report No. 53, California Department of the Youth Authority, Division of Research, October.

MOSTELLER, F. (1968) "Rerandomization," in D. L. Sills (ed.) International Encyclopedia of the Social Sciences. New York: Macmillan/Free Press.

MUTHEN, B. (1983) "Structural equation modeling with categorical variables." Annals of Applied Econometrics (Journal of Econometrics).

———(1982) "Structural equation modeling with ordered categorical and continuous latent variable indicators." Presented at the annual meeting of the psychometric Society, Montreal, June.

———(1979) "A structural probit model with latent variables." Journal of the American Statistical Association 74: 807-811.

———(1978) "Contributions to factor analysis of dichotomous variables." Psychometrika 43: 551-560.

———and C. Christoffersson (1981) "Simultaneous factor analysis of dichotomous variables in several groups." Psychometrika 46: 407-419.

OVERALL, J. E. and J. A. WOODWARD (1977) "Nonrandom assignment and the analysis of covariance." Psychological Bulletin 84: 588-594.

PORTER, A. C. (1967) "The effects of using fallible variables in the analysis of covariance." Ph.D. dissertation, University of Wisconsin, Madison.

RIECKEN, H. W., R. F. BORUCH, D. T. CAMPBELL, N. CAPLAN, T. K. GLENNAN, J. W. PRATT, A. REES, and W. WILLIAMS (1974) Social Experimentation: A Method for Planning and Evaluating Social Programs. New York: Seminar.

RINDSKOPF, D. M. (1976) "A comparison of various regression-correlation methods for evaluating nonexperimental research." Ph.D. dissertation, Iowa State University, Ames.

ROSELLE, R. M. and D. T. CAMPBELL (1969) "More plausible rival hypotheses in the cross-lagged correlational technique." Psychological Bulletin 71: 74-80.

RUBIN, D.B. (1976a) Assignment to Treatment on the Basis of a Covariate (ETS RB 76-9). Princeton, NJ: Educational Testing Service.

———(1976b) "Multivariate matching methods that are equal percent bias reducing, I: some examples." Biometrics 32: 109-120.

———(1976c) "Multivariate matching methods that are equal percent bias reducing, II: maximums on bias reduction for fixed sample sizes." Biometrics 32: 121-132.

———(1975) "Bayesian inference for causality: the importance of randomization." Proceedings of the American Statistical Association, pp. 233-239.

———(1974) "Estimating causal effects of treatments in randomized and nonrandomized studies." Journal of Educational Psychology 66: 688-701.

RUFFIN, J. N., J. E. GRIZZLE, N. C. HIGHTOWER, G. McHARDY, H. SCHULL, and J. B. KRISHER (1969) "A cooperative double-blind evaluation of gastric "freezing" in the treatment of duodenal ulcer." New England Journal of Medcine 281: 16-19.

RUTMAN, L. (1977) Evaluation Research Methods: A Basic Guide. Beverly Hills, CA: Sage.

RUTSTEIN, D. D. (1969) "The ethical design of human experiments." Daedalus 98: 523-541.

SCHEIRER, M. A. and E. L. REZMOVIC (1983) "Measuring degree of program implementation: a methodological review." Evaluation Review 7: 599-634.

STROMSDORFER, E. W. and G. FARKAS [eds.] (1980) Evaluation Studies Review Annual, Vol. 5. Beverly Hills, CA: Sage.

STROUD, T. W. F. (1972) "Comparing conditional means and variances in regression model with measurement errors of known variance." Journal of the American Statistical Association 67: 407-412.

TROCHIM, W. M. K. (1982) "Methodologicaly based discrepancies in compensatory education evaluation." Evaluation Review 6: 443-480.

WARREN, W. Q. (1967) "The Community Treatment Project: history and prospects," in S. A. Yefsky (ed.) Law Enforcement, Science, and Technology. Washington, DC: Thompson Books.

WEIKART, D. P. (1972) "Relationship of curriculum, teaching and learning in preschool education," in J. C. Stanley (ed.) Preschool Programs for the Disadvantaged Children. Baltimore: Johns Hopkins University Press.

WILEY, D. E. (1976) "Approximations to ceteris paribus: data adjustment in educational research," in W. H. Sewell, R. M. Hauser, and D. L. Featherman (eds.) Schooling and Achievement in American Society. New York: Academic.

WORTMAN, P. M. and R. G. ST. PIERRE (1975) The First Year of the Educational Voucher Demonstration: A Secondary Analysis of Student Achievement Test Scores. Research report, Northwestern University, Psychology Department, Methodology and Evaluation Program.

YINGER, J. M., K. IKEDA, and F. LAYCOCK (1977) Middlestart: An Experiment in the Educational Enrichment of Young Adolescents. Cambridge: Cambridge University Press.

6

INCREASING THE LIKELIHOOD OF INFLUENCING DECISIONS

Carol H. Weiss

After all the rigors of conducting a good evaluation research study, evaluators hope to see the results affect program decisions. Novice evaluators often assume that attention to study results will be automatic: Why would an agency sponsor an evaluation if it didn't intend to put the results to use? All they have to do, they assume, is do a competent study and perhaps make a greater effort than usual to communicate the results clearly and simply, and then the report will become the basis for program decision-making.

Alas, 'tis not so. Experience shows that evaluation results often go unheeded. Many factor intervene between the completion of an evaluation study and its application to practice. For evaluators who want to increase the utility (and the likelihood of agency use) of evaluation results, it is well to understand the range of factors that may, and often do, impede utilization. Only with understanding of the manifold obstacles can evaluators plan a sensible course to deal with them.

RITUALISTIC EVALUATION

One set of obstacles arises when the agency had no interest in using evaluation results from the outset. The agency supported the study for reasons that had little to do with its informational contribution. Agencies may find evaluation useful for a variety of reasons extraneous to its purported purpose. For example, an agency may fund an evaluation study as a ploy to delay action on a difficult issue; managers fend off demands for action with the excuse that a study is being done and they are waiting for results before they can act. Occasionally an agency supports an evaluation to gain recognition for what the managers are sure is a "successful" program. They expect the evaluation to document the success, and they plan to use the results for public relations and fund-raising. Should the study show anything else, they have little interest in paying attention.

On occasion, agency managers support an evaluation study to "paper over" certain known deficiencies in program operation. Suchman (1967) called this the "whitewash" tradition in evaluation. Managers select certain good features of the program for careful review and try to screen from view those aspects of the program that are problematical.

More often, agency managers undertake an evaluation research study with the intent of using the results as ammunition in bureaucratic contests. They expect that the results will come out "their way," and then they can brandish them as backup for the position they espouse. In this game evaluation is a tactic in the struggles and negotiations that attend controversies within organizations.

Sometimes agencies undertake evaluation studies because evaluation is a rational thing to do. Managers face no particular issues, nor do they have any particular need for information. Rather, they want to appear, and to be, responsible and rational administrators. Evaluation is reputed to be the "right" course of action; it will present them to the outside world as rational actors. Accordingly, they go through the approved ritual (Feldman and March, 1981).

Perhaps even more frequent is the undertaking of evaluation research because the agency funding the program requires evaluation as a condition of program support. Local managers who have little interest in evaluation themselves go through the motion of complying with the mandate. If that is the only way to ensure continued support for program operations, it seems a harmless enough price to pay.

In all these cases, the agency has little or no interest in paying attention to evaluation findings. Should the evaluation show weaknesses when the expectation was for program success, a first line of defense is usually to file away the report in the expectation that nobody else will want to know. When there were no expectations at all, but just ritualistic adherence to "correct procedure," few agency people can be expected to read even the executive summary. Careful analysis of evaluation findings is rarely likely under any of these conditions.

EVALUATIONS WITH INFORMATIONAL INTENT

Of course, there are many occasions on which agencies undertake evaluation with conscientious intentions to consider results in decision-making. That is a good first step. In fact, it can be argued that unless such initial commitment exists, evaluators are well advised to ply their trade elsewhere. When agency people have real questions in mind and real decisions to face, they are more likely to pay attention to evaluation findings. Nevertheless, even in these cases a host of obstacles may intrude. It is important for an evaluator to understand the organizational and political conditions in the decision-makers' environment that constrain attention to evaluation research. It is useful, too, to understand the conditions that affect evaluators, particularly those who come from the social science tradition, who sometimes assume that they are neutral, objective, and free of all outside influences. Only with sensitivity to the factors that constrain the several parties to the evaluation does it become possible for the evaluator to act wisely to increase the utility and usability of evaluation results.

The time to begin planning for utility is in the planning phase of the study. It is part of the process of choosing the appropriate evaluation questions, focusing on salient issues, developing measures that make sense to people in practice, and designing appropriate comparisons. Many evaluators begin to think about the use of evaluation results only when the study is almost over. Then they start hatching schemes for preparing short, jazzy reports and mailing them to lists of key people (Weiss with Bucuvalas, 1980: 202-204). But increasing the utility of evaluations cannot rely only on communication, however expert. It must also involve supplying the kinds of information people want or need. Planning for use has to begin early, and it should be grounded in a realistic apreciation of the dynamics of the program context.

ACTORS IN THE
EVALUATION-INTO-USE PROCESS

EVALUATORS AND DECISION MAKERS

Let us begin the analysis of the use of evaluation research with a brief introduction to the major actors: the evaluator and the program decision maker (see Figure 6.1). Evaluators may be staff members of the federal or state department sponsoring the program or of a local agency running the program; they may be outside researchers, in consulting firms, research institutions, or university academic departments. Program decision makers may be officials of the federal or state agency supporting the program, state or local officials or foundation officers who have a say about whether and how the program shall continue, or managers of the local agencies who operate the program.

Wherever they sit, evaluators and decision makers are members of different institutional worlds. They respond to the norms of their own institutions. Any attempt to link the spheres more closely has to take account of the varying structural conditions under which they work.

Evaluators are often faculty members of a university. As such, they respond to the academic reward system. Rewards are based on publishing research results in books and journals and hewing close to the mainline interests of their discipline. They are affected by the interaction patterns in academia—the people they work with and talk to, the meetings they attend within and outside their own institutions. Their career goals—climbing the rungs of the ladder to tenure and full professorship—press toward an emphasis on methodological sophistication and tend to give short shrift to the distractions of ongoing contacts with program agencies or dissemination of results to practitioners.

Other evaluators work in research organizations heavily dependent on competitive contracts. Staff are employed on a project-by-project basis, without much security of employment. Continuity and career rewards hinge on a succession of successful bids for new studies, so that writing winning applications takes precedence over competent completion of current evaluations. Both their superiors and their colleagues reinforce the emphasis on proposal-writing and rapid execution of current work.

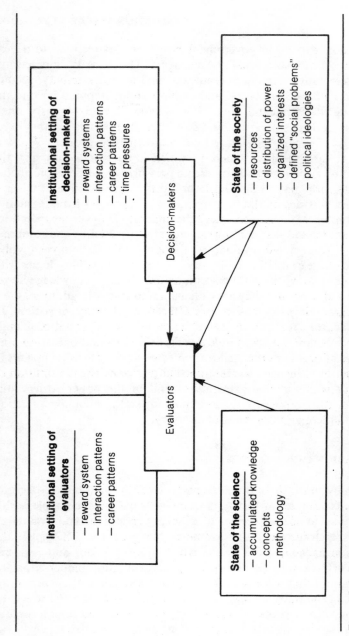

Institutional setting of decision-makers
— reward systems
— interaction patterns
— career patterns
— time pressures
—

Decision-makers

State of the society
— resources
— distribution of power
— organized interests
— defined "social problems"
— political ideologies

Evaluators

Institutional setting of evaluators
— reward system
— interaction patterns
— career patterns

State of the science
— accumulated knowledge
— concepts
— methodology

Figure 6.1 Influences on Key Actors in the Evaluation–Decision System

163

Decision makers in government bureaucracies respond to a very different set of institutional arrangements. The rewards, interactions, and career patterns in the bureaucracy tend to foster activity, accommodation with other actors, and caution about stepping beyond the prevailing departmental line. Bureaucrats have to satisfy their superiors and consult with a range of interested parties in other executive agencies, the legislature, and constituency groups. Work is geared toward the fiscal year, in which annual budgeting and the calendar of expiring legislation create pressures to get decisions made. When decision makers are legislators, they are responsive to the special characteristics of their environment—pressures of the legislative leadership, local constituents, and the imperatives of the next election.

Evaluators and decision makers are also affected by the resources available to them. For evaluators, the most salient resources involve the state of the evaluation craft—the concepts and methodologies with which they can work and the accumulated research knowledge about the kinds of programs they are called upon to study. In addition, they, like program decision makers, are affected by the state of society. In particular, they respond to prevailing definitions of social problems, what are and are not acceptable standards of program operation, and the types of problems that call for remedial action. Decision makers in addition are influenced to an important degree by the distribution of authority within their organizations and in the larger society, the nature of the resources at their command, and the bounds on action set by political and organizational policy.

EVALUATION FUNDING AGENTS

In many cases, there is a third party in the evaluation-into-decision process: the funder of the study (see Figure 6.2). Some people in this category sit in special offices of planning, research, and evaluation within the department that supports the program. They plan the evaluation agenda, often decide which studies to do, and issue requests for proposals (RFPs) to potential evaluation bidders (that is, organizations that will respond to the RFP with competitive proposals to conduct the study). They review the incoming proposals, select the most appropriate proposal on a variety of criteria, and fund it by contract for the specific task. Other funding agents come from private organizations or foundations that support the program, and they may or

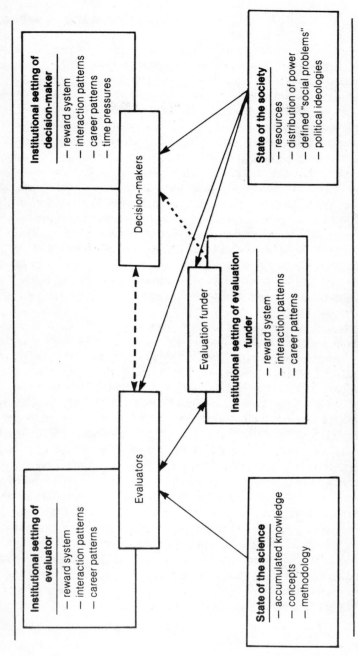

Figure 6.2 Influences on Key Actors in the Evaluation-Decision System

may not engage in the same kind of competitive bidding. Once in a while, a legislative committee or a superordinate body, such as a state commission, mandates and funds the evaluation.

Funding agents, too, respond to the settings in which they work. Their motivations and rewards are likely to differ from those of both program decision makers and evaluators. When funders are members of research and analysis staffs, they may adopt an academic orientation and view their role as championing the methodological excellence of studies that are done. In other research offices tied closely to policy-making officials, they are likely to be responsive to the pressures of practical political choices. In such cases they can become enmeshed in "firefighting"—handling the emergencies of the moment —and try to use evaluation as a tool in these activities. Still other funders aim to develop and fund studies that are relevant to longer-term decisions, studies that address not only the hot topics of the day but also try to enlarge understanding of the dimensions of social problems and the aptness of alternative programmatic schemes for coping with them.

Although funding agents, rather than program decision makers or program managers, often initiate an evaluation study, they are not likely to be its direct users. The best they can do is call the study to the attention of people who are potential users. But in many research and evaluation offices, this task is perpetually scanted. Funders spend so much of their time planning new evaluations, developing detailed specifications for these evaluations, reviewing proposals, and monitoring the contractor's conduct of the evaluation that they have little time for deciding what to do with incoming reports. Furthermore, they are sometimes poorly informed about who the program people are and what they need to know. They are isolated from program debates and unaware of which officials can use the information that is being reported. The report goes into the file, or is routed to a staff member whose interest may be peripheral, or is recorded as testimony to the funder's own qualifications and sterling performance on the job.

When the major actors in the evaluation-to-decision process have such disparate concerns and motivations, small wonder that the fit between research and decision is often poor. Each set of actors may be playing in the same game, but they are likely to be playing by different sets of rules.

OBSTACLES TO THE USE OF EVALUATION

We can analytically distinguish three major stages in the evaluation-to-decision process:

(1) *Evaluation formulation.* Questions for evaluation are identified. This involves understanding the salient issues about which knowledge is needed, selecting which facets of program operations to study, translating the knowledge needs into evaluation questions, operationalizing the concepts that will be used (e.g., what concretely is meant by "needs service," "works well," "learning," etc.), and determining how the evaluation will be carried out.

(2) *Conduct of the study.* Data sources are selected, measures are developed and refined, samples are drawn, data are collected and analyzed, and conclusions are drawn.

(3) *Implications for decision.* Evaluation results are translated back into the arena of policy. At this stage, the implications of the results for the future of the program are made explicit, and results (and often recommendations) are disseminated to potential users.

Most of the circumstances that impinge on the utility of evaluation to program decision makers occur in phases 1 and 3, where the research world interacts with the world of practice. It is in the same phases, at the boundaries between the two domains, that most obstacles arise.

Obstacles to the use of evaluation tend to be of two kinds: (a) intellectual and cognitive and (b) social and structural. The first set has to do with limits on knowledge; the second has to do with the limitations imposed on actors by the institutions in which they work. Figure 6.3 provides the framework for analysis of the kinds of difficulties that can interfere with the use of evaluation research. Cells A and B deal with the transition from the world of policy and practice, where programs operate and questions arise, to the formulation of an evaluation research study. Cells C and D deal with the transition from evaluation back to the world of program and policy decision-making. (The second phase—the actual conduct of the study—does not appear in Figure 6.3 because the problems that arise there are largely technical and methodological, and as Coleman [1972] has said, these problems have less effect on use.)

Stages of the Evaluation-Decision Process	Intellectual/ Cognitive Domain	Social/Structural Domain
From Policy Issue to Evaluation Formulation	A Specification of the Evaluation Problem	B Institutional Pressures on Policy Makers and Evaluators that affect specification
From Evaluation Findings to Policy Action	C Interpretation of Evaluation Findings	D Application of Evaluation to Policy

Figure 6.3   Sources of Difficulty in Applying Evaluation to Policy

SPECIFYING THE EVALUATION PROBLEM

Cognitive Limits

Some of the problems that bedevil the utility of evaluations arise from actors' inability to specify the appropriate kinds of data to collect. Among these problems are the following:

1. Decision makers find it difficult to know and articulate the kinds of information that will make a difference to their decisions. They find it even harder to specify the particular data or statistical relationships that would clarify an issue. Such cognitive limitations are by no means unique to decision makers. All of us have problems identifying which specific pieces of information will make a difference when we have to make a complex set of choices. In schools, for example, people often say they want data on students' test scores, because school people are expected to place highest priority on academic achievement. Yet in the event, test scores may be irrelevant to whether a program is continued, changed, or abandoned.

Since decision makers are usually uncertain about what they hope to get from evaluation, evaluators have to ferret, guess, and improvise. If they are particularly well versed in the program field, their estimates may turn out to be close to the mark. But there is considerable danger that the evaluator's specification of the central issues for study will be issues that concern the evaluator and be only marginally relevant to the concerns of decision makers when the point of choice arrives. When surrogates for decision makers, such as staff in evaluation offices, define the evaluation questions, they may be no better able than the evaluator to gauge decision makers' real information needs.

2. Evaluation takes time. Often two, three, or four years elapse between the initial decision to undertake an evaluation and the point at which results are ready. Therefore, the people who are formulating the study plan have to try to forsee what issues will be relevant fairly far into the future. Problems in prediction are legion (Duncan, 1969) and compound the difficulty of specifying appropriate questions for study.

3. Doing a relevant evaluation requires choosing appropriate research methods. But often evaluators conceptualize issues and select methods in terms of the methodologies in which they are proficient. They do not necessarily pick the research method that best fits the issues; almost unwittingly, they may see the aspect of the issue that is addressed best by the methodology with which they are familiar. Whether their specialty is experimentation, survey research, or econometric modeling, they tend to formulate evaluation questions in terms for which their methodology is suitable.

Institutional Pressures

Since the key players work in different institutional systems, they respond to the demands and rewards of the different spheres they inhabit. Thus the social and structural imperatives of their organizations can introduce obstacles such as these:

1. Location in different institutional positions creates variant perceptions of which of the issues facing the program are central. For example, evaluators may be engaged by the desire to test a hypothesis about the types of programming that best serve a particular target population, or they may wish to develop new methodological strategies for analyzing longitudinal data. Analysts in the Office of Management and Budget may see as the primary issue the need to cut program costs. Legislators may want to know whether the program should be continued or eliminated. Program managers will often want to know which kinds of modifications will make the program work

better. The issue deemed worthy of study varies with the position people hold. So, too, does the rapidity with which answers are wanted, which cut at the program should be taken, and which factors in the situation are seen as fixed and which are subject to policy alteration.

2. Mechanisms of funding also affect the definition of the evaluation. When the evaluator takes the initiative in developing the evaluation and receives a grant to fund the study, he or she has considerable latitude in framing questions in terms that fit his or her view of priority issues. These may or may not be the concerns of policy makers. When an agency specifies the focus of the evaluation and either hires its own evaluator or awards an evaluation contract through competitive bidding, the agency has major say in the formulation of the study. In the latter case, the evaluation is likely to have a shorter time frame and a more practical orientation. But that does not necessarily mean it will turn out to be more useful. The agency's conventional assumptions and restricted view of alternative programming strategies may restrict the range of questions that are addressed.

3. Bias intrudes in various ways. When the agency operating the program initiates the evaluation, it may seek to emphasize questions that deal with daily operations and minor adjustments to things as they are. On the other hand, an evaluator who perceives his or her role as advocate for the program's clients may raise larger questions that could lead to fundamental restructuring of the whole pattern of program arrangements.

4. The piecemeal nature of most evaluations limits the continuity of research and the cumulation of knowledge. Evaluations, even of the same program, tend to be undertaken on a project-by-project basis. In each period, a different research organization usually does the study, and each new team of evaluators has to start anew to learn the program field, the issues, the political constraints, and the range of available options. This type of disjointed research often leads to a series of modest and even flawed studies and limits the opportunities to build on prior knowledge. Rather than widening and deepening the understanding of effective programming, episodic evaluations take different cuts at the issues and at times contribute more to confusion than to enlightenment.

INTERPRETING EVALUATION FINDINGS

Intellectual-Cognitive Limits

After the study is finished, evaluation results are transmitted to people in the sphere of action. Among the problems that affect the ease of transmission are the divergent intellectual orientations of people in the domains of evaluation research and program decision-making.

1. Evaluators often write reports in a style that appeals to their research colleagues. Decision makers find their prose turgid, laden with jargon, filled with complicated mathematical data, and hard to understand. This is a familiar complaint, and if language were all that was at issue, it would be an easy problem to solve. However, "jargon" is often a whipping boy for more serious cognitive obstacles. Decision makers are often unfamiliar with the social science concepts that are embedded in academic language. They may not grasp the discussion of "redistributional effects" or "learned incapacities." More important, they may fail to share the conceptual assumptions on which the evaluation was based. For example, an evaluator may have taken for granted that class, ethnicity, and occupational position inevitably influence the gains that program participants could achieve, whereas a decision maker who believes that each individual is in control of his or her own destiny may find these assumptions untenable.

2. Evaluation findings are often ambiguous. Relations in the data may be small or inconsistent; the variables studied may account for only a small fraction of the variance in outcomes. No clear highway to recommendations, no obvious course of action, opens up. To move from this kind of shapeless evaluation to action is a heavy intellectual burden. It is not at all clear what decision makers should do.

3. Each evaluation studies a particular realization of a program concept in a specific time and place. Studies do not evaluate "compensatory education"; they evaluate a specific compensatory program with particular staff members using particular techniques and materials in a concrete setting teaching specific students. Whether the results that are observed in one instance will generalize to other programs is usually unclear. It is also unclear whether outside conditions that affect the program will be the same in the future as they are in the

present. Therefore, moving from the results of one evaluation study to prescriptions for future action is plagued by cognitive uncertainties.

Social-Structural Obstacles to Application

Disjunctions between the domains of evaluation research and program decision-making are especially obtrusive at the point when decision makers are expected to take action on the basis of evaluation results. Evaluation reports may not reach appropriate users; decision makers may attach different meanings to results than do the evaluators; they may have different awareness of the options that are organizationally feasible; organizational conditions can constrain their capacity to put the results into practice.

1. One structural feature that frequently blocks the use of evaluation results is lack of appropriate dissemination. Results do not reach the people who could use them. Even when an evaluation is specifically commissioned by a prospective user, it sometimes fails to reach him or her. The failure can occur because the incumbent of the position changed since the start of the study, because funding intermediaries neglected to send on the report, because the report was completed so late that people were no longer interested, or for any of a number of other reasons. When the study was requested at a further remove from the user—for example, when it was required by the terms of a federal grant—the chances that evaluative information reaches the appropriate audience are even lower.

2. Institutional location makes a difference in the interpretation of study results. In looking at a set of data, the evaluator will highlight certain findings and interpret them in one way, whereas a decision maker may find that the same data tell a different story. What to the evaluator looks like "only 20% of the participants" may become in the eyes of an experienced program manager "fully 20% of the participants."

There is likely to be an even bigger gap when the report moves from the "is" to the "ought." An evaluator may conclude from findings of low rates of success that there should be a major overhaul of the program. A program decision maker may find such a conclusion neither feasible nor necessary.

3. Not infrequently, the putative decision maker has no particular decision to make. The program is operating and faces no crisis or turning point. Following the time-honored dictum, "If it's not

broken, don't fix it," program managers let the program proceed along its accustomed course.

Much of the time in most organizations, decisions to make a change in direction are rare events. The usual pattern of organizational life is one in which many people in many offices take minor steps in the course of doing their jobs. Over time, these small and uncoordinated steps almost imperceptibly move the organization down certain paths and close off others. No one is consciously aware that they—or the organization—is "deciding" on a policy. It is only in looking back that people realize that the organizational direction has changed— that, in effect, through a series of small acts, a decision has been made. When a decision "happens" through such diffuse and amorphous processes, there are few opportunities to consider the results of evaluation. People do their jobs and take action on the basis of the information they have at hand. Because they are not aware that what they are doing is making decisions, they rarely take the time to consult new information sources.

4. Another structural obstacle to the use of evaluation is fragmentation of authority. In most program agencies, particularly large ones, no one person or small group of people has the exclusive authority to make decisions. Staff in many offices have to be consulted, outside constituencies have to be accommodated; sometimes legislative action is required to appropriate requisite funds. The dispersion of authority means that even if one group of users finds evaluation conclusions persuasive, their stand may be altered in the negotations with collateral groups.

On occasion, the agency for which the evaluation was done has little authority to implement the actions that appear needed. For example, an evaluation suggesting that children's school learning will be improved by better health care suggests action that is outside the school's bailiwick. Or an evaluation showing that the performance of a local agency would be improved by changes in eligibility rules for clients implies the need for change that can be made only at the federal level. The lack of fit between the import of evaluation conclusions and agency authority can seriously constrain the possibility of application.

5. Limited resources are another constraint on the use of evaluation. The main shortage is usually money, but it may also be shortages of facilities, qualified staff, or motivated managers. When an agency lacks people with the necessary qualifications to run a program more effectively, it is likely to neglect evaluation conclusions.

6. Staff turnover affects the use of evaluative information in a number of ways. When the person who initiated the study and was committed to its completion leaves the agency, his or her successor may lack the same enthusiasm. Moreover, many staff members know that they will be in their positions for only a short time. This is particularly true of political appointees. In such cases, they have less concern with following through on evaluation results; the results of reform will come to fruition long after they have left the scene. They tend to concentrate on takeoffs, such as launching new initiatives, rather than on landings.

In sum, a formidable array of obstacles beset the use of evaluation results. Intellectual and structural limitations are particularly intrusive at the time the evaluation is being developed and again when results are ready for action. Let us now look at some possible strategies for overcoming the difficulties we have discussed.

REASONABLE EXPECTATIONS

Given the difficulties that litter the path between the initial plan for evaluation and the application of results to decision-making, it is little wonder that clear-cut uses of evaluation findings are rarely found. Direct use of evaluation results requires an unusual concatenation of circumstances: decision makers facing a clear decision point who have specific questions in mind, an evaluation study that is appropriately designed and conducted to supply evidence on those questions, unambiguous results, clarity and timeliness of presentation to the appropriate audience, congruence of values, relevance of results to the contemporary local situation, lack of external pressures that constrain the choices made by decision makers, sufficient resources to apply the findings in the program context, and authority to act. The likelihood of all these conditions falling into place simultaneously is painfully low. Most of them are beyond the capacity of the evaluator to create, or even to influence substantially.

Therefore, the first lesson to be drawn from this review is this: Moderate your expectations for the kinds of use you expect from evaluation research. To anticipate that the findings from one study will switch a decision from course A to course B is usually unrealistic. Even the most sympathetic and willing managers have to attend to many considerations beyond the application of research results. Not the least of their jobs is to reconcile the conflicting demands placed on them by diverse interests, constrained budgets, public desires, staff capacities, client wants, and needs for continuity of operation.

Perhaps a realistic level of aspiration for the influence of evaluation research would be that officials *attend* to the results of evaluation research and take them into account in their deliberations. The action they take may not represent full-scale acceptance of evaluation findings and recommendations, but it will be based on better evidence about the program and its context. They will be better informed of the kinds of problems that come up in program implementation, the nature of outcomes, and alternative strategies for dealing with the situation. They will take action with more conscious awareness of the trade-offs involved and what they are giving up for the sake of accommodating organizational and political pressures.

This sounds like a modest level of expectation for the use of evaluations, but I believe it is a reasonable one. I also think that it is preferable to the view that evaluation results should always prevail. To expect evaluation to *determine* policy implies a technocratic view of the world that is incompatible with democratic decision-making.

Moreover, the expectation that evaluation should prevail assumes that evaluation provides "the right stuff." We all know that most, if not all, research studies fall short of methodological perfection. And even when an evaluation study is done competently, it presents good evidence on the process and outcomes of a program in only one of its realizations, under one set of conditions, using one type of design and set of measures. Furthermore, it inevitably deals with only a limited subset of the issues that have to be taken into account in program decision-making. It is a partial account of issues and concerns, with many important factors unrepresented, such as budgetary constraints, staff competencies, client demands, and political feasibilities. Experienced decision makers have to consider a broader array of concerns than the typical evaluation deals with.

All evaluations, like all other research, are based on a series of value choices—choices of goals, criteria, measures, analytical assumptions—as well as prescriptions for what to do about program shortcomings. The notion that the values and assumptions embedded in the evaluation should play a dominant role in decision-making in effect undermines the principles of multi-interest participation and negotiation in the decision-making process. It implicitly places the evaluator in the position of Plato's philosopher-king—or at least that of his single trusted advisor.

Good evaluation studies deserve a hearing. If that is a modest definition of use, it still is no minor achievement. Recent investigations have demonstrated that when research gets a hearing, it can have far-reaching effects. Even when results do not sway immediate decisions, they lay down a sedimentation of ideas, concepts, generalizations, and findings that affect the way in which people look at programs. People assimilate the ideas into their view of how the world works. When findings from a number of different studies converge, they gradually alter people's conception of which issues are important and need to be addressed, which facets are amenable to change and which are "sticky" and resistant, where priorities lie, and the range of options that are worth considering in dealing with program concerns (Aaron, 1978; Alkin et al., 1979; Berg et al., 1978; Caplan et al., 1975; Cherns, 1972; Cohen and Weiss, 1977; Frankel, 1975; Knorr, 1977; Patton 1978; Pelz, 1978; Rich, 1980; Weiss with Bucuvalas, 1980).

This conceptual model of research use has been called "enlightenment" (Crawford and Biderman, 1969; Janowitz, 1970; Weiss, 1977). It represents a contribution to understanding. Over time, shifts in understanding can have significant consequences. What people do is influenced by what they "know" to be true, and what they learn from evaluation studies can alter agency agendas, agency priorities, and the types of actions that are considered and implemented. The process may be slow, but in the long run it may be profound. Of course, some evaluations come and go without leaving a mark. But others contribute findings, concepts, and ideas that percolate into courses of major reform.

PRACTICAL STEPS TO INCREASE THE LIKELIHOOD OF USE

Many prescriptions have been advanced for improving the chances that evaluation results receive a hearing in councils of action. Here is a review of some of the more promising ideas. None of them will work every time, and most of them depend on a certain degree of hospitality in the environment. Nevertheless, each is probably worth consideration.

(1) Plan the study with users in mind and, if possible, with their participation. Involving the people who will make decisions about the program in the planning of a study can accomplish three desirable ends: (1) It can help to ensure that the study is directed at the issues that matter to the people who will have a say about the program's future; (2) it can increase the realism of the evaluation's assumptions about what the program is actually working to achieve—its "real" goals rather than its rhetorical goals, and (3) it can help to win a degree of interest in and commitment to the study. When the people who have a stake in the program help to shape the questions that are asked, they are more likely to find the results pertinent at the end. When they are given a chance to explain the circumstances under which the program operates, they give the evaluator a better understanding of the potentials and limits of possible outcomes. Program people are also a wonderful resource for identifying problematics in the situation. They can identify those issues that are in contention, where information will have particular leverage (Patton, 1979; Rothman, 1980; Schulberg and Jerrell, 1979; Smith and Caulley, 1982).

To involve program stakeholders in planning the evaluation requires the ability to identify who the stakeholders are (Gold, 1983; Stake, 1983; Weiss, 1983). In the past many evaluators have invited participation from agency managers, who clearly are interested parties. But they have been much less likely to invite participation from other groups that also have an interest, such as operating staff, clients of the program, and staff of agencies with correlative or conflicting missions. Another set of possible stakeholders are people from outside agencies who might want to adopt the program if it proves to be successful (or abandon a smiliar program they already run if evaluation shows that effects are negative). It is difficult to figure out how to identify such people in advance and involve them in the planning of the evaluation. Other prospective users, such as people who enact legislation or control budget allocations, are also difficult to engage in the planning process.

Even when they are invited to join in evaluation planning and agree to do so, decision makers may engage in only token participation. It appears that some prospective users find the planning process uncongenial. They do not feel skilled in the kind of technical discussion that goes on; they assume that research planning is the task they are paying the evaluator to do; or they may just be too busy (Farrar and House,

1983; Murray, 1983; Zweig, 1979). Maintaining a lively level of participation in evaluation planning is easier said than done.

When prospective users cannot or do not participate, it is still possible for the evaluator to keep their concerns in mind. This may require frequent conversations with interested parties to learn about the matters that are on their minds. In more systematic fashion, evaluators may use the procedures of multiattribute utility analysis (Edwards et al., 1975; Guttentag, 1973) to gather data on which issues and which values matter most to different groups of stakeholders. Perhaps the most reliable device for learning about questions and program realities is for the evaluator to observe the program in action. By periodically watching what goes on, the evaluator is better equipped to gauge the salience of questions and to set realistic criteria for program success. "Hanging out" can be valuable; systematic observation may be even better.

There is considerable consensus among evaluators that close involvement with the program, its practitioners, and clients is a valuable source of information for evaluation planning. But it is by no means a foolproof scheme for ensuring utility. To their consternation, some evaluators who were fully engaged with the program still found at the end of the study that their conclusions went unread. The evaluator may have paid attention to some groups of stakeholders but failed to attend to others who had the real say when decisions were made. Or program conditions changed during the course of the study. At the outset, when the study was being planned, one set of issues may have been uppermost in people's minds. But in the year or more while the study was in progress, new factors emerged, old ones lost their salience, and the original study was out of synch with current conditions. (For enlightening accounts, see Deitchman, 1976, and Kogan and Henkel, 1983.)

Nevertheless, planning an evaluation with users in mind often has value. At the very least, it protects the study from addressing issues that are important only to the evaluator and have little relevance to the sociopolitical environment in which program decisions are made.

(2) Staying close to the scene. The need to understand the program and its people doesn't end when the planning is done. If evaluators are to keep the study relevant, they need ongoing information about (a) what is going on in day-to-day program activities, (b) whether new questions arise that the evaluation will be expected to

answer, and (c) whether conditions change (e.g., funding levels, staff assignments) so that the program is actually trying to achieve different goals from those originally set. If the program undergoes considerable shifts, the evaluation may be called on to change direction as well. Of course, this is difficult to do with a quantitative before-and-after design; the preprogram measures limit the kinds of changes that can be examined. But a number of helpful modifications can still be made (e.g., Weiss, 1972: 94-98; Cook and Reichardt, 1979). Adapting the evaluation to changed circumstances is much easier if it is designed as a qualitative, "illuminative" inquiry (Hamilton et al., 1978) based more heavily on observation and sequential interviews.

Clearly, there is little point in adhering to an original design that addresses issues that no longer matter. Evaluators should be close enough to the program scene to find out about changes as early as possible, so that they can take whatever steps are feasible to adjust the study to new informational needs.

Another advantage of maintaining contact with program people during the course of the study is the opportunity to feed back study data. Evaluators may find it useful to keep program managers informed about preliminary findings. As one program manager said in an investigation of evaluation use (Patton, 1977), the last thing he wants is surprises at the end. Early warning about things that are going wrong, client dissatisfaction, and the like can aid managers in making midcourse corrections. Evaluators worry that early feedback will "contaminate" their data, but often such worries are unfounded. Improvements in program operation—that is, helping the program to do better what it was intended to do in the first place—is not likely to be a contaminating influence.

When the time comes for final analysis of study data, evaluators have occasionally invited participation from program staff in making sense of the findings. This, of course, cannot be an invitation to them to censor negative results or give undue weight to the elements they like. It can be an opportunity to learn from program staff which findings are important and deserve elaboration, as well as an occasion to learn from them about possible reasons for the pattern of results that emerged. It may be, for example, that they know that little time or attention was actually paid to the achievement of certain of the stated program goals; effort was concentrated elsewhere. Or they may be able to explain why certain kinds of program participants benefited more from the program than others. Encouraging their input, while preventing possible self-serving interpretations from prevailing, can be a useful adjunct to the analysis.

(3) Concentrate the evaluation on conditions that can be altered. One of the dicta that is often suggested for increasing the usability of an evaluation is to stick to manipulable variables—those conditions that can be changed by the people who make decisions about the program (e.g., Coleman, 1972). Advocates of this prescription say that there is little value in exploring the effects of conditions that lie outside decision makers' jurisdiction, such as the sponsorship of the program, the gender of participants, or other such "givens." Program people do not have the authority to alter many of the conditions that affect program success, and if a study devotes a large fraction of its resources to demonstrating the influence of such variables, its results cannot be put to use.

In a similar vein, purveyors of advice suggest that whatever implications the evaluators draw from the data should stay within the realm of the feasible. They should take into account the limited opportunities and resources at the disposal of program decision makers and not make recommendations for drastic overhaul of the programmatic structure. Even if the program is shown to be of little value to its participants, in this view evaluators are advised to concentrate on the few opportunities for modification that program people have the jurisdiction to make.

These counsels of caution sound plausible. If the evaluation comes up with recommendations that are not feasible to implement, they are likely to go unused. But such strictures assume that the only kind of use is immediate and direct application of results by the people involved in the one program under study. As much of the earlier discussion in this chapter has indicated, immediate and direct application of results in the local case is usually limited by a host of constraints. If the evaluator abides by the limitations constraining this one set of decision makers, he or she foregoes the opportunity to say things relevant to programs of similar type in the larger context. It will often be of major importance to know whether intensive services work better than less frequent service in this kind of program, whether highly trained professionals do better than people with lower levels of training, whether program site or program auspices matter, and so on. In the context of the program at hand, perhaps nothing much can be done to alter these conditions, but in the larger program world, much can be done to reshape the premises of effective programming. Planners and program developers elsewhere can learn which operating conditions make a difference in increasing the likelihood of success. It may be particularly significant to learn how much of the variance in outcomes is attributable to external conditions that no program decision maker—local, state, or federal—can alter, so that reasonable expectations can replace grandiose dreams.

Given that so much of the use of evaluations that does occur takes place at a remove from the immediate program site, injunctions to "stay feasible" should be treated with considerable caution. In some cases they make good sense. But in others an emphasis on feasibility is likely to set unnecessary limits on the learning that can accrue from evaluation research. At their peril evaluators forego the opportunity to explore the range of variables that have an impact on program effectiveness. For it is a broad-gauged understanding of how and when programs work well that is likely to be the most useful knowledge evaluation can contribute.

(4) Clear, well-written, timely reports. When evaluators want to communicate with managers and practitioners, they need to write clearly and simply. Graphs and charts can dramatize findings. Complicated statistical presentations can be relegated to the appendix. A short summary at the beginning should present the key results without blurring the necessary qualifications. It is helpful to be clear and concise but without sacrificing discussion of the limitations of the study (e.g., inconsistent results from different data sources, missing information, limits on generalizability). Managers need to know what the study cannot tell them as much as they need to know what it can confidently say.

Timeliness is important if there is a clear decisional point coming up. For example, when the program is a demonstration, funded for a finite time to find out whether it will improve service, the evaluation report is more useful if it is finished before decisions about continuing the program are made. Often it is the legislative cycle that marks the significant decision point. Whether or not to reauthorize the program, and at what level of appropriations, are decisions that can be informed by evaluative evidence. In such cases it is crucial that the report be submitted on time. But sometimes a program faces no obvious point of choice. Things are likely to go along much as they have been going. Adhering to an arbitrary deadline will make little difference in how much attention the report receives.

Moreover, on major issues about lines of programming, decisions are rarely made once and for all. If the issues are important, they will

come up year after year. Repeated opportunities arise to take account
of evaluative evidence in modifying eligibility rules, modes of service,
intensity of effort, and other program features. Missing one budget
cycle need not signal the end of a study's usefulness. It may be more
vital to complete a thoughtful analysis than to rush out a report that
does scant justice to the data in hand.

On the other hand, lateness has no intrinsic merit. Evaluators, like
most researchers, have a tendency to stretch out the data-analytic process. They want to be sure that they have analyzed every plausible con-
figuration of variables before they consider the job done. When they
become enchanted by the opportunity to perform every type of statistical procedure in the book, their report may appear when the issues
that motivated the study have lost their salience, when the conditions
that were studied have already changed under the press of events, and
when interest in the evaluation has receded. Promptness may not be
the highest virtue, particularly if it involves skimping on the analysis,
but comprehensiveness of analysis at the expense of timeliness is not
intrinsically meritorious either. Some reasonable accommodation is in
order.

(5) To recommend or not to recommend. Should evaluators make
explicit recommendations on the basis of their data if they want decision makers to pay attention? Certainly dramatic recommendations
will have eclat. Whether they will be followed is more problematic.

Perhaps the most reasonable answer to the question about whether
to make the leap from data to recommendations is a contingent one. It
depends first on how specific and clear-cut the data are, and second on
how much the evaluators know about the program and its environment.

Evaluations sometimes show clear differences in outcomes between
participants who received one version of the program and those who
received a different kind or level of service. Under this circumstance,
the implications for decision-making are obvious. More commonly,
evaluative data show ambiguous results: Most people received limited
benefits from participation; older people did better than younger ones
under one version of the program, but only if served by certain types
of staff; participants in some sites did better than others, although
none of the measured variables identifies unique features of more effective sites. What kinds of recommendations do evaluators draw
from such muddy patterns? If they are experts in the program field—
familiar with prior research and program experience—and know a

good deal about outside conditions that impinge on the program, they may certainly want to offer their insights to decision makers. But if they are research specialists and program novices, they may be better advised to present the data as clearly and forcefully as they can and leave it to program specialists to draw appropriate implications. As noted earlier, a joint effort of interpretation may be a way to draw on the special expertise that each group brings to the endeavor.

(6) Get the results out. Dissemination of evaluation results is essential. Submission of a 400-page typed report is almost a guarantee that nobody will read the results. Evaluators should see that a short, well-written summary gets to everyone who has a say about the program: not only the funding organization and agency managers but also agency staff, clients, and perhaps legislators, foundations, and the media as well. Each of these groups can take steps that will be better informed for knowing what the evaluation tells.

Personal contact with prospective users often engages attention more effectively than written reports. Evaluators can take advantage of opportunities to attend meetings where future actions are being considered. They may be able to make presentations at staff meetings, interorganizational conferences, training sessions—all the opportunities to get the findings assimilated into agency practice. Continued meetings with decision makers in local, state, and federal offices can keep the results of the evaluation on the docket over a period of time. This is time-consuming stuff, but if utilization is a key value, the effort is worthwhile.

Nor do opportunities for dissemination stop with the particular agencies whose programs were evaluated. Some of the most important prospective users are located at agencies with similar missions, who would be interested in adopting the program if results proved positive and equally interested in avoiding this type of program if the results showed little success. Perhaps the best route to reach such audiences is to get information about the evaluation into professional publications that such people see—journals that reach social service administrators, school superintendents, health care agency directors, and so on.

Another audience is the evaluation community. Papers given at professional meetings or published in professional journals can alert fellow evaluators to a range of issues that they are likely to care about: useful measures, feasible designs, reasonable estimates of how much change occurs when service of various kinds is provided, and special conditions that enhance or limit program effectiveness.

(7) Fitting the evaluation results into the larger picture. One of the most useful ways to get evaluation results a hearing is to integrate them with other research and evaluation about the program area. "Evaluation synthesis" is becoming a recognized and valued activity (Light and Smith, 1971; Light, 1979; Glass et al., 1981). It involves review of a series of evaluations that have addressed programs with similar goals, and an effort to make sense of the range of results that have been observed.

If all studies showed roughly similar findings, synthesis would be an easy endeavor. However, studies of substantially similar programs —even programs with the same label (such as Head Start programs or Community health centers)—often show strikingly divergent outcomes. Therefore, the key synthesis task is not just to present the diversity of results, but to try to account for the differences. When each evaluation presents data on such intervening variables as characteristics of participants, amount of service provided, experience and education of staff, costs of service per participant, and other internal and external conditions, it becomes possible to disaggregate overall figures on program success and examine outcomes for subgroups served under different conditions. The synthesis thus may be able to identify the features that distinguish successful from unsuccessful programs.

Even in the absence of sufficient data to account for differential outcomes reliably, it is often useful to show how one program compares with others that have been evaluated. If the particular job training program under study has much higher rates of success than similar programs, that is valuable for decision makers to know. It provides an empirical standard of comparison that can be more informative than comparison with the statement of the program's official goals (which may have been set more for their value in winning support than with expectations of actual achievement). Comparison with the outcomes of other programs offers decision makers a basis for realistic levels of expectation.

Evaluation syntheses generally have been undertaken by federal agencies (e.g., General Accounting Office, 1983) or by academic scholars interested in a practice field. To expect the evaluator of a single program to embark on a major review of this kind sounds unrealistic. Nevertheless, even the harried evaluator of one program, beset by problems and deadlines and a limited budget, might set aside time to see how results relate to the results of other evaluations. In fact, Cronbach et al (1980) make the sensible recommendation that review of previous evaluations be undertaken *before* beginning an evaluation study. In the interests of evaluation utility, even the end of the study is not too late. Showing decision makers where their program falls in the distribution of outcomes can be a real contribution. With sophistication and some luck, it may be possible to do more—to identify those program conditions that are associated with higher rates of success.

Synthesis activities give evaluation a chance to generate durable generalizations and contribute to the development of theory. Any one evaluation is hostage to the particular time and conditions under which it was done. Comparison of data from dozens of parallel evaluations makes it possible to understand not only what has happened under a variety of conditions but to begin to examine why things happen as they do. When that level of understanding is approached, the utility of the enterprise is considerably enhanced. Almost as a matter of course, empirically supported generalizations will be incorporated into program lore and, if disseminated to appropriate scholars, will find their way into the textbooks on which the next generation of professionals will be raised.

(8) High-quality research. Executing a study that meets high standards of research competence is not usually seen as a tactic to increase its level of use. Nevertheless, there are indications that quality counts (Caplan, 1976; Dunn, 1980; Patton et al., 1977; Weiss with Bucuvalas, 1980). Decision makers who turn to evaluation for direction rather than relying on less scientific sources of guidance want to know that the evidence is trustworthy. They are engaged in making decisions that have major consequences for their agency, their reputation, and the people they serve. Relying on a flawed study will put these things in jeopardy. People who turn to evaluation to support their position in intra-agency debate want to be sure that the evidence cannot be discredited by people who hold contrary positions. They want a strong case that can withstand methodological scrutiny (Weiss, 1980).

Some investigators of research use have found scant relation between the quality of a study and its level of use (Useem and DiMaggio, 1978; van de Vall, 1975). In some cases, apparently, users of research and evaluation are either not qualified to judge the quality of a study or are ready to use congenial findings regardless of their validity. Nevertheless, users with some sophistication about research and those who believe that the evidentiary basis for their positions will undergo hostile examination have a real stake in the competence of the evaluation.

Evaluators, too, have an investment in good research. As professionals and social scientists, they want to produce reputable reports, and they want the respect of future sponsors. But on occasion they are so beset by problems in the conduct of a study that they cut corners. Many evaluators are apparently unwilling or unable to take a firm stand and demand the cooperation necessary to do competent research. Too ready a concession to unacceptable conditions not only jeopardizes the evaluator's professional reputation but also on occasion reduces the likelihood that the study will be taken seriously.

When an evaluation study is done well, it also has a chance of lasting influence. It is much more likely to be published and thus becomes available to people who can refer to it for a variety of purposes. Not the least of the long-range uses will be to contribute to the development of generalizations about the prerequisites for effective programming, which may turn out to be the information most likely to be used.

CONCLUSION

We have discussed the many obstacles that interfere with the translation of evaluation results into program decisions and a series of proposals for improving the translation of evaluation into action. How well do the proposed "solutions" match the obstacles that were identified? Figure 6.4 shows how the proposed solutions fit the disjunctures identified in Figure 6.3

Two of the prescriptions seem to help, if only marginally, to overcome intellectual-cognitive problems in the formulation of an evaluation study. Two address the social-structural problems that arise during formulation, but both have obvious limitations. Four have some promise of making inroads on the intellectual-cognitive problems that affect the translation of evaluation back into the policy sphere. Two prescriptions, of doubtful efficacy, have to do with social-structural problems in the transition of results into action.

It would appear that traditional advice to evaluators about improving the use of evaluation, while probably worth attending to, will not

	Intellectual/ Cognitive Domain	Social/Structure Domain
From Policy Issue to Evaluation Formulation	**A** Plan with users in mind Stay close to the scene	**B** Plan with users Concentrate on manipulable variables
From Evaluation Findings to Action	**C** Clear, well- written reports Dissemination: get the results out Evaluation synthesis High quality research	**D** Translate findings into recommendations Make recommendations feasible to implement

Figure 6.4 Match of Prescriptions to Obstacles

lead to massive breakthroughs. Little can probably be done about some of the most intractable problems:

— Policy makers find it difficult to identify their informational needs in advance.

— Agencies' self-interest in policies and programs constrains their ability to engage in adequate formulation of evaluations.

— Evaluators' tendency to see the problem in terms of the concepts and methodologies with which they are familiar reduces their receptivity to alternative formulation of evaluation questions.

— Much evaluation research comes to ambiguous or inconsistent conclusions.

— The findings of a single study are of doubtful generalizability to other situations and to the future.

— Resource constraints and status quo proclivities limit agency implementation of results, especially those that imply fundamental restructuring.

— Decisions are often made through gradual and amorphous processes in which evidence is rarely considered.

— Evaluation results are only one input into complex bargaining around the interests and ideologies involved in social programs.

Only one of these problems is within the evaluator's control. Most of them are unsoluble, at least in the sense that any solution would be worse than the problem it aims to solve. A democratic society does not want technocratic solutions imposed on decision makers; a pluralistic society does not want political controls on the freedom of research. Nobody truly wants evaluators to determine the future course of social programming for the nation. The continuing tension between policy makers, who hold positions that authorize them to set direction, and evaluators, who press for rational consideration of the evidence, can be fruitful and creative.

At this point, the courses of action most readily available to evaluators are improvement of the quality of evaluation research and improved modes of dissemination. If all the varied groups that have a stake in social programs have good information about program process and program outcomes, opportunity is widened for informed discussion on issues that matter. That is no small contribution.

REFERENCES

AARON, HENRY J. (1978) Politics and the Professors: The Great Society in Perspective. Washington, DC: Brookings Institution.

ALKIN, MARVIN L., RICHARD DAILLAK and PETER WHITE (1979). Using Evaluations: Does Evaluation Make a Difference? Beverly Hills, CA: Sage.

BERG, MARK R. et al. (1978) Factors Affecting Utilization of Technology Assessment Studies in Policy Making. Ann Arbor: Institute for Social Research, University of Michigan.

CAPLAN, NATHAN (1976) "Social research and national policy: what gets used, by whom, for what purposes, and with what effects." International Social Science Journal 28: 187-194.

CAPLAN, NATHAN, A. MORRISON and R. J. STAMBAUGH (1975) The Use of Social Science Knowledge in Policy Decisions at the National Level. Ann Arbor: Institute for Social Research, University of Michigan.

CHERNS, ALBERT B. (1972) "Social sciences and policy," in A. B. Cherns, R. Sinclair, and W. I. Jenkins (eds.) Social Science and Government: Policies and Programs. London: Tavistock.

COHEN, DAVID K. and JANET A. WEISS (1977) "Social science and social policy: schools and race," in Carol H. Weiss (ed.) Using Social Research in Public Policy Making. Lexington, MA: D. C. Heath.

COLEMAN, J. S. (1972) Policy Research in the Social Sciences. Morristown, NJ: General Learning Press.

COOK, T. D. and C. S. REICHARDT [eds.] (1979) Qualitative and Quantitative Methods in Evaluation Research. Beverly Hills, CA: Sage.

CRAWFORD, E. T. and A. D. BIDERMAN [eds.] (1969) Social Scientists and International Affairs. New York: John Wiley.

CRONBACH, L. J. and associates (1980) Toward Reform of Program Evaluation: Aims, Methods, and Institutional Arrangements. San Francisco: Jossey-Bass.

DEITCHMAN, S. J. (1976) The Best-Laid Schemes: A Tale of Social Research and Bureaucracy. Cambridge: MIT Press.

DUNCAN, OTIS DUDLEY, (1969) "Social forecasting: the state of the art." The Public Interest 17: 88-119.

DUNN, WILLIAM N. (1980) "The two communities metaphor and models of knowledge use." Knowledge: Creation, Diffusion, Utilization 1: 515-536.

EDWARDS, WARD, MARCIA GUTTENTAG, and KURT SNAPPER (1975) "A decision-theoretic approach to evaluation research," in E. L. Struening and M. Guttentag (eds.) Handbook of Evaluation Research. Vol. 1. Beverly Hills, CA: Sage.

FARRAR, ELEANOR and ERNEST R. HOUSE (1983) "The evaluation of Push/Excel: a case study," in A. S. Bryk (ed.) Stakeholder-Based Evaluation. Beverly Hills, CA: Sage.

FELDMAN, M. S. and J. G. MARCH (1981) "Information in organizations as signal and symbol." Administrative Science Quarterly 26: 171-186.

FRANKEL, CHARLES [ed.] (1976) Controversies and Decisions: The Social Sciences and Public Policy. New York: Russell Sage.

GENERAL ACCOUNTING OFFICE (1983) The Evaluation Synthesis. Washington, DC: Author.

GLASS, GENE V., BARRY McGAW, and MARY LEE SMITH (1981) Meta-Analysis in Social Research. Beverly Hills, CA: Sage.

GOLD, NORMAN (1983) "Stakeholders and program evaluation: characterizations and reflections," in A. S. Bryk (ed.) Stakeholder-Based Evaluation. Beverly Hills, CA: Sage.

GUTTENTAG, MARCIA (1973) "Subjectivity and its use in evaluation research." Evaluation 1: 60-65.

HAMILTON, DAVID, CHRISTINE KING, DAVID JENKINS, MALCOLM PARLETT, and BARRY MacDONALD [eds.] (1978) Beyond the Numbers Game. Berkeley, CA: McCutchan.

JANOWITZ, M. (1970) "Sociological models and social policy," in Political Conflict: Essays in Political Sociology. Chicago: Quadrangle.

KNORR, KARIN D. (1977) "Policy makers' use of social science knowledge: symbolic or instrumental?" in Carol H. Weiss (ed.) Using Social Research in Public Policy Making. Lexington, MA: D. C. Heath.

KOGAN, MAURICE and MARY HENKEL (1983) Government and Research. London: Heinemann.

LIGHT, RICHARD J. (1979) "Capitalizing on variation: how conflicting research findings can be helpful for policy." Educational Researcher 8: 7-11.

———and PAUL B. SMITH (1971) "Accumulating evidence: procedures for resolving contradictions among different research studies." Harvard Educational Review 41: 429-471.

MURRAY, CHARLES (1983) "Stakeholders as deck chairs," in A. S. Bryk (ed.) Stakeholder-Based Evaluation. Beverly Hills, CA: Sage.

PATTON, MICHAEL Q. (1978) Utilization-Focused Evaluation. Beverly Hills, CA: Sage.

———P. S. GRIMES, K. M. GUTHRIE, N. J. BRENNAN, B. D. FRENCH, and D. A. BLYTH (1977) "In search of impact: an analysis of the utilization of federal health evaluation reseach," in C. H. Weiss (ed.) Using Social Research in Public Policy Making. Lexington, MA: D. C. Heath.

PELZ, DONALD C. (1978) "Some expanded perspectives on the use of social science and public policy," in J. M. Yinger and S. J. Cutler (eds.) Major Social Issues. New York: Free Press.

RICH, ROBERT F. (1981) Social Science Information and Public Policy Making. San Francisco: Jossey-Bass.

ROTHMAN, JACK (1980) Social R&D: Research and Development in the Human Services. Englewood Cliffs, NJ: Prentice-Hall.

SCHULBERG, HERBERT C. and JEANETTE JERRELL (1979) The Evaluator and Management. Beverly Hills, CA: Sage.

SMITH, NICK L. and DARREL N. CAULLEY [eds.] (1982) The Interaction of Evaluation and Policy: Case Reports from State Education Agencies. Portland, OR: Northwest Regional Educational Laboratory.

STAKE, ROBERT E. (1983) "Stakeholder influence in the evaluation of cities-in-schools," in A. S. Bryk (ed.) Stakeholder-Based Evaluation. Beverly Hills, CA: Sage.

SUCHMAN, EDWARD A. (1967) Evaluative Research: Principles and Practice in Public Service and Social Action Programs. New York: Russell Sage.

USEEM, MICHAEL and PAUL DiMAGGIO (1978) "An example of evaluation research as a cottage industry: the technical quality and impact of arts audience studies." Sociological Methods and Research 7: 55-84.

van de VALL, MARK (1975) "Utilization and methodology of applied social research: four complementary models." Journal of Applied Behavioral Science 11: 14-38.

WEISS, C. H. (1983) "Toward the future of stakeholder approaches in evaluation," in A. S. Bryk (ed.) Stakeholder-Based Evaluation. Beverly Hills, CA: Sage.

———(1980) "Knowledge creep and decision accretion." Knowledge: Creation, Diffusion, Utilization 1: 381-404.

———(1977) "Research for policy's sake: the enlightenment function of social science research." Policy Analysis 3: 531-45.

———(1972) Evaluation Research. Englewood Cliffs, NJ: Prentice-Hall.

———with M. J. Bucuvalas (1980) Social Science Research and Decision-Making. New York: Columbia University Press.

ZWEIG, FRANKLIN M. [ed.] (1979) Evaluation in Legislation. Beverly Hills, CA: Sage.

7

THE ART OF IMPLEMENTATION

Ross F. Conner

Students of program evaluation and evaluation research typically read a variety of evaluation studies, each focusing on a different type of program and each using a unique mix of methods (e.g., Freeman and Solomon, 1982). These studies generally do not give many details explaining exactly how the study was implemented. Although this omission is understandable from the authors' perspective, it presents a real problem for the student who is trying to learn how to execute an evaluation or for the experienced evaluator who is interested in expanding his or her repertoire of evaluation techniques. Without an understanding of exactly how, for example, the final evaluation design evolved from a preliminary design or how program staff members were involved in the development of the evaluation, it is difficult for the reader to understand how he or she would implement such an evaluation. The purpose of this chapter is to ameliorate this problem by focusing centrally on the implementation of program evaluations.

This chapter has two main goals: first, to present a general conceptual model that describes the process of implementing an evaluation and, second, to illustrate this model with an actual evaluation study. The conceptual model describes the process of doing an evaluation, from the first day the evaluator begins to work with a program until the last day when he or she completes the evaluation. Because program evaluations vary greatly, the steps in the model are generic ones, meant to describe a typical evaluation study. Although the sequence of the steps is fairly fixed, the length of these steps and the period between steps can vary. The purpose here is not to provide a listing of activities that, if followed by an evaluator, will result in a perfect evaluation. Instead, the aim is to describe and illustrate the sensibilities and sensitivities that are second-nature to an expert evaluation researcher. The model and illustrative example presented here will be especially useful to a new evaluator who is not able to serve an apprenticeship with an experienced evaluator and, thus, cannot as easily develop his or her skills in the art—as well as in the science—of implementing evaluations.

A MODEL FOR
EVALUATION IMPLEMENTATION

There are seven main steps to follow in implementing a program evaluation. These steps, presented in summary fashion, are learning, creating, briefing, revising-elaborating, initiating, monitoring, and utilizing. All of these steps are followed in a program evaluation, although some steps receive relatively more attention at different points during an evaluation. It is important to note that the reason for these differences in attention is not that the evaluator can overlook the particular steps. Rather, steps can be deemphasized because they have been well covered at earlier or concurrent stages. Each of the steps is described and discussed below.

LEARNING ABOUT THE PROGRAM

The first step in implementing an evaluation is learning about the program. Even if an evaluator has some preliminary ideas about and understanding of the program, he or she should approach the program as if he or she knows next to nothing. The evaluator should collect and review all the printed material that is available—for example, budget submissions, relevant legislation, annual reports, internal reviews, minutes of important committee meetings, and organizational charts. In addition, the evaluator should meet with key people associated with the program: the director, funders, related decision-makers, some clients and staff, other researchers, and other people with some connection to the program. Indeed, the most important aspect of this step is involvement with all types of program personnel. Moreover, the most important aspect of this involvement is listening to what these people say about the official goals of the program, the unofficial goals, the way the program is supposed to operate, the way it actually operates, and so forth.

The evaluator's task at this stage, then, is not simply to take in the program world. The evaluator must go beyond what he or she sees or hears to look and listen for clues to the underlying dynamics of the program. Sometimes what an evaluator sees on the surface matches what he or she identifies from deeper soundings of the program's dynamics. Frequently, however, these do not match, often for reasons that have less to do with hidden agendas or motives and more to do with the complex process that characterizes the creation and maintenance of social programs. If the evaluator does not understand the real dynamics of the program, he or she can develop and implement an evaluation that is not appropriate or relevant to the actual program even though the evaluation may fit the "theoretical" program (that is, the program described in legislation or in official program documents).

This "lisening and looking" phase requires a significant amount of the evaluator's time. In addition to the formal meetings with project personnel, the evaluator should plan on spending a considerable amount of time in informal meetings as well as simply "hanging around." In addition to participating in the ordinary office routine, the evaluator should occasionally join the staff and other program-related people on coffee breaks, over lunch, or for an after-work drink. The evaluator will need to be sensitive to the program's social network and to use his or her judgment about the appropriateness of participating in these types of activities. The evaluator should not force his or her participation but instead should be available for these opportunities and receptive to them when they arise. During these informal contacts, the evaluator must be careful to avoid making any public judgments about the program or its personnel. To maintain the appearance and reality of objectivity and independence, the evaluator must assume a posture of openness and receptivity without judging what he or she is told.

Through these formal and informal contacts with people associated with the program, the evaluator not only learns about the proposed and actual operation of the program but also builds credibility and rapport with project personnel. Depending on their past experience, evaluators vary in the amount of credibility they bring to a project. However, credibility-building or reconfirming is required for each new evaluation, even to an evaluator with high credibility and respect among program staff for his or her past evaluation work. Staff members know the program better than a new evaluator, and they want to see some of this same understanding develop in the evaluator. In this first phase of evaluation implementation, an evaluator can build his or her credibility by learning quickly about the program and then by demonstrating this learning to the staff in direct and indirect ways.

Along with credibility, the evaluator will be developing rapport with program personnel. Whereas credibility relates to the evaluator's professional competence, rapport relates to the evaluator's personal competence. In conducting most evaluations, evaluators require some degree of extra work by staff and frequently a good deal of additional patience as well. Staff will make these extra efforts for someone whom they respect and like. Consequently, rapport-building is a necessity if an evaluator hopes to complete his or her work.

CREATING THE EVALUATION PLAN

Once the first learning step is well under way, an evaluator can begin the next step: creating the evaluation plan or framework. This step can start sooner for the experienced evaluator, later for the novice. In either case, however, the evaluator must be careful not to begin this step too soon; otherwise, premature closure may cause the evaluation plan to be incomplete or misguided. Due to the variety of situations and circumstances among programs, it is impossible to give a standard rule about the point where learning becomes secondary and creating primary. In general, however, the evaluator should be at a point where he or she receives confirming information about various aspects of the program from several staff, independently of one another. For example, the complete goal set offered by one staff member should roughly match that given by another staffer (although there may be differences in their ratings of the importance of the goals). Another rough indication that the transition point between learning and creating has been reached is that the evaluator can anticipate or predict what a likely answer might be to his or her question or what the missing link might be in his or her understanding of a particular issue.

When the evaluator is ready for the creative step to begin, the first task is to conceptualize the general goals for the evaluation. Whether the evaluation will have primarily a quantitative approach or a qualitative one, the evaluator must decide on the main areas for assessment, depending on the primary goals and activities of the program, the evaluation funds available, and the time constraints for the study.

It is helpful to write down the main assessment areas, then sketch out various evaluation designs that could address each of these areas. It is useful to include among these designs the most rigorous design that could be used to address each of the main evaluation questions, ignoring for the moment political and situational realities. The reason for doing this is that it gives the evaluator a standard for his or her planning, against which the effects of design trade-offs necessitated by political and situational realities can be assessed.

For example, let us assume that the main evaluation goal of a special math program for elementary school students is to assess the increase in math knowledge due to the program. The most rigorous design the evaluator could use would be a true experimental design with two randomly assigned groups, only one of which receives the program. Both groups would be tested on math knowledged before the program began and again at its conclusion. Any changes in knowledge for the experimental group beyond those for the control group would indicate the effects of the special program.

Once the evaluator has sketched out this rigorous design, he or she then adapts the design to situational realities. One such reality could be a requirement that all of the school's 100 eligible students must receive the program. The evaluator's adaptation of the rigorous design should be guided by an awareness of the standard set by the true experimental design: the importance of a comparison in determining the change in math knowledge due to the program. Several different adaptations may be possible that meet or come close to meeting this standard. For example, another situational reality of the special math program may be that the program can be given to only 50 students at a time. Consequently, the 100 eligible students could be selected randomly to be in the group receiving the first offering of the program or in the group receiving the second offering. This second, delayed treatment group would serve as the untreated control for the first group, thus providing the comparison necessary to determine math knowledge change. Alternatively, a quasi-experimental comparison group may be available from another, similar school. This adaptation of the design also would provide a comparison, albeit a less ideal one, against which to measure change.

Once designs have been selected that, in view of situational and political realities, best address the main evaluation areas, the next task is to determine the general kinds of measures to be used for each of the main assessment areas. The goal is not to develop specific measures at this point: instead, the evaluator should formulate the general focus of measures (e.g., math ability) and the general measurement approach (i.e., standardized test, questionnaire, interview).

At this stage of the implementation model, the evaluators will have completed what others have described as evaluability assessment (Rutman, 1980; Wholey, 1977; see also Chapter 2 in this volume for a full discussion of this concept). That is, the evaluator now would know what could and should be assessed and he or she also would have some concrete ideas about how the assessment should be undertaken. The next step is sharing this knowledge with the program.

BRIEFING PROGRAM STAFF ABOUT THE EVALUATION PLAN

During the creating step, the evaluator works largely on his or her own, drawing what was learned in the first learning step and on professional evaluation training. Once the evaluation design or designs and the associated measures are selected, the evaluator is ready to consult again with the program personnel for the crucial feedback step.

The feedback step is a more formal process than the learning step, although its success depends to a large extent on the rapport and credibility developed informally by evaluator during the learning step. In most cases the evaluator will schedule a meeting with the program director to review the proposed evaluation plan. In some cases, the entire staff may be involved in the initial meeting or, alternatively, may be briefed following the evaluator-program director meeting. The evaluator will have to rely on his or her developing sensibilities in determining the best participants in the feedback meeting.

Prior to the meeting, the evaluator should plan carefully what he or she wants to say and how it can best be said. A general agenda would be to present (a) the main program goals and activities, (b) the associated main focuses of the evaluation, and (c) the particular designs and measures for each of the areas to be evaluated, including an implementation plan of when and how the parts of the design and the measures will occur.

The evaluator's presentation of the main program goals and activities should be brief, not only because the staff is familiar with this but also because the evaluation plan should be the main focus. The evaluator may want to prepare and hand out a listing or diagram of the program's goals and activities. (See Chapter 2 for a suggested format.) This listing, which should be condensed to one page if possible, can aid the evaluator in his or her presentation and demonstrate, in a concrete way, the evaluator's understanding of the program. Given that the staff already knows about the main program goals and activities, the purpose of the first part of this agenda is to provide an opportunity for the evaluator to demonstrate his or her knowledge of the program and, in so doing, to further the development of his or her credibility. Even though the staff is familiar with the program, many staff members like to hear a brief overview of the program's goals and activities, perhaps because they become so caught up in day-to-day events that they lose perspective on the overall effort. If the evaluator presents the program well, he or she not only can refresh the staff's attitude toward the program but also can convince the staff to listen seriously to the evaluation proposal.

The second and most important part of the general agenda is to present the main focuses for the evaluation. At this point, the evaluator begins to introduce the staff to new material as he or she presents the proposed evaluation. Because the details of the evaluation will be unfamiliar and may be somewhat complex, a second handout is useful to supplement this part of the agenda. It is advisable to organize the presentation of the evaluation plan around the main parts and goals of the program, even if this will mean some duplication, in order to facilitate staff understanding. Essentially, the task is to tie each part of the evaluation plan to the relevant part of the program. For each of the main parts of the program, the evaluator describes the associated evaluation goal, the evaluation method to be employed (i.e., the research design), the general tools to be used in achieving the evaluation goal (i.e., the research measures), and how these parts will tie together in practice.

Assume, to continue the earlier example, that we are evaluating an educational program with the main goal of improving performance in math by teaching elementary school students via a team-teaching approach, with one teacher and four aides. Secondary goals of the program are to make teachers more receptive to team-teaching and to make children like math. Assume further that the evaluation plan selected for the program entails two parts: a quantitative control group study of the changes in the children's math knowledge and attitudes, and a qualitative open-ended interview study of changes in teachers' attitudes.

In presenting this evaluation plan, the evaluator would begin with the main goal of increasing math knowledge. The associated evaluation goal would be to assess changes in math knowledge. The method will be to compare changes in math knowledge from start to end of the program in two student groups: those randomly selected to participate in the new program and those who remain in the traditional math program. (Here, the evaluator will need to explain why a comparison is required by translating the evaluation research jargon of "plausible rival hypotheses" to concrete examples of likely change-producing confounding factors.) The tool to be used to assess change in the groups will be a standardized test of math knowledge, which the evaluator might reference and from which he or she could provide illustrative questions. (It probably would be unnecessary to pass out a copy of the test because the purpose at this point is not to have the staff focus on small details but instead to understand and react to the overall plan.)

Next, the evaluator addresses the second program goal, to make teachers more receptive to team-teaching. The evaluation goal is to assess teachers' attitudes toward team-teaching, and the associated method is interviews over the course of the study with the team-teaching teachers and other singly teaching teachers in the same school. The tool would be an interview guide with a listing of discussion topics and selected questions. Again, the evaluator may want to describe, in jargon-free ways, the pros and cons of informal interviews and the types of discussion topics that may be covered.

Finally, the evaluator discusses the tertiary program goal of making the children like math more. Here the associated evaluation goal is to assess changes in children's attitudes, and the method is the same as that for the first goal; a control group study using the same randomly constituted groups. The tool would be different (an evaluator-developed survey of students' attitudes toward math) but would be administered along with the standardized math test. This is an example of the type of duplication that may occur but that is necessary if program staff members are to follow easily the presentation of the proposed evaluation plan.

One caution for the novice evaluator is to avoid giving a mini-research design class during the explanation of the methods that are proposed for each part of the evaluation. Although it will be tempting to do so, the challenge is to focus any "instruction" on specific aspects of the plan and to give explanations in jargon-free terms. Explanation via good and bad examples is often a successful approach.

The title of this step, briefing, has two aspects: the evaluator feeding back to the staff and the staff feeding back to the evaluator. Once the evaluator has presented his or her plan, the staff must have the opportunity to give its reactions, suggestions, and comments. There are different ways for the evaluator to receive this feedback (e.g., from the group as a whole or in individual meetings, verbally or in writing); the method or methods selected should assure candid and complete feedback. If the number of staff and other interested parties is large, the evaluator may want to form an advisory board or committee that would work closely with him or her at this stage of the evaluation and for the following stages as well. (An evaluator-created advisory board can be useful, too, if the conduct or outcome of an evaluation is expected to be politically sensitive.)

Once the evaluator has received feedback on the evaluation plan from all interested and affected parties, he or she should assure these parties that their comments have been heard and understood. This may take the form of a simple follow-up call to the interested individuals (if their number is small) or a more detailed letter or memo summarizing the comments. As with other activities in earlier steps, this follow-up provides an additional opportunity for the evaluator to increase his or her credibility by increasing staff members' confidence that they have been accurately heard.

REVISING AND ELABORATING THE EVALUATION PLAN

Based on the comments, reactions, and suggestions of those individuals involved in the previous step, the evaluator is ready to revise the original evaluation plan. If the evaluator has conducted the previous steps well, the amount of revision will be lessened. Nonetheless, some revision is almost assured because the staff will be seeing the proposed evaluation plan for the first time, along with its designs and measurement approaches. Indeed, the evaluator who receives no or few suggestions for changes has good cause to worry about his or her credibility and rapport with the program staff.

In the revising process, the evaluator needs to incorporate as many of the suggested changes as possible without compromising the design's basic integrity. Compromise is inevitable, but the evaluator

may come to a point where his or her judgment as a researcher con-
flicts with the program staff's judgment. This is one of the times when
the evaluator must rely on the credibility he or she has developed. The
evaluator can use this credibility to argue for certain design and measurement features that are essential if the evaluation questions of interest to the program are to be answered.

An equally important part of this phase is elaboration of the evaluation plan, particularly the measures. This is the point at which detailed measures are adopted or developed. For a more quantitatively
focused evaluation, if the evaluator is lucky, he or she can draw on
off-the-shelf measures already developed for particular measurements. If measures have not been developed, the evaluator will have to
draft and pilot test his or her own. For a more qualitatively oriented
evaluation, the evaluator must decide on the types of information to
collect and the particular collection methods to be used. Once they are
formulated, these measures should be shared with the program staff
to assure acceptability.

In the revising and elaborating process, the evaluator must be clear
about the limits to design and measurement changes, beyond which
the soundness of the evaluation plan becomes questionable. With this
understanding firmly in mind, the evaluator can make compromises
that do not go beyond this limit. The evaluator's role is to argue for
the most powerful design and measures that will answer the evaluation
questions of most importance to the program. The staff usually knows
little about evaluation and will look to the evaluator to provide this
knowledge and to blend it with programmatic realities and requirements.

The revising and elaborating process requires a constant dialogue
between the evaluator and staff or other interested parties. Because of
the technical nature of parts of most evaluation plans and the conse-
quent need to reflect on and creatively adapt scientific requirements
and progarm realities, the evaluator probably will not want to "ham-
mer out" changes in working sessions with staff. Instead, an iterative
process usually works best, where the evaluator responds to the most
recent suggestions with a changed plan, discusses the revised plan with
staff to obtain additional suggestions, makes further revisions in the
plan, and so forth. This process continues until all parties are generally pleased with the result. A similar, albeit shorter, iterative process
usually occurs in the final work on particular measures.

INITIATING THE EVALUATION PLAN

Now, the evaluator is poised to initiate and implement the plan. As a preliminary step, he or she probably will pilot-test certain of the evaluation measures and make whatever adjustments are necessary before full implementation. Once these changes are made, the evaluation plan is ready.

This part of the art of implementing program evaluation is closest to the science of program evaluation with which most novice evaluators are familiar. During the initiating phase, the evaluator may randomly assign potential program clients to different study groups, may interview program staff, may administer questionnaires to participants, may code and analyze clients' responses, and the like. Although these research tasks certainly are not easy in the field, most evaluators already know what to expect. If the previous steps in this model for implementing program evaluations have been carried out successfully, the initiating step can be the least problematic. The main reason for this is not surprising: Thorough planning pays off in better implementation. There is a second and almost equally important reason: Good rapport with staff pays off in greater staff flexibility and adaptability. When the unexpected arises, staff members who feel this rapport are more likely to inform and to consult the evaluator about adjustments that may be necessary. If this rapport does not exist, the evaluator may be informed after the fact—or not at all—about new developments, at which point it is too late to make changes that accommodate the new reality and also preserve the integrity of the evaluation plan.

MONITORING THE EVALUATION

Although technically part of the initiating step, monitoring is important enough to set out as a separate phase. Just as many comprehensive evaluations include process monitoring of a program (Rossi and Freeman, 1982), so an evaluation plan should include monitoring implementation of the plan. Although an evaluation plan may be well conceived, unexpected developments and changes can occur that necessitate adjustments. The evaluator cannot rely on the staff to notify him or her of these new developments because staff, lacking knowledge of the scientific restrictions of an evaluation, may not even realize that a development has occurred that, from a scientific viewpoint, is significant. Consequently, the evaluator has to monitor the implementation of his or her evaluation to identify these unexpected developments.

The basic requirement in monitoring implementation of the evaluation plan is participating directly in the implementation. If the evaluation planner also is the sole implementer, this direct participation will occur automatically. However, if there is an evaluation staff, even a small one, the evaluation planner may not be centrally involved in client intake, questionnaire administration, and the like. In this case, it is wise for the evaluation planner to be involved directly to some extent, particularly at the outset. Once the evaluation planner and the evaluation and program staff learn what is and is not a "significant new development" from an evaluation standpoint, less frequent monitoring is sufficient.

UTILIZING THE EVALUATION

Like monitoring, utilizing also is a phase of the initiating step and also important enough to list as a separate step. The old view of utilization, as something that occurred after an evaluation was completed, has given way to a different view of utilization in evaluation research, as a continuous process beginning almost the first day of evaluation planning (Weiss, 1977). During the evaluation planning process and the evaluation implementation stage, information is generated and passed on to the program staff that may be as useful as or more useful than the final evaluation results. Evaluators not only should be aware of this fact but also should seize on and plan opportunities to provide useful information. By doing so, the evaluator further builds his or her rapport and credibility as someone with valuable input. These activities also undercut the stereotype of an aloof outside researcher, someone really more comfortable in a laboratory coat, who is tight-lipped until the end of the study, when a large, convoluted (and probably tardy) report is created—a tome the staff promptly puts on a high dusty shelf.

Providing useful information does not mean compromising a promise of confidentiality to clients or providing pretest data that may cause program changes to be made prematurely. Frequently the evaluator can give the staff low-level intake information (e.g., on numbers and types of clients) or information about staff activities that can be useful to program staff. Rather than hold this information until the final report phase, the evaluator can feed it back for immediate staff use.

AN EXAMPLE OF EVALUATION IMPLEMENTATION

The second main goal of this chapter is to provide an example of how an actual evaluation is implemented. The description and discussion that follow give an insider's view of an actual evaluation project, with details on how different stages were planned to occur and how they actually occurred. The discussion follows the steps of the model outlined in the previous section. The evaluation project described here illustrates all of the steps in the model; however, the project provides better examples of some steps than others due to the particular course the evaluation planning and implementation took. This is inevitable when any individual evaluation project is analyzed in terms of a generic model developed across many different evaluations.

The example discussed is one of my own studies because I can describe it accurately from an insider's view. Although the example is one with which I have been involved, the concepts from the model generalize across my and others' evaluation projects. The concepts are applicable to quantitatively oriented evaluations as well as to qualitatively oriented evaluations, based on my more limited direct and indirect experience with these latter types of evaluation studies. The writings of those investigators who are more familiar with qualitative studies (e.g., Patton, 1980) echo many of the same concepts and sensibilities that make up the model.

THE CITIZEN DISPUTE SETTLEMENT PROJECT

Program Background

In 1974, the American Bar Association began an experimental program in criminal justice reform known as BASICS: Bar Association Support to Improve Correctional Services. This new program was created to improve correctional services and to encourage bar associations to take an active leadership role in bringing about and operating social change programs.

BASICS invited all state and local bar associations to participate in its program. A grant solicitation brochure was sent to associations asking them to apply for small planning grants to be used for conducting studies on local or state correctional problems. Over 100 responses were received, and BASICS funded 80 planning projects in 40 states. After approximately three months of planning, 62 bar associations applied for larger grants of up to $35,000 to implement their correctional reform ideas. BASICS awarded "action" program grants to 20 bar associations so they could put their study findings to work and build correctional improvement efforts.

One of these awards was given to the Orange County (Florida) Bar Association to create a citizen dispute settlement (CDS) program. This program, designed as an alternative to the court system, provides impartial hearings to residents of Orange County, Florida who have complaints involving ordinance violations and misdemeanors.

This concept of informal hearings can be traced to the early function of the Justice of the Peace, who served as an informal hearing officer for citizens involved in minor disputes. Today, police officers often play this role when they are called to quiet a neighbor's barking dog or to end a family dispute. Yet police officers are often unable to resolve the dispute. Too often minor disputes left unresolved can develop into major disputes, adding more frustration for the people involved and more cases to an already overburdened criminal justice system.

The project began in the fall of 1975 after a project director was hired. CDS was administered by the county bar association through an executive board that directed general policy and long-term development. Daily decisions and short-term plans were made by the CDS project director. The director, an intake counselor, and several part-time aides comprised the project staff. The largest portion of CDS workers was the volunteer attorneys from the Orange County Bar Association who served as hearing officers at CDS hearings.

Program Operation

The main goal of the Orange County Bar project was to conduct effective hearings for citizens involved in minor disputes (i.e., simple assault, menacing threats, trespassing, disorderly conduct, harassment, breach of peace, property damage, neighbor dispute, family dispute, petty theft, animal control, littering, and bad checks). Citizens with any of these complaints either were referred to the program by city or county law enforcement officers or presented their complaint on their own initiative.

When a citizen presented a complaint, he or she was interviewed by CDS to obtain information about the dispute as well as information about the complaint. A date was then set for the hearing, usually within a week. The other party involved in the dispute, the respondent, was notified by mail of the date, place, and purpose of the hearing.

Each hearing was unique. Some were as short as 30 minutes, others extended for two or three hours. The complainant, respondent, and a hearing officer were present at some hearings; at others the complainant and respondent were joined by family, friends, and witnesses if this was permitted by the hearing officer. If the parties reached an agreement, they signed a statement listing the terms of the agreement. Copies of the statement were then given to both the complainant and the respondent.

STEPS IN DEVELOPING THE EVALUATION PLAN

Learning

My first contact with the CDS project was a one-day visit following the BASICS planning phase but before the start of the action phase. As one of two project evaluators for the entire BASICS program (Conner and Huff, 1979), I was asked by the BASICS National Management Board to visit half of the 20 action grantees to discuss the board's desire to have each grantee include an evaluation component in its program. During these visits, I also discussed ways in which this activity could be accomplished (e.g., working with a local university-based evaluator), as I was doubtful that grantees could accomplish this extra task without additional help. The board was prepared to provide intensive evaluation assistance and resources through our evaluation team to only 4 of the 20 action projects. Consequently, another purpose for this initial visit was to learn enough about the potential of the projects to make a recommendation to the board concerning the advisability of intensive evaluation help.

The first meeting with the CDS project director, who was just beginning to develop his program, was cordial and useful to the project director and to me. The project director was receptive to the need for evaluation, in part because he was still in the early stages of establishing the program and also because the program that served as a model (the Columbus, Ohio Night Prosecutor Program) had conducted some evolution and urged even more thorough evaluation of new programs. The project director was interested in the general evaluation ideas we discussed and in the possibility of obtaining nearby evaluation assistance. I benefited from our meeting because I saw the opportunities for conducting a rigorous evaluation of a program that had the potential for duplication by other bar associations. The planned project lent itself to rigorous evaluation because the director genuinely wanted to know whether his program solved the disputes and because he expected to have many more potential clients than he could serve. These conditions presented a perfect opportunity for selecting clients randomly from the waiting list, thereby solving a practical problem for the director (i.e., how to select clients equitably from the large pool of potential clients) and, at the same time, providing control and experimental groups for the evaluation.

This first meeting lasted about three-fourths of the day, including a relaxed, informal lunch. I spent the last part of the day visiting the only other person involved with the project at this early time, the head of the Orange County Bar Association committee that sponsored the grant. I had met this person during the planning phase at a regional workshop and wanted to renew our acquaintance and learn how he perceived the project at this stage. He and the project director agreed on the project's goals and proposed activities. Soon after my visit, I sent the director a letter thanking him for his time and telling him I would notify him of the board's decision on the four projects selected to receive intensive evaluation help.

About a month later, the board selected the CDS Project for intensive evaluation assistance. I quickly called the project to arrange another meeting. This second meeting was quite important because, by this time, the director had hired a secretary-clerk and was beginning to train volunteer lawyers as hearing officers. The appearance of the first clients and the start of services were not far away. I knew that I would need on-site research assistance no matter what direction the evaluation might take. Consequently, I telephoned ahead to a colleague at a nearby university to request the name of a qualified, experienced graduate student who might want to work on the project. He suggested Ray Surette, whom I interviewed over the phone and then arranged to meet in Orlando on my second visit.

The primary purposes of this second visit were to strengthen the rapport and trust between the director and me, to introduce the new research assistant to the project, and to learn more about the direction the program was taking as it moved from conceptual to actual implementation. My assistant and I identified no major disparities between the official and unofficial goals of the program or between the planned and actual activities. Rather, we noted several small changes intended to strengthen the intervention (e.g., the plan to have written agreements for successfully resolved disputes signed by all parties, including the hearing officer). The main reason for the absence of any significant disparities in this case probably was related to the fact that the project director had not been involved in developing the initial plans for the project but instead was hired to carry out specifically what was in the proposal. Given that the proposal writers (a volunteer subcommittee of the bar association) turned the project over almost totally to the new director, the proposal itself became the main guide. In addition, the project was based on a similar, ongoing program. Consequently, the planning proposal could be quite specific about anticipated activities, thereby lessening the slippage between planned and actual activities.

During this and subsequent visits, the formal and informal contacts between me or my research assistant and the project staff continued to build the rapport established at the outset of the project. Because the first contacts had been positive ones, it was easy to be accepted by new staff and to strengthen the rapport with continuing staff as we demonstrated our sincere interest in learning about the project. Following my second visit and additional visits by my research assistant, I had enough information to move to the next phase of evaluation implementation.

Creating

The first step in creating the evaluation was to develop the general goals for the evaluation. It was clear from the first meeting with the project that it would be important to assess the types of complaints that were brought for resolution and the outcomes, both short- and long-term, from the dispute resolution hearings. Consequently, the primary aims of our evaluation plan were (1) to monitor the characteristics of clients and their complaints and (2) to measure the effectiveness of the hearings.

From our discussions with the program creators and staff, we began to see that the CDS program was being viewed, and to some extent promoted, as an alternative to parts of the local criminal justice system. For this reason a secondary objective established for the evaluation plan was to analyze the impact of the program on the local criminal justice system.

Once the general evaluation goals were established, we began the creative process of formulating possible evaluation designs. Monitoring the characteristics and complaints of clients did not require a research design; we needed simply to develop a client intake form that could be used to collect the necessary information.

Assessing the effectiveness of the hearings required our most creative design work. Because the program director was genuinely interested in the effectiveness of his program, we naturally focused first on a control group-true experimental design for the project, with randomly selected treatment (i.e., hearing) and control (i.e., no hearing) groups. Our consideration of possible designs could stop at this point due to an important reality of the expected operation of the program. The director anticipated a large surplus of clients; consequently, he had a need to select equitably among the clients to determine which would be allowed to use the program's services first. The main requirement of the control group design, that potential clients be assigned at random to either the treatment or the control group, solved his problem of equitable selection. The plan was to have all prospective clients complete an intake form and then to select randomly a specific number of clients for hearings. Those clients not selected would be placed on a waiting list and served on a space-available basis, probably in several weeks. Any complaints of an urgent nature would be served immediately. Our plan was to compare the dispute resolution rates between the served group and a sample of the not served-waiting list group about a month later. In addition, we planned to follow up several months later with a sample of the served group to see if the situation causing the dispute had been changed over the long term.

Finally, our plan to evaluate the impact of the CDS program on the local justice system involved two components. First, to assess the caseload impact, we planned a time-series analysis of the number of misdemeanor cases filed with the local state attorney's office for the two years prior to the start of the program and for a period after the beginning of the CDS program. Since the project anticipated handling cases similar to or less serious than misdemeanors, a review of the state attorney's office records would show any impact on reducing misdemeanor filings. Second, to assess the cost-effectiveness of the CDS project relative to the state attorney's office, we planned to calculate a per case figure for CDS processing and for state attorney's office processing. If feasible, we wanted to calculate a figure of cost per successfully resolved case for both settings because these figures would incorporate an adjustment for unsuccessful cases, allowing us to address true cost-effectiveness.

In sum, we formulated a variety of designs for our different evaluation research goals. Because of certain program realities (e.g., the expected surplus of clients, the ready availability of misdemeanor case filling data), we were able to plan our evaluation designs easily and quickly. In other instances, once various design options have been formulated, an evaluator might have to collect additional information (i.e., return to the learning step) to know whether some options are feasible.

Briefing the Program about the Evaluation Plan

Just as we were making the final decisions about the evaluation plan and beginning preparations for briefing the program, the program director took another job and left the program. His position was quickly filled by a person who had been working locally in the Orange County criminal justice system. The new director had only a vague idea about the evaluation plans when we contacted him to arrange the briefing on the proposed evaluation plan.

Because of this unexpected turn of events, our briefing was somewhat different from the one we would have planned had the previous director still been in place. In particular, the briefing began with a longer-than-usual explanation of our contacts with the previous director and of the reasons for some of the preliminary understandings we had with him about the main focuses of the evaluation. In addition, we asked the new director to reeducate us about the program as he was now implementing it. Because we had had no opportunity to establish rapport with the new director at this point, we had to rely on our description of the rapport we developed with the previous director, hoping that this would positively influence the new director's readiness to learn about and accept our evaluation plan. We were aided in this special task by positive comments the previous director had passed on to the new director.

Apart from this crucial extra preliminary step, our presentation of the evaluation plan was similar to that for the more usual situation. We described our understanding of the program's goals and operations and then presented the aims of the evaluation, linking them with each of the program's focuses. Our task was facilitated by the director's previous, albeit limited, experience with evaluation research on criminal justice programs. Because of this knowledge, the director had a general sense of needs and benefits of evaluation, as well as of the costs and occasional complications associated with evaluation activities.

The director accepted our evaluation plans and was ready to have us implement them. However, there was one critical reality that the program was just beginning to recognize and that we also would have to face: The large numbers of clients expected for the program did not match the reality of a limited number of clients appearing at the program's doorstep. It appeared, according to the director, that the program not only would be able to process all interested clients but also would have to serve all clients to maintain intake figures at a minimally acceptable level. It was clear, therefore, that the control group design we proposed to assess the effectiveness of the program would not be feasible. Although this design had appeared earlier to be quite appropriate, the new developments with the program now ruled out this option.

Because the new director still was interested in whether his program was effective, we discussed various alternative comparison group designs to replace the control group design. We discovered that another reality of the program's current operation provided an opportunity for a comparison group: Only about two-thirds of the scheduled hearings resulted in hearings. That third of the cases where no hearing was held could serve as a comparison group against which to evaluate the effectiveness of the cases in which hearings were conducted. This strategy did not provide an ideal comparison, however, because prospective clients self-selected themselves into hearing and no-hearing groups, resulting in some inequalities between groups aside from the occurrence or nonoccurrence of a hearing. Nevertheless, this plan would allow a quasi-experimental assessment of impact and conformed to the new program realities.

We left the briefing sessions with the director's endorsement of the revised impact study plan as well as of the other components of our proposed design (i.e., monitoring clients' characteristics and complaints, analyzing the CDS Program's impact on the local criminal justice system, and assessing the cost-effectiveness of the program relative to locally available alternatives). We were ready now to make final revisions in the plan and develop the measures fully.

Revising and Elaborating the Evaluation Plan

We began our design revisions during the feedback session with the new director when the new situational realities required us to redesign the impact study plan from a control group design to a quasi-experimental comparison group design. The impossibility of the originally planned design and the absence of any more planning time necessitated an instant revision rather than simply a promise to the director that we would reconsider and contact him the next week. This experience, incidentally, is a good example of how skills such as flexibility and quick creativity frequently are required for a successful evaluation and of how these skills develop—namely, with increased practice in a variety of situations.

In other evaluation projects, usually there is more time for the evaluator to return to his or her drawing board, revise the designs in such a way that the basic integrity is not compromised, then repeat the previous briefing stage. This sequence would continue until both the program staff and the evaluator were satisfied with the evaluation plan. During the revision process, the evaluator must maintain a clear understanding of the goals of his or her evaluation so that any revisions will continue to meet these goals. For example, in the CDS Project, one of our goals was to assess the impact of the hearings. The quasi-experimental comparison group design that we devised in our revision process satisfied this goal, although it was less rigorous than the originally planned design. Had we instead agreed to interview a small sample of participants in hearings, we would have compromised the integrity of the evaluation goals because an interview plan could not give us the comparative information necessary to assess impact.

The rapport and credibility the evaluator has built may need to be marshalled during the revising stage to convince program staff that certain critical design features are necessary to accomplish particular evaluation goals. This is the kind of special expertise an evaluator brings to a program; it serves as the basis for arguing in favor of particular design considerations. Indeed, given an acceptable set of evaluation goals, an evaluator has a responsibility to argue for what he or she knows to be required to meet the goals and to educate the program staff as to why certain requirements apply. The evaluator's attitude is not "I know the right way and this is it!" Instead, it is "Based on my experience and training, this approach is what's required to meet the goals we've set out. Let me explain the reasons for this."

TABLE 7.1   Response Categories for Client Intake Form Question, "Income During Last Month"

None
$ 100 or less
$ 101 to $200
$ 201 to $300
$ 301 to $500
$ 501 to $800
$ 801 to $1,000
$1,001 to $1,500
$1,500 or more

Like many other evaluators, we had to develop new measures for this study. Consequently, the main focus of our activities during this phase was creating a series of instruments especially for the needs of the CDS program evaluation.

The first and easiest instrument we created was the intake form used to monitor complainants' characteristics and complaints. Another of our evaluation goals was to assess the impact of the program on the local criminal justice system, so the categories we used for the 18 questions on the intake form matched those used by the justice system to characterize its clients.

In some instances the categories were not those we would have preferred; nonetheless, for purposes of comparability we followed the local justice system's model. For example, the categories associated with the question of "income during last month" were not as detailed as we would have liked (see Table 7.1). The "$301 to $500" and "$501 to $800" categories were too big; we would have preferred a further breakdown in $100 increments. (The eventual study results showed that nearly half of the clients fell into one of these two categories; a more detailed breakdown would have allowed us to characterize the median income level with more certainty.)

We also had to develop short- and long-term measures of the impact of the hearings. The short-term measure was a simple two-question rating form asking the complainant, respondent, and hearing officer to rate their satisfaction with the settlement that had been reached and the likelihood that the problem would be solved. They made these ratings independently at the conclusion of all hearings using 7-point scales (1 = "very satisfied" or "very likely" to 7 = "very unsatisfied" or "very unlikely," respectively). We kept these measures short and limited because of the program director's concerns that these participants not be burdened with too much extra work and that the hearings be as short as possible. In retrospect, I wish that we had asked a few more questions about the hearing and that we had asked the complainant and respondent a few questions prior to the hearings about their expectations.

The long-term follow-up measures, given to a sample of complainants and respondents approximately three weeks later, were nearly identical with the short-term measures: satisfaction ratings with the settlement reached and judgments about whether the presenting problem had been solved, both made on 7-point scales. This latter measure also was to be given to the no-hearing comparison group complainants and respondents. Again, our original concern and that of the program staff was to keep extra work to a minimum for the clients; consequently, we kept the number of questions small. Based on the wisdom of hindsight, we wish that, here too, we had asked more questions, particularly in view of the effort it required to track down those people we wanted to interview.

There were two additional measurement areas we had to address: the way we would compare the impact of the CDS Program on the local criminal justice system and the way we would approach the cost-effectiveness analysis. In the former case, the approach was straightforward. We planned to record the number of misdemeanor cases filed monthly at the Orange County State Attorney's office, beginning two years prior to the program's start and continuing for a year after its beginning. In the latter case, we also thought the approach would be direct and simple: Assemble the cost per case for the State Attorney's Office and compare it to the cost per case for the CDS Program. As explained below, this turned out to be not nearly as simple as we, as well as the program director, had at first thought.

Initiating the Evaluation Plan

With planning, revision, and elaborating completed, we were ready to initiate the evaluation. The first important step was pilot-testing our measures. The intake form was acceptable as planned, largely because it was based on the form currently in use by the local justice system. Their form had no doubt undergone a good deal of pilot-testing and revising, so we were able to capitalize on these prior efforts.

The satisfaction rating scales used by clients and hearing officers, simple as they appeared, underwent several changes during pilot-testing. As originally designed, the scale was set horizontally and went from 1 = ("very unsatisfied) to 7 = ("very satisfied"). Pilot-test clients told us that they understood a vertical scale better and that 1, not 7, ought to be associated with the best rating. We made these changes, then learned from other pilot-test clients that it would be helpful to anchor the general positive and negative ends of the scale. After further work, we indicated to the side of scale points 1, 2, and 3 that these were "good" ratings and we added a smiling face to make this apparent at first glance. Likewise, points 5, 6, and 7 were labeled "bad" ratings and a frowning face was added. These changes pleased clients and greatly improved the validity of this simple scale.

The information on monthly State Attorney's Office intake was obtained easily. The cost-effectiveness data on the same office, however, turned out to be impossible to collect. The problem was not so much in obtaining expenditures as in trying to determine the costs attributable only to the misdemeanor-related functions of the office. When we realized that there was no possible way of collecting comparable costs on the State Attorney's Office and the CDS Program, we were forced to abandon this part of the evaluation plan.

The implementation of our impact assessment of the hearings progressed smoothly, aided by an understanding, supportive staff. The rapport we had worked so hard to establish paid off in the ease of implementation of our plan. The longer-term follow-ups we undertook with the sample of complainants and respondents, as well as the contacts with the no-hearing comparison group individuals, proved to be extremely time-consuming. Fortunately, we had several energetic and determined interviewers who tracked down nearly everyone. (Of those with hearings, we reached 91% of the complainants and 93% of the respondents. Among the no-hearing comparison group, we contacted 93% of the complainants and 73% of the respondents.)

Monitoring the Evaluation

Our monitoring of the evaluation occurred through regular visits of my research assistant, regular updates between us via telephone, and my occasional site visits to observe the program and the evaluation. Had I not had the on-site assistant, I am certain that the evaluation would not have been carried out as successfully as it was. For example, my assistant and the program staff developed procedures to record the dates of and participants in hearings, as well as the names and addressses of the no-hearing clients. These procedures greatly facilitated our timely identification of those we needed to interview.

Utilizing the Evaluation

In line with the newer view of utilization as something that occurs throughout the conduct of an evaluation, not simply at the end, we attempted to provide useful information whenever we could without compromising clients' confidentiality or the integrity of our research design. Periodically we gave the director summaries of the intake information so that he would have a better idea about the composition of his clientele. This assisted him in describing and promoting his program.

We also gave the director general summary reports on the satisfaction ratings of the complainants and respondents. At the conclusion of our study we presented detailed data on this information. During the course of the program, the director was interested only in the general level of satisfaction, perhaps because he was so familiar with many of the hearings (via reports from the attorney hearing officers and from occasional observation of actual hearings) that he knew that agreements usually were reached and clients generally were satisfied.

The long-term follow-up information, presented at the end of our study, was less useful to the director because he thought the three-week follow-up period was too short a time for change. (His view on this perhaps was colored by our finding that, in terms of long-term problem solution, the hearings did not seem to be particularly effective. More details are presented below.)

The evaluation served an additional purpose: In applying for continuation funding, the director found it beneficial to inform potential donors that an independent evaluation was being conducted and to give details about some of the formative data we generated during the course of the evaluation. The director secured funding and reported that the fact and substance of our evaluation assisted him.

CONCLUSION

Before we move to some concluding thoughts about the model and about the art of implementing program evaluations, some readers may wonder what the results of the study were. Although the findings are not our main focus here, the conscientious reader deserves a brief overview of these outcomes. (Complete details can be found in Conner and Surette, 1980.)

STUDY RESULTS

The intake data showed that for the 10-month period of the study, 306 complaints were presented for settlement, of which 194 (63.4%) resulted in hearings. Over half of the presenting complaints were harassment or simple assault, indicating that the program was dealing with serious cases. The median age of complainants was 36 years, and nearly two-thirds were female.

The short-term ratings complainants, respondents, and hearing officers made at the end of the hearings indicated that all these participants generally were satisfied with the settlements reached. Among complainants, 69% gave positive ratings; among respondents, 79%; among hearing officers, 64%. Complainants and especially respondents also generally thought that the problem that underlay the complaint had been solved. Hearing officers were much more cautious in their assessments.

The long-term follow-up with those complainants and respondents who had a hearing showed continued high satisfaction with the hearing. On the issue of whether the problem had been solved, a majority of both complainants and respondents reported that the problem had been solved. Substantial minorities of both groups, however, reported that the problem remained unsolved.

The meaning of these latter results requires the comparative ratings from the no-hearing complainants and respondents. The no-hearing complainants gave approximately the same report as those who had had a hearing, indicating that the hearings may not have been solving underlying problems. The respondent ratings could not be compared because of suspected validity problems. Nearly all of the no-hearing respondents reported that the problem had been solved. Based on interviewer reports, these high ratings reflect respondents' desire to avoid the problem or a hearing altogether. This seems clear to us now ("common sense," some would say) but was not obvious at the time.

We found, largely due to its relatively limited intake, that the CDS Program was having no noticeable impact on the State Attorney's Office misdemeanor filings. The time-series line we generated showed a gently decreasing trend of misdemeanor filings prior to the CDS Program and a stable or slightly increasing trend following its introduction.

CAUTIONARY THOUGHTS ON THE MODEL

There are three cautions the reader must keep in mind when attempting to apply the model described and illustrated in this chapter and diagrammed in Figure 7.1.

First, the stages of the model are not discrete but blend into one another. This type of merging between stages of the implementation process is not uncommon, since the stages are not discrete steps separated

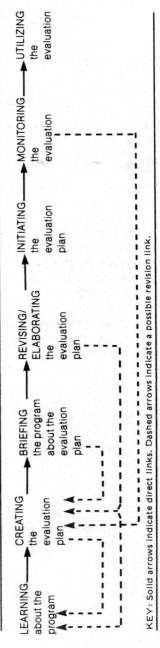

KEY: Solid arrows indicate direct links. Dashed arrows indicate a possible revision link.

Figure 7.1 A Model of Evaluation Implementation

one from the next. Instead, the stages of the process blend into one another, sometimes with a clear transition between stages and other times with no apparent break between stages. Occasionally, as in the CDS Program example, several stages are involved at once. The novice evaluator should not expect the stages necessarily to occur as distinctly separate events.

Second, progress through the stages may be forward, then backward, then forward again. Movements back to earlier stages (for example, from briefing back to creating or even to learning) do not necessarily reflect failure on the part of the evaluator. Indeed, greater insights and understanding may send the evaluation researcher back to earlier stages.

Finally, this model has not been tested experimentally. It is a conceptual model, intended as a heuristic. That is, this model should serve as "an aid to learning, discovery or problem solving by experimental and especially trial-and-error methods" (Webster's definition for "heuristic"). The intent is to give the reader, particularly the novice evaluation reader, enough of an idea about implementing evaluations to begin the trial-and-error process of actual implementation through which real learning and insights occur. If this chapter has built the novice evaluator's confidence to a point where he or she feels ready to try it for himself or herself, the model will have served its purpose. For it is only through the trial-and-error process, particularly the error phase, that the art and science of program evaluation and evaluation research come together.

REFERENCES

CONNER, R. F. and C. R. HUFF (1979) Attorneys as Activists: Evaluating the American Bar Association's BASICS Program. Beverly Hills, CA: Sage.
CONNER, R. F. and R. SURETTE (1980) "Processing citizens' disputes outside the courts: a quasi-experimental evaluation." Evaluation Review 4: 739-768.
FREEMAN, H. E. and M. SOLOMON [eds.] (1982) Evaluation Studies Review Annual, Vol. 7. Beverly Hills, CA: Sage.
PATTON, M. Q. (1980) Qualitative Evaluation. Beverly Hills, CA: Sage.
ROSSI, P. E. and H. E. FREEMAN (1982) Evaluation: A Systematic Approach. Beverly Hills, CA: Sage.
RUTMAN, L. (1980) Planning Useful Evaluations: Evaluability Assessment. Beverly Hills, CA: Sage.
WEISS, C. H. [ed.] (1977) Using Social Research in Public Policy Making. Lexington, MA: D. C. Heath.
WHOLEY, J. S. (1977) "Evaluability assessment," pp. 41-56 in L. Rutman (ed.), Evaluation Research Methods: A Basic Guide. Beverly Hills, CA: Sage.

8

AUDITING EVALUATION ACTIVITIES

Joe Hudson and Hugh A. McRoberts

This chapter deals with auditing or evaluating program evaluation activities. Our focus is broad and covers the audit of a variety of evaluation activities as these might be organized and carried out in government departments or agencies. Because program evaluation generally is either carried out by government departments or funded and sponsored by them, we believe that examining evaluation activities within such organizational contexts is an appropriate way of approaching the subject.

We first introduce and define the central elements of auditing, relate them to the audit or evaluation of evaluation activities, and describe some examples of such metaevaluations or audit examinations. We then identify major types of program evaluation activities potentially subject to examination, and suggest an approach to planning and carrying out an audit of them.

THE CONCEPT OF AUDITING

The need to audit began when the first property owners left their affairs in the hands of overseers, who were then required to account for their handling of the properties. As the owners probably soon realized, there was no necessary relationship between the accounts given by the overseers and the true state of affairs. If it were to their advantage to do so, they could conceal the truth from the owners. The owners could, of course, return to the property and verify the accounts for themselves, but that would be largely self-defeating. The solution was for the owners to hire an independent third party to review the overseers' accounts and give assurance about the degree to which they represented the true state of affairs completely and without bias. This is how the profession of auditing evolved, with all its surrounding procedures and protocol (Normanton, 1966).

There are common elements to all audits, regardless of the type of account examined. First, there must be an audit client. This is a person or group—the owners—responsible for some function or activity, unable to exercise close control over it, and therefore forced to rely on accounts rendered by other parties. In the public sector, for example, the client is the public or electorate represented by the legislative branch of government.

The second element common to audits is the auditee; that is, the manager or group of managers to whom continuing responsibility for the operation of an activity has been delegated. In the public sector, managers are represented by the executive branch of government. They supply information to the owners as an accounting for their activities. The value of the accounting information given by managers is likely to be related directly to its accuracy, completeness, and relevance. It also depends on the ability of the owners and the time at their disposal to assess and interpret this information.

The third element is the auditor, who acts on behalf of the owner or audit client and is independent of the manager or auditee. The auditor is expected to be familiar with the business and the procedures used in preparing the accounts and, on the basis of this knowledge, to examine the management accounts and provide assurance to the owners about the reliability of the information. The auditor is therefore not as concerned with creating new information about an auditee's activities as with verifying the information reported. The objective is to determine the degree of correspondence between the auditee's operation, reports on it, and established standards or criteria (Schandl, 1978).

Audit criteria or standards are the fourth element of auditing. Criteria are used as a basis for comparing the audit evidence or information collected so as to arrive at a judgment or audit opinion. Without criteria, there is little systematic basis for comparison or for giving audit opinions.

The most common type of accounting information is contained in financial statements, and auditing has been concerned primarily with the procedures involved in giving opinions on this type of account. The information contained in financial statements, for example, consists of a series of assertions: that the enterprise has cash, receivables, inventories, and so on. The accounting statement further asserts that these items are appropriately disclosed and described and that their classification accords with an acceptable interpretation and application of generally accepted accounting principles.

Not only financial accounts but also almost any type of statement conveying information from one party to another can, in principle, be audited. Confronted by a demand for broader-based audit information on more than the traditional fiscal auditing provided, most government audit officials have begun to carry out a variety of audits dealing with such matters as the efficiency and effectiveness of government operations.

There are two quite distinct ways in which program evaluation plays a role in the more recent, broad-based audits of program efficiency and effectiveness. Most commonly the term "program evaluation" is used synonymously with auditing. To carry out an audit of program effectiveness is, from this perspective, simply another way of referring to an evaluation of program effectiveness. This is, for example, the way the terms are applied in various state legislative audit bureaus (Brown, 1979).

There is a second, less common way of using the terms "audit" and "evaluation." The distinction made in this usage is specifically that of program evaluation and metaevaluation. To audit program evaluation, from this perspective, is to examine and arrive at opinions about program evaluation activities carried out by, or for, government agencies. Examples of this approach can be found in the audit authority given to the Auditor General of Canada (Auditor General, 1977) as well as the provincial Auditors General in Alberta and Ontario. Audit opinions are given on the assertions contained in both financial and nonfinancial (program evaluation) accounts rendered by government.

AUDITING PROGRAM EVALUATION ACTIVITIES

Various authors give different meanings to the term "metaevaluation" and suggest different ways to carry out such work. Cook and

Gruder (1978), for example, discuss seven models of metaevaluation, four that are carried out after an evaluation has been completed and three that are done simultaneously with the evaluation. For audit purposes, the three simultaneous models (consultant metaevaluation, simultaneous secondary analysis of data, and multiple independent replications) are not likely to be particularly useful. Auditors, unlike consultants, usually carry out their examinations after the fact. Therefore, the four models identified by Cook and Gruder that can be used subsequent to the primary evaluation are likely to be of more practical use for audit purposes.

These four models represent different ways of doing metaevaluation work. The first, for example, amounts to an essay review of evaluation work. The second is a review of literature about a particular program. The third approach to metaevaluation is an empirical reevaluation of an evaluation study. This consists of reanalyzing the data contained in the primary evaluation study and testing the conclusions reached or examining additional questions. The fourth model is an empirical reevaluation of multiple data sets about the same program. Other authors have referred to this approach as a "meta-analysis."

Each of these ways of doing metaevaluation can be used in an audit of evaluation activities in government departments and agencies. Clearly, however, the audit of such activities can consider a broader set of concerns than simply evaluation studies. An additional focus, for example, is the organizational framework and the management procedures used in government departments to plan, carry out, report, and use the results of evaluations. A number of such metaevaluation studies have been carried out over the past decade or so by academics, professional institutes, and government audit organizations. A brief review of these may help illustrate the type of concerns potentially subject to examination.

EXAMINATIONS OF GOVERNMENT
EVALUATION AGENCIES

An early examination of U.S. federal-level evaluation activities was reported by the Urban Institute in 1971 (Wholey et al., 1971). This study covered fifteen programs of four agencies during 1968-1969.

The major conclusion reached in the study was that the evaluation of social programs in the U.S. federal government during this time was "almost non-existent." The study found that there was no comprehensive federal evaulation system and that, even within agencies, orderly and integrated evaluation opertions had not been established.

Bernstein and Freeman (1975) reported an examination of American federally funded evaluation research activities under way during 1970. Information was collected and analyzed on approximately 1000 federally funded evaluation studies. Approximately half of the studies measuring program impacts were found by the investigators to be deficient either in design, sampling, or validity of measures.

The General Accounting Office (GAO, 1982) recently completed a different type of study of federal evaluation activities. The purpose was to provide a description of evaluation activities in federal departments and aencies during 1980. Information provided by Cabinet departments and agencies in response to a mailed questionnaire showed that during fiscal year 1980, the total amount of resources devoted to program evaluation was approximately $177 million. Departments reported available evaluation resources ranging from $10,000 to approximately $23 million, with over half reporting resources of approximately $30,000 or less. About 1300 full-time professionals were reportedly engaged in program evaluation activities in the 164 departments and agencies, although over half the departments also reported devoting 5 or fewer full-time professional staff to program evaluation. A total of 2362 evaluations were reported as active in fiscal year 1980; approximately two-thirds of these were carried out by in-house staff, the remainder by contractors.

A more recent study of federal evaluation activities was reported by the Auditor General of Canada (Auditor General, 1983). This audit covered program evaluation activities in the Canadian federal government, based on an examination of 19 departments. It examined the organization and management of departmental program evaluation activities, including the planning, conduct, and reporting of program evaluation studies. The audit concluded that significant progress had been made in establishing program evaluation activities in federal departments and agencies. All 19 departments had established program evaluation units, and most had prepared program evaluation plans to evaluate all departmental programs on a cyclical basis. Of the 19 departments, 17 had evaluation studies in progress, and a total of 86 evaluation studies had been completed at the time of the audit. Improvents were identified in the quality of completed evaluation work, but significant weaknesses were found in the methods used to carry out and report it.

AUDIT SCOPE

Each of these studies examined and reported on program evaluation within particular organizational contexts. In this respect they are forms of metaevaluation. Each has a different focus; together they cover three broad categories of concerns. The first is the organization and management of program evaluation within particular agencies; the early study done by Wholey and his associates concentrates on this. The second is the quality of evaluation studies and reports produced by an agency; the Bernstein and Freeman study deals specifically with this category of concerns. The third is the transmittal and use of information produced by evaluation studies; the Auditor General's audit of federal-level evaluation in Canada deals extensively with this concern.

Program evaluation activities in government agencies can be considered in each of these categories. The scope of an audit might include any or all of the three categories.

Auditing the organization and management of program evaluation activities. In this category of evaluation activities audit attention can be given to management procedures and controls governing the whole process of planning, collecting, reporting, and using program evaluation information. Specifically, an audit might examine such areas as the organizational mandate for the program evaluation function in the department, evaluation planning procedures, staffing, resourcing, and contracting. A key audit question to be addressed is whether satisfactory management systems and procedures have been established to ensure comprehensive, systematic, and objective evaluations of departmental programs.

Program evaluation measurements and reports. This category of evaluation activities subject to audit deals with the quality of program evaluations actually carried out, as well as the quality of their reports. The previous category of activities involves an examination of the organization and management of the program evaluation function in a specific departmental context; here attention is given to the planning and conduct of studies and their reports. The comprehensiveness of the measurements used in the evaluations would be examined, along with their quality. An assessment of the quality of measures focuses on their objectivity, validity, and reliability, whereas evaluation reports would be assessed in terms of accuracy, balance, and comprehensiveness.

Reporting and using program evaluations. This category of evaluation activities covers the transmittal and use of program evaluation studies. Auditors might examine how promptly and regularly program evaluation informtion is provided to the clients, recommendations made as a result of the evaluation study, and progress made at implementing recommendations.

AUDIT CRITERIA

Criteria are the standards or norms for making audit judgments that are reported as audit opinions about the particular subject examined. The audit evidence collected is considered in relation to the criteria in arriving at these judgments.

Several sets of standards for program evaluation have been proposed, including those of the General Accounting Office, the Joint Committee on Standards for Educational Programs, Projects and Materials, the U.S. Evaluation Research Society, as well as by Eleanor Chelimsky at the Institute for Program Evaluation of the GAO.

The GAO standards, issued as an exposure draft in 1978, are designed specifically for the assessment of impact evaluations. Fifty items are listed that can be applied to evaluations of a broad range of programs. Standards are proposed for planning, data collection, data analysis, reporting results, and data disclosure.

There are 30 Joint Committee standards (Joint Committee, 1980) grouped according to four attributes of an evaluation—its utility, its feasibility, its propriety, and its accuracy. To assist in interpretation of the standards, 178 guidelines are proposed covering potential pitfalls and caveats. Standards, guidelines, pitfalls, and caveats are covered in 369 statements about the proper conduct of educational evaluation.

The U.S. Evaluation Research Society (1980) standards cover a variety of different types of evaluations, including evaluability assessments, process evaluations, impact evaluations, monitoring evaluations, and metaevaluations. They are grouped under six headings: formulation and negotiation, structure and design, data collection and preparation, data analysis and interpretation, communication and disclosure, and utilization. A total of 55 statements are made in these standards.

Eleanor Chelimsky (1983) at the Institute for Program Evaluation (GAO) has written about an approach for determining the quality of evaluations as it is being used in that agency. Two components of quality are proposed—technical adequacy and usefulness—each encompassing several elements. The technical adequacy of an evaluation is made up of three factors: the appropriateness of an evaluation design for answering the questions posed within its time and cost constraints; the appropriateness of the evaluation's execution to the design selected and the resources available; and the absence of major conceptual errors, inappropriate technical procedures, and improper conclusions or inferences. Usefulness, the second component of evaluation quality, covers the factors of relevance, timeliness, presentation, and impact.

These different approaches to evaluation standards overlap considerably. Any of them might serve as appropriate criteria for auditing program evaluation activities. Clearly, however, the nature of the evaluation activities taking place within a particular jurisdiction may make certain of the standards inappropriate or irrelevant. In the final analysis, quality standards are always relative to a particular situation and the variety of circumstances interacting with evaluation activities. Therefore, to a considerable extent, criteria need to be developed to fit the relatively unique organizational arrangements within a particular jurisdiction. Besides being relevant, audit criteria should possess other qualities, including internal consistency, comprehensiveness, acceptability, and logical organization.

A set of audit criteria might, ideally, be organized in a form resembling a triangle. At the base the criteria are detailed and specific. Moving upward, they are summarized and more general. Finally, at the top of the pyramid is the single, most generalized criterion. In this way, the implications of not meeting detailed criteria become evident as one moves to more general criteria.

Different sets of criteria are required to arrive at judgments on the three sets of program evaluation activities—categories that could potentially be subject to audit. For example, criteria for the organization and management of departmental evaluation activities might be stated as follows, beginning with the most general criterion:

Government departments should have an organizational capability to plan, implement, and report program evaluation information.

This can be broken into five more specific criteria, which, in turn, break into further sets of even more detailed criteria. For example, the second-level criteria can cover the policy mandate and the resources assigned to a program evaluation unit; the systematic and comprehensive coverage of departmental programs; the integration of program evaluation within the organization with other management, accountability, and information system functions; the management of resources for program evaluation activities in the organization; and the objectivity with which program evaluation activities are carried out within the organization. More detailed criteria can then be identified for each of these sets.

The logic of moving from a general criterion to more detailed criteria can also be illustrated in relation to the second category of evaluation activities potentially subject to audit: evaluation measurements and reports. The most general criterion used to audit this set of concerns could be stated as follows:

Program evaluations should be state-of-the-art and cost-justified.

This breaks into five sets of more detailed criteria, relating to the focus of the evaluations being audited. These cover the relation between program impacts and effects and program outputs and activities; the validity of measurement procedures used; the reliability of the measurement procedures; the accuracy, completeness, and balance of the evaluation report; and the documentation available in support of the evaluation report.

For the third category of matters potentially subject to audit, reporting and using evaluations, the highest-level criterion might be stated as follows:

The results of program evaluations should be considered for use in making program decisions.

This might be divided into two sets of more detailed criteria. One might be concerned with the completion of evaluation reports on a timely basis for meeting the information needs of relevant organizational decision makers, the other with reporting the results of evaluations on a timely basis to relevant decision makers outside the organization.

AN APPROACH TO AUDITING EVALUATION ACTIVITIES

The work involved in auditing the evaluation activities of government organizations should be carried out on a phase-sequential basis encompassing discrete activities, specific objectives, and unique work products. Somewhat arbitrarily, three phases to an audit of evaluation activities are proposed.

Phase One: Obtaining an overview and identifying matters for examination. The objective of this initial phase in an audit of evaluation activities is to gain an understanding of the particular organization subject to audit and the organization of program evaluation activities in it. On the basis of information collected, the auditor determines the specific matters to be pursued in subsequent audit work.

In this initial phase, information is collected on the mission, operations, and organizational structure of the department being audited, along with information on the organization and operation of the program evaluation unit in that department. The area covered is relatively broad, including information collection on such questions as the following:

— What is the legal mandate for this department?

— How is the department organized on program and accountability lines?

— What are the major sets of issues confronting this department?

— How is the program evaluation function organized in this department?

— What program evaluations have been carried out by the evaluation unit in this department?

Data collection procedures for answering these questions involve reviewing documents and interviewing departmental officials. Three types of documents could be reviewed by the auditor. In the first category are the key organizational documents, such as legislation and major amendments, that establish and direct the work of the department, and strategic and operational plans. In the second category of documents are files on previous audit work carried out on the department. These should be reviewed with particular attention to the observations and recommendations made and the departmental response to them. In the third category are the documents relating specifically to the organization and operation of program evaluation activities in the department. These include the mandate or policies on program evaluation, organization charts and planning documents for this function, budgets, expenditures, staff complements, and program evaluation studies completed.

Audit information can also be collected by interviewing key department officials, particularly those with responsibility for the program evaluation function. These interviews can serve several purposes. They provide an opportunity to learn about and arrange to collect other relevant documents; to collect additional information arising from the review of documents; and to give the auditee full information on the purpose, scope, and timing of the audit work.

At the end of this initial audit phase, the information collected should be reviewed and assessed in order to determine the specific matters that should be examined in the next phase of the audit.

Phase Two: Preliminary examination. The objectives in this audit phase are to collect additional information and conduct a preliminary analysis on those matters of concern identified in the initial phase. This assessment should lead to the most important matters, which will be the subject of detailed examination.

The organization and management of the departmental program evaluation function is examined first. A preliminary examination can then be carried out on the evaluation reports produced by the departmental evaluation unit. Finally, the procedures for transmitting evaluation reports and for monitoring action recommended in them should be documented and assessed. On the basis of these preliminary assessments, the auditor should have an adequate information base to identify those matters requiring more detailed examination in the final audit phase.

To examine the procedures for organizing and managing program evaluation in the department, the auditor should carry out an assessment of the adequacy of the departmental mandate for program evaluation, the organizational structure and resources established for planning and carrying out program evaluations, and the procedures followed for reporting evaluation results and acting on them.

In making a preliminary examination of the program evaluations completed in a department, the auditor should examine the planning that was done before the evaluation study was undertaken, the methods used, and the results reported. Both essay reviews and reviews of the literature are carried out in this preliminary examination.

For example, planning reports for program evaluations could be assessed according to the following types of concerns:

— Does the evaluation planning report provide an understanding of the program? Were key program documents reviewed by the evaluators? Were interviews carried out with relevant program officials about program objectives, operations, and program resources?

— Was an assessment carried out by the evaluators to examine the plausibility of the link between program activities and expected results? Was the pertinent evaluation literature reviewed?

— Were potential evaluation questions identified by the evaluation client, ranked in order of importance, and appropriately translated into topics for study?

— Were measurments of performance for each of the evaluation questions developed on the basis of reviewing previous work done in comparable programs, identifying relevant indicators or sets of measures, and identifying appropriate data collection, sampling, and analytic procedures? Were alternative approaches to measurement suggested?

— Were estimates given on the amount and type of resources required for the different measurement approaches considered?

In assessing program evaluation study reports, the auditor should consider the validity and reliability of the data collected, the internal validity of the study design, and the accuracy and balance of the findings reported. Critical audit questions include the following:

— Was the information collected by the evaluators relevant to the measurement purpose? Was it objective, reliable, and complete?

— Did the analysis carried out by the evaluators examine the relation between program outputs and activities and program objectives and effects compared with estimated or measured objectives and effects of alternative programs or delivery systems?

— Were the analytic procedures used by the evaluators appropriate to the nature of the data? Were they adequate to determine both the specific results and the strength of the relation measured?

— Does the evaluation study report provide an adequate description of the measurement purpose, the data collection and analytic procedures used, and the findings?

— Does the evaluation study report contain a balanced presentation of the findings, including any methodological limitations and their implications?

Examination of these types of questions forms a basis for identifying matters for detailed examination in the final phase of the audit. The specific matters identified potentially may be positive or negative. Matters of both types need to be examined in the audit so that a balanced audit report can be made to the client. Also, it is important to carry out a detailed examination of mattters that are positive as well as those that are negative because a matter judged as satisfactory on the basis of a preliminary examination may, on the basis of further audit work, be found to be unsatisfactory.

A number of factors are considered in identifying potentially significant matters to be pursued in the final audit phase. The following are examples:

— whether program evaluations were reported to senior officials in or outside the department;

— whether a well-established professional literature exists for evaluating comparable programs;

— whether the matter is a known or probable concern to the audit client;

— whether the preliminary audit examination revealed potentially significant problems meriting further examination;

— whether there are significant audit risks associated with giving a positive opinion based solely on the preliminary examination.

Phase Three: Detailed examination. The objective of the third phase is to conduct sufficient work to substantiate the matters of potential significance in order to report the findings to the audit client.

Audit work is carried out on the three major categories of departmental program evaluation activities and the specific matters of potential significance identified in respect to them. Initial attention is given to examining program evaluations identified as needing detailed examination. Their use is examined next. The auditor can, at the same time, test the extent to which the procedures for organizing and managing the program evaluation function in the department are followed.

For example, because program evaluation study reports can be considered outputs of the organizational and management procedures established for the departmental evaluation function, they can be examined to determine whether the organizational and management procedures were actually carried through in the planning and conduct of the study.

Detailed audit examination would involve, at a minimum, assessing the departmental working paper files for the evaluation studies under consideration. For information on audit issues related to the quality of evaluations, various types of working paper documentation may be examined by the auditor, including sample or population listings, minutes of meetings, record or edit checks, data processing code books, and data tabulations. The importance of the matter being examined should dictate the amount and type of audit evidence required.

Interviews are not likely to be used extensively in the final audit phase. Where they are used, it is primarily to expand tentative audit findings and provide audit information to officials in the department.

Interview evidence is used less than documentation simply because it is less strong, although it can be "hardened" by having interview notes signed off by the interviewee.

In addition to examining working paper files, the auditor may want to obtain a copy of the actual measurement data used in the evaluation and carry out an independent analysis of it. The purpose of this re-analysis would be to compare the evaluation results reported with those obtained from the audit test. A sample of data tables from the evaluation can be analysed by the auditor and the tabulations compared. This type of audit work addresses the adequacy of the methods used for data collection and analysis as well as the accuracy and completeness of their treatment in the evaluation study report. This kind of analysis is necessary where there is reason to believe that negative or unpopular findings that are present in the data have not been examined adequately or disclosed in the report.

Examining the transmittal and use made of evaluation information during the final audit phase involves a relatively broad set of potential concerns. These include the accuracy and balance of derivative or secondary reports of evaluations, the recommendations made in the reports, the implementation status of these recommendations, and the follow-up procedures used to monitor implementation of the recommendations in the department.

In particular, the auditor needs to examine the accuracy and balance of the secondary reports on the results of evaluation studies, including the Executive Summary and evaluation findings reported in strategic plans and reports by the department. Audit attention is given to assessing how well the information presented in the original report coincides with that presented in reports derived from the original. The question of concern is whether the study findings are reported accurately in various secondary documents.

Considerable care needs to be exercised by the auditor in giving audit opinions about the use of program evaluation information. It may not be appropriate for the auditor to make judgments about what the specific nature of the use of evaluation information should be. This may fall within the domain of policy matters and therefore not be within the scope of the audit. If it is subject to audit, giving an opinion will require considerable care and caution. Program evaluations are only one source of information to be considered in making policy or program decisions. At the same time, however, failure to use the results of program evaluations may indicate that due regard for economy is not being given in the department. The auditor must therefore examine the extent to which the results of evaluations have been reported to appropriate decision makers and used by them in making management decisions. Such questions as the following emerge: Have procedures been established to follow up and review the results of evaluations? Are these procedures carried out in a satisfactory manner? Are there alternative procedures that are feasible and should be implemented?

AUDIT JUDGMENTS

Table 8 .1 shows the set of logical possibilities represented by the categories of evaluation activities conceivably subject to audit and the specific audit questions that could be addressed in respect to them. The row heading in Table 8.1 refers to the feasibility of implementing additional or alternative evaluation procedures; the column headings address questions about the relative quality of the evaluation procedures in place. In short, this table summarizes concerns about both the quality of what is in place and what feasibly should be in place. The six composite audit findings would then amount to the following:

(1) Satisfactory procedures are in place and it is not reasonable and appropriate that others be implemented. In short, the criteria of sufficiency and quality have been met.

(2) The procedures in place are judged to be satisfactory, but it is reasonable and appropriate that others be implemented. In short, the quality of evaluation activities is satisfactory, but these activities are not sufficient.

(3) The quality of the procedures in place are not satisfactory, but it is not feasible that other procedures be implemented. This amounts to the best of a bad lot; the evaluation activities are found to be of poor quality but not much else can feasibly be done. The question for the auditor then becomes whether the evaluation activities that are being carried out amount to a waste of resources.

(4) The evaluation procedures in place are found to be of poor quality and it is feasible to implement other evaluation activities. This is the worst of all words, where what is there is found to be bad, and it is quite reasonable and appropriate that better-quality evaluation activities be carried out.

(5) There are no evaluation activities in place and it is not reasonable and appropriate that any be established. This situation is likely to apply only rarely.

(6) There are no evaluation activites in place and it is quite reasonable and appropriate that additional procedures be implemented.

SUMMARY AND CONCLUSIONS

This chapter has presented an approach to the audit of program evaluations in the context of government departments and agencies. We began with a discussion of the generic nature of auditing through an exploration of the audit triad; the producer of information, the receiver of information, and the auditor. We showed how this applied in the most developed area of auditing—financial attest auditing—and contrasted that with the audit of program evaluations. We noted that there was much in common between the audit of program evaluations and certain types of what Cook and Gruder (1978) have labeled metaevaluation.

We then briefly reviewed some of the literature on the state of program evaluation within the government context. This review suggested that in the case of program evaluation in government the nature of the organizational context within which the work was carried out was an important audit consideration, paticularly with respect to the reporting and use of individual studies, and the continuity of the function in the organization.

The essence of auditing involves making judgments, and thus the standards or criteria used by the auditor lie at the very heart of audit work. If the standards are fair and logically sound and if they are applied properly, the audit is likely to be useful and credible. If they are

TABLE 8.1   Quality of Organization and Management, Measurements and Reports, Transmittal and Use

	Feasibility of Implementing Other Procedures	
	Not Reasonable and Appropraite	*Reasonable and Appropriate*
Satisfactory procedures in place	(1)	(2)
Unsatisfactory procedures in place	(3)	(4)
No procedures in place	(5)	(6)

Quality of organization and management, measurements and reports, transmittal and use.

not, then the audit process is likely to add to the noise already in the information channel between the producer of information and the receiver. We briefly described some attempts made to set standards for program evaluations. On the basis of this review we concluded that in government three matters are fundamental: the need for a stable organizational capability for program evaluation; the technical quality of the studies; and the need for procedures to ensure that key decision makers have the opportunity to consider and use the results of evaluations. We proposed a generic structure for criteria to deal with each of these matters.

We next described the mechanics of carrying out an audit of a program evaluation function, suggesting a staged approach beginning with a broad overview and working from there in an ever more focused fashion.

Finally, we briefly described the nature of the audit judgments to be made in writing an audit opinion. In particular, we note that in addition to comments on the adequacy of what is present, the auditor is also obligated to alert the client to things that ought to be done and that in the circumstances could reasonably and appropriately be done.

To be of value, information must not only be as correct and complete as possible but must be believed to be so by the person receiving it. Judgments about the former matters are technical in nature. The opinions about the latter are social, in that they arise out of the complex millieu of circumstances that surround the preparation and transmission of the information; the medium is in this sense part of the message. To the extent that a message contains information on an issue where the receiver's and sender's interests diverge, there is a learned tendency on the part of receivers to downgrade the credibility of the information.

This tendency on the part of the information receivers to downgrade information is compounded when the information speaks to important matters and is prepared in ways that are not well understood. Statisticians, for example, are no more or less honest than the general run of the population; however, their messages are more often misunderstood. Program evaluators are in danger of joining statisticians in the pantheon of "great liars" unless ways are found to make the information they produce credible to those to whom it is sent.

Accounting, of course, suffered from the same problem. Indeed, jokes about the abilities of the "creative" accountant abound. Their solution to the problem, as we have already discussed, is the audit that assures the receiver that the information being presented has been prepared in a dependable way and may be relied on. In short, it gives the information credibility with the receiver. Auditing offers a similar promise for program evaluations. It represents an independent review by professionals. If carried out in a consistent and professional way, such reviews can give the receiver of information the assurance needed to view the evaluation as credible. In turn, if decision makers get information they believe is credible, perhaps they will make use of it.

REFERENCES

Auditor General Act, 1977, Ottawa, Canada.

Auditor General of Canada (1983) Report of the Auditor General of Canada to the House of Commons. Ottawa, December.

BERNSTEIN, ILENE N. and HOWARD E. FREEMAN (1975) Academic and Entrepreneurial Research. New York: Russell Sage.

BROWN, RICHARD E. [Ed.] (1979) The Effectiveness of Legislative Program Review. New Brunswick, NJ: Transaction.

CHELIMSKY, ELEANOR (1983) "The definition and measurement of evaluation quality as a management tool," in R. G. St. Pierre (ed.) Management and Organization of Program Evaluation. San Francisco: Jossey-Bass.

COOK, T. D. and C. L. GRUDER (1978) "Metaevaluation research." Evaluation Quarterly 2: 5-15.

Evaluation Research Society (1980) Exposure Draft: Standards For Program Evaluation. Potomac, MD.

Joint Committee on Standards for Educational Evaluation (1980) Standards for Evaluation of Educational Programs, Projects & Materials, New York: McGraw-Hill.

NORMANTON, E. L. (1966) Accountability and Audit of Government. New York: Praeger.

SCHANDL, CHARLES W. (1978) Theory of Auditing. Houston, TX: Scholars Book Company.

U. S. General Accounting Office, [GAO] (1982) A Profile of Federal Program Evaluation Activities, Washington, DC: Government Printing Office.

——— (1978) Assessing Social Program Impact Evaluations: A Checklist Approach. Washington, DC: Government Printing Office.

WHOLEY, JOSEPH S., JOHN W. SCANLON, HUGH G. DUFFY, JAMES S. FUKUMOTO and LEONA M. VOGT (1971) Federal Evaluation Policy, Washington, DC: Urban Institute.

ABOUT THE AUTHORS

ROBERT BORUCH, Professor of Psychology and Education and Director of the Methodology and Evaluation Research Division at Northwestern University, is author of over 100 articles and books on research methods and policy. He serves often as member or chair of committees of the U.S. National Academy of Sciences, the Social Science Research Council, and the U.S. National Research Council. Boruch's interests are in applied social research and applied statistics, and information policy. His recent book with Joe Cecil on assuring *Confidentiality of Data in Social Research* (Pennsylvania Press) reflects that interest.

ROSS CONNER is Associate Professor and Associate Director, Program in Social Ecology, University of California, Irvine. Most recently he has written about the use of control groups in evaluation and about the reasons for the use and nonuse of evaluation findings in public policymaking. He is the editor of the forthcoming *Evaluation Studies Review Annual, Vol. 8.* To be sure he practices what he preaches to policymakers, he serves as a planning commissioner for his city.

THOMAS D. COOK is Professor of Psychology, Education, Urban Affairs, and Public Policy at Northwestern University. His publications include the books *Sesame Street Revisited* and *Quasi-Experimentation,* and he has co-edited *Evaluation Studies Review Annual, Volume 3* and *Qualitative and Quantitative Methods in Evaluation.* His interests are in metascience and in public policy research, especially evaluation and the utilization of social science research and theory.

JOE HUDSON is a Principal in the Office of the Auditor General of Canada. He received his Ph.D. and served on the faculty of the University of Minnesota. He has held a number of positions with the Minnesota Department of Corrections, including director of research and development, comprehensive planning, and victim services. He is co-author of *Considering the Victim* (1975); *Restitution in Criminal*

Justice (1977); *Offender Restitution in Theory and Action* (1978); *The Serious Juvenile Offender* (1979); *Perspectives on Crime Victims* (1980); *Justice As Fairness* (1981); and the author of numerous articles in the areas of restitution, victim services, evaluation, and auditing.

MELVIN M. MARK is Assistant Professor of Psychology at The Pennsylvania State University. He received his Ph.D. from Northwestern University in social psychology in 1980. He is co-editor of *Social Science and Social Policy* and of *Evaluation Studies Review Annual, Volume 3.* In addition to his interests in the use of social science research in policy processes, Dr. Mark's research focuses on relative deprivation and the social psychology of justice.

HUGH A. McROBERTS is a Principal in the Office of the Auditor General of Canada and an Adjunct Professor of Sociology and Anthropology at Carleton University, Ottawa. He received his Ph.D. from Carleton and was a full-time member of the faculty there until 1981. His research has been primarily in the area of social stratification with a focus on the issues related to occupational mobility and intergenerational status attainment models. He has published a number of papers in this area and is the coauthor of a forthcoming book, *Ascription and Achievement: Studies in Mobility and Status in Canada* (Carleton University Press).

MICHAEL QUINN PATTON is on the faculty of the University of Minnesota, where he has been Director of the Minnesota Center for Social Research (1975-1980) and where he was named outstanding teacher of the year in 1976 for his innovative evaluation teaching. His Ph.D. in sociology is from the University of Wisconsin. He has done evaluation at local, county, state, national, and international levels, including a two-year project at the University of the West Indies (Trinidad) during which he completed *Practical Evaluation.* He is the author of numerous articles, reports, and conference papers on evaluation, as well as the following books: *Utilization-Focused Evaluation* (1978); *Qualitative Evaluation Methods* (1980); and *Creative Evaluation* (1981).

DAVID RINDSKOPF is Associate Professor in the Educational Psychology and Psychology Departments at the City University of New York Graduate Center. His research interests include evaluation and policy analysis, especially work that improves the methodology of those areas. His current research concentrates on the application of latent variable models in medical research.

LEONARD RUTMAN has national responsibilities for the program evaluation practice of Price Waterhouse in Canada. He received his B.A. and M.S.W. at the University of Manitoba and his Ph.D. from the University of Winnipeg. Currently he is on leave from the School of Social Work at Carleton University. He has consulted extensively for several departments in the provincial and federal governments in Canada and has done some work for UNESCO. He is the author of *Planning Useful Evaluations: Evaluability Assessment* and co-author (with Dick de Jong) of *Federal Level Evaluation,* (with Andrew Jones) of *In the Children's Aid,* and (with Goerge Mowbray) of *Understanding Program Evaluation.* Rutman also edited the first edition of *Evaluation Research Methods: A Basic Guide* (1977).

CAROL H. WEISS is Senior Lecturer and Senior Research Associate at the Harvard University Graduate School of Education. She is author of *Social Science Research and Decision-Making* (Columbia University Press, 1980), *Evaluation Research: Methods of Assessing Program Effectiveness* (Prentice-Hall, 1972) and other books on evaluation research and the utilization of research in policymaking. She has published scores of papers in such journals as *Evaluation Review, Policy Analysis, New Directions in Program Evaluation, Journal of Higher Education, American Sociological Review,* and *Public Administration Review,* and serves on the editorial boards of *Society, American Behavioral Scientist, Policy Studies Journal,* and *Knowledge: Creation, Diffusion, Utilization,* among others. The winner of the Evaluation Research Society's Myrdal Award for Science in 1980, she is president of the Policy Studies Organization (1983-1984) and was the first Congressional Fellow of the American Sociological Association (1983).

Evaluation research
  methods : a basic guide